ALLAN BORDER

Beyond Ten Thousand

ALLAN BORDER

Beyond Ten Thousand

MY LIFE STORY

Souvenir Press

"I was pleased to learn that Allan Border has now become the highest scorer in Test cricket.
Not only does this recognise his skill as a batsman, it is also a tribute to his physical fitness and tough character because it has taken many years of toil to reach such a milestone.
Australians look upon Border as a typical Aussie battler who has served his country well.
I join in congratulating him on his feat."

SIR DONALD BRADMAN, *Adelaide, February 26, 1993*

PAGE 2: A favourite stroke, the cover drive, during my century against the West Indies at the MCG in 1992.

OPPOSITE: A favourite place to play, England. Square-cutting, early in the 1989 Ashes tour.

I would like to dedicate this book to my darling wife Jane, whose love and support have been the main contributors to my longevity in this great game.

Designer: Stan Lamond, Lamond Art & Design
Editor: Dawn Cockle

First published in Australia by
Swan Publishing Pty Ltd, Dalkeith, Western Australia

First British Edition published 1994 by
Souvenir Press Ltd, 43 Great Russell Street,
London WC1B 3PA

ISBN 0 285 63200 0

Printed in Australia by
McPherson's Printing Group

CONTENTS

FOREWORD

It was fitting that Allan Border's final tour of England to defend the Ashes should be the most important of his cricketing life, though whether or not he agrees is another matter. He has done a great deal for Australian cricket over a 15–year span, and I've no doubt he has enjoyed most of it. For 1993 in England though the Australian selectors made him guardian of the cream of Australian cricket's youth with an eye to the end of the 20th century. It is not given to everyone to be so trusted as there have been only slightly more than 40 captains of Australian cricket in the entire 116 years the game has been played at Test match level.

There are many types of cricketers—flamboyant ones who capture the headlines for a variety of reasons; ambitious ones who trumpet for all to hear that their destiny lies in greatness. There are others, some wonderful, some not so.

Allan is one of the players I would always want to have in my team. As I would also be very happy indeed to play under his captaincy, you might gather that I reckon him not only to be a hell of a player but also a team man through and through. That has always counted a great deal with me and there has been no better example of it than in the way he took on the captaincy of Australia.

After Kim Hughes resigned at the Gabba in 1984, Border was shanghaied into the captaincy. Some players covet the captaincy. Some are reluctant. It was typical of Border that, reluctant though he might have been, once he accepted the job he gave it precisely 100 per cent.

I've seen Allan play in all his home Tests and limited-overs internationals, and all the international matches he has played in England. On the score of 'wish I had been there' the match I'm sorry I missed is the 1984 battle for a draw against the West Indies in Port-of-Spain, Trinidad. A century, a 98 and a draw may be low down in the statistical list of Test cricket excitement, and it is a performance impossible to explain to someone who walks into a room knowing nothing about cricket.

I'm just sorry I missed it!

So far as batting statistics go, Border's name is at the top of all players who have ever walked onto a cricket field to represent their country at Test level. It is an astonishing achievement, but not one on which I intend to dwell, as Allan is the only person who has been there for every one of those runs. To me the most incredible thing is that it has been achieved by an Australian, in the same way as Dennis Lillee, when he was the world's greatest wicket-taker in Tests, had achieved something quite remarkable. Normally Australians don't play all that much cricket and you have to be quite outstanding to achieve something of this kind. For me, more astonishing than the actual runs though, is the fact that when Border passed Sunil Gavaskar's previous aggregate, he did it with a batting average in excess of 50 per Test match innings.

That puts him in a very short list with Gavaskar, Vivian Richards, Javed Miandad and Sir Garfield Sobers who, by a whisker, may just have been the best of the group. To be in this company sums up perfectly for me why Border has been such a wonderful cricketer and captain for Australia.

Two friends of mine, Barry Knight, a fine cricketer and an outstanding cricket coach, and Frank Twiselton, a great friend of Australia and Australians, had, in different ways, a considerable influence on Allan's career. They talked to me about him in the 1970s, many years ago and when few had heard of him. I was very impressed with him as a player as far back as 1981 when he was the Australian batting star of a lost series against England, a foretaste perhaps of what we now know of him, that he is often at his best when the going is tough.

A cricketing life though is not just a matter of numbers. With Allan what you see is what you get! There is no subterfuge, no saying one thing and meaning another. In fact, there have been times which he might look back on and regret having said exactly what he has. Then again he might not. The one thing you know is that he is honest and I can assure you, to his team and cricket followers around Australia, that means a great deal.

Sitting in the commentary box watching, and often learning something new about the game each day, is one of the most interesting things in my life. You see and hear players, followers of the game, captains of industry, fellow media people and administrators of sport. They pass by on the stage in the same way as commentators, some performing in memorable fashion, some not.

I've been lucky to see them all as a player, a captain, a commentator and a journalist and Border is one who has always impressed me. He was Australian of the Year and it was as much for being an Australian, and being proud of it, as it was for anything else, because he is equally at ease talking with a prime minister as he is with an Australian follower of the game who might just have taken it into his head to phone him in the Headingley dressing room during a rain break in a Test match, as one fan once did!

There are many parameters by which people are judged in all walks of life. In cricket it has always been my view that anyone who graces the stage for a certain amount of time will, in some way, put something back into the game. Someone who has been around for a longer period, I believe, has an obligation to leave a legacy for those who are to follow.

Allan started at the time of the split between the establishment and World Series Cricket and he will finish when the time is right. When he retires he will leave a legacy for those who follow in Australian cricket and, because of that, it is a pleasure and a privilege to introduce this book to sports lovers the world over.

RICHIE BENAUD

Chapter One

OVER THE FENCE, AND ON THE WAY

*The very young Allan Border, but not
too young to hold a cricket ball.*

---

*I enjoyed a youth that certainly wasn't misspent, but
as you will see, it was a youth that guaranteed I would be
more likely to trouble the cricket scorers than any of
industry's head-hunters.*

STARTING OUT

Fifteen minutes by road from the Sydney Harbour Bridge, and just about dead north of the famous 'Coathanger', is the suburb of Mosman, leafy and green, where I was born and enjoyed my sporty and carefree youth.

The family, my mum Sheila, my dad John, and the boys, Mark, me, John and Brett, lived in a red-brick, grey slate-roofed Federation style house, so typically Australian, yet named 'Omaha'.

Dad hailed from Coonamble, up in the dry, hot north-west of New South Wales, and later worked as a wool classer. His main sporting interest had been swimming, but as I grew up I found out he also slogged the cricket ball to 'cow corner' when he turned out at weekends with the Ramsgate RSL.

Mum ran a little shop—one of those mixed goods stores where you could buy anything from a boiled lolly to a bar of soap—in busy Military Road, the main thoroughfare through Mosman.

It was the early 60s and the newspaper headlines of the time were all about Sydney's notorious Bogle-Chandler murders, the first James Bond movies, Australian Margaret Court's first Wimbledon crown, Britain's Great Train Robbery and the JFK assassination.

It all passed me by; as an eight-year-old all I remember is big brother Mark thrusting a small bat into my hands.

'Omaha' was what you might call an 'open house'; it was central, and therefore an ideal meeting place, and as time went by its reputation for a friendly welcome was surpassed only by my brother Johnno's reputation as a maker of rock cakes. On occasions it was nothing for there to be as many as 20 kids in at one time, and plenty of them were there just for Johnno's rock cakes.

Mum would watch all these kids rolling in, and it would go something like this, as they filed past her at the door: "Hello Mrs Border, how are you? ... Johnno's going to make rock cakes this afternoon."

One New Year's Eve about 300 people passed through the house; and another time Johnno's church group went on a bushwalk and came back to our house— about two cricket teams of them. Mum looked like a traffic cop, waving her arms, directing them to "bread over there, milk over here, there's the biscuit tin ..."

One of the girls there turned to me and said, "If I did this to my mother she'd kill me."

But that's how it was at 'Omaha'; Mum and Dad had country links and had never lost sight of that great Australian bush tradition, the hospitality house.

Across the road from 'Omaha' was Mosman Oval, the home of the Mosman first-grade cricketers, and baseballers, and beyond that under tall poplar trees, Mosman Public School.

Ask my dad and he may tell you that at school I never showed much interest

Going to Sunday School with Johnno. Mosman Oval is in the background.

Ready for backyard baseball with Johnno.

in anything other than cricket. It wasn't that I was ordinary at my schoolwork—in fact in my last year at public school the headmaster, Harold Reece, presented me with a special prize that encompassed scholastic performance, sport and leadership. Harold likened it to his school's version of the Rhodes Scholarship.

I was a prefect, along with three other boys, two of whom were Rob Hirst, who went on to become the drummer for the band Midnight Oil, and Tom Burlinson, most recently chosen as the voice of Frank Sinatra for the movie of Old Blue Eyes' life.

Neither acting, nor music, were exactly strengths of mine. I had a small part with Tom in the school's *My Fair Lady* production, saying, from memory, two words—but I've forgotten what they were!

When I was nine the piano in the living room caught my eye, and I informed Mum that a trial of tickling the ivories would be in order. A music teacher was hired to come to our house, and after school once a week, lessons began. There was a significant problem: sitting on my piano stool, if I looked out the window and across the road, I could see all my mates hitting a cricket ball around. I thought, 'Great, and here I am practising my scales.'

Brother Mark, Mum, Dad, Johnno and me in 1960.

After a year I passed my first exam at the Conservatorium, but even then I knew in my heart I wasn't going to be a pianist. And it had nothing to do with the short, podgy Border fingers—have you ever seen Elton John's?

I had a problem with asthma, and it seemed the attacks were more common when I practised piano. The doctor my parents consulted came to the conclusion that I was doing too much, which was causing stress, which was triggering the asthma. He told Mum, "Something has to go, either the piano or the sport."

Mum looked at the doctor, then looked down at me, and replied, "Well … we can't ask him to give up his cricket."

To this day, when I hear people discussing stress, I always think, 'Yeah, I know what stress is—practising the piano inside while you can hear your mates outside hitting a cricket ball around.'

My career in rugby was a shortlived one, too; it had blossomed momentarily at primary school, where I was a speedy breakaway in the seven-stone division. But once the guys got taller, wider and heavier and I found myself covering my head at the bottom of some of those stomping rucks, I started to think, 'AB, maybe this isn't the game for you.' When they started punching I knew it definitely wasn't for me!

In my last couple of years at high school I wasn't all that keen on the scholastic side of things, either. There were mornings when I enjoyed a couple of hours

The Class of '67. Actor Tom Burlinson is in the back row, second from left,
and Midnight Oil band member Rob Hirst in the front row, second from left.
I'm front row, right. The teacher is Harold Reece.
Opposite: *A lot of runs later. At Mosman Oval in 1993. The house in the*
background is 'Omaha', just a good pull shot away.

under the Moreton Bay figs in the park across the road from school in preference to a double-period of history. Some days I wouldn't even bother turning up, instead I'd pack my cossie in my school bag and head for Balmoral Beach. But I never missed Wednesday—that was sports day. And I never missed a day when the football team was playing, so I could cheer my mates.

It had become clear, the only thing I really liked was the sporting side of life.

SORRY MISS CHEESEMAN!

When I was very small the family once set off in the car for Adelaide and by late in the day we were heading due west along the gunbarrel-straight highways in the south-west of the State. The setting sun was a perfect red ball, so big that I wanted to touch it. Mum still tells the story of how, despite being offered any one of at least half a dozen balls in the car, I kept pointing at the sun saying, "I want that big red ball in the sky."

I was ball-crazy.

I'm the only left-hander in the family, although both my grandmothers stood on the 'wrong side of the milk churn'. That used to worry me a bit early on, because when I first rolled up to school I noticed that every other kid seemed to be right-handed. I decided to try to conform, to be 'one of the mob'. So, if I happened to be at someone else's place I'd watch the way they used their right hand and I'd try to copy the things they did. That's why I eat right-handed today.

But one day when a teacher was showing us how to catch a ball I decided no change was necessary when it came to sport.

"Catch it in your right hand, Allan," she'd say. And I did, as did just about everyone else. But when we got to the "catch it in your left hand" part I was the only one who could do it.

Two great men had an early influence on my sporting instincts: John Sykes, who was a first baseman with Mosman Baseball Club and the father of my best mate, Marcus Sykes; and Tom Fleming, an elderly gentleman with a stiff leg and a demeanour to match, who was my early cricket instructor.

John used to let Marcus and I toss around his old baseballs from the time we could walk; over the years he instilled in me ball skills and a sense of team spirit. In youth cricket, those of us who had worked with John Sykes were always the superior fieldsmen. And, coincidentally, I later became Mosman baseball's first baseman.

Tom Fleming coached the Mosman Under-12s, and was very big on discipline. He sometimes organised Sunday matches at the Mater Children's Home for his young charges, suggesting to us that we take a look around because "that's what life can be like if you don't behave yourself". Just a gentle reminder

Change in lifestyle. In 1956 a rocking horse and a cloth cap, in 1992 a cricket bat and a hard hat.

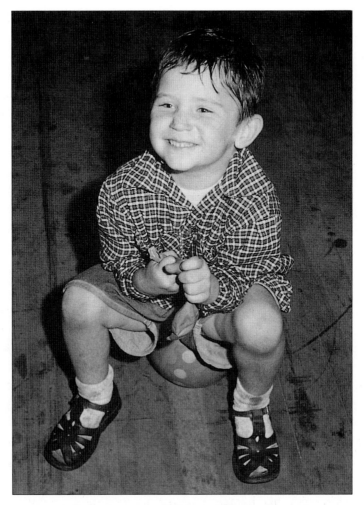

Ball crazy—even if it is something to sit on!

that we should do as we were told and sit and watch our teammates during the game on Saturday mornings: no running around and climbing the trees at Primrose Park, our home turf.

You had to put the stumps up the right way for the game and make sure you always packed them at the bottom of the kit after the game, and if you didn't there was a promised "swift kick in the backside" from Tom.

He never stopped stressing how important it is to get the basics of the game right. Tom insisted that we only call him "Mr Fleming", a rule that inevitably led to a bit of mischievous by-play. We'd call out "Hey Tom ... " and Tom, hopping on that bad leg that had been injured in a motorbike smash, would shout back "You just wait!"—but he'd do it with the hint of a smile.

For a long time most of my cricket was played in the Border backyard, on lawn down the side or out the back on a concrete slab. We held intensely competitive 'Test matches' between myself, Johnno and Brett.

Any more players and we went across the road to Mosman Oval. That was the scene of The Tornado Test of 1969, not the stuff Wisden is made of, but pretty dramatic anyway.

A mini-tornado struck Mosman, sucking windows out of cars, bringing down powerlines and darkening the sky. But at Mosman Oval play went on at a stage when the light was merely fading quickly and the breeze from the scoreboard end only strengthening.

I was bowling to David Mankey. We were using a tennis ball because my little brother Brett, only eight years old and knee-high to a grasshopper, was playing. He was fielding at mid-on. I bowled the ball, and the wind caught it and swerved it straight back at me!

David's startled look suddenly gave way to a cry, "Hey, look at Brett!" I turned to see little Brett wheeling towards me, airborne, picked up by the wind. I grabbed him by the legs, then laid on top of him. Might be the best catch I've ever made!

Our backyard 'Tests' were usually played with a stump and either a ping-pong ball or one of those plastic practice golf balls with the holes. The hard ball was banned because insurance premiums on damage to the property next door had reached Everest proportions.

This house next door had been converted into flats, and among the tenants was a lovely elderly lady, Miss Cheeseman. I'd often hear her say, "Oh Mrs Border, I do so love to hear the boys enjoying themselves."

The only trouble was that her window was nearest to our place and was more often broken than not. We must have done wonders for the bank balance of an old chap named Mr Long. He was retired, and sort of a local handyman. The tinkle of breaking glass had hardly died away before I'd hear Mum on the phone. Mr Long had a daughter called Joyce, who always answered with, "Oh it's you

In the backyard at 'Omaha', and for once the window behind me isn't broken!

Mrs Border, you'll want to speak to Dad. The boys been playing cricket again?"

Our substitute hard balls were the young, green grapefruit from our backyard tree; they were as hard as any cricket ball, shiny and either skidded or bounced from the concrete slab, a true test of any batsman's technique.

Even in the worst wet weather we played; our field was the beautifully long and wide hallway of 'Omaha', the bowler coming from the other side of the dining room. And there were no problems recruiting fieldsmen in a house that could cater for a few hundred people on a New Year's Eve!

Mum maintains I was so competitive in these backyard contests that in victory I would burst through the door shouting "I am the champion!" I don't know about that—but I've always liked winning more than losing.

Such was my enthusiasm for the game, and the promise I showed at the Mosman junior coaching classes, that at the age of nine I was invited to play with the Under-12s.

The family anticipated the need for a pair of batting gloves to go with the bat brother Mark had already given me. Mum came back from Cummings local sports store with a pair, but not knowing anything about batting gloves and thumb guards, she came back with a pair of right-handers.

My left-handedness had finally got me into a spot of bother in sport.

The Under-14s All Stars baseball team, 1968, John Sykes and me.

Aged nine, front row, second from left, in the Mosman Under-12s team.
Tom Fleming is on the right.

SHOP CLOSED, SON AT THE CREASE

My parents more or less lived in the car at weekends, what with three young boys, all of us playing at different times at different venues. As we grew up it was nothing for them to have to travel the length and breadth of Sydney in one day. I have a vivid recollection of the car—yes, the Kingswood! a brand new Holden station wagon, ten days old.

We were playing backyard baseball and Johnno hit a home run to left field, right onto the roof of the carport. I'd never been on the carport roof before and discovered it was made from fibro, very thin fibro, because I crashed through right into the roof of the new car. It's a tribute to the good nature of my parents that they whisked me straight off for X-rays; a check on the damage to the car, and a ban on roof climbing came later in the evening.

Some parents dote on their children's sporting talent. My Dad used to umpire our games a bit—I never thought I had a hope of getting a leg before, but I used to give it a good shout just in case.

Dad was always reserved in his thoughts about my play. He liked my style, and he'd now and again tell others he hoped I might play for Australia one day—but he always said it with a smile, and never when I was around. He knew the drill; not many out of one generation make it when you think about it.

Dad was watching the day I made my first century, for Mosman Under-12s, at Cammeray, a suburb near Mosman. As I neared the nineties, he showed supreme faith in my ability by getting into the Kingswood and driving back to Mosman to get Mum to close the shop and come down for a look.

That must have been a first in business—a sign saying "Shop Closed, Son at the Crease". I was 11 years old.

A season later I had to endure the less glorious side of batting—a fight for survival. I was in the Under-14s and had broken a toe, but had to bat when a collapse left us struggling. We couldn't win, but we didn't lose.

My ability outstripped my height. The Mosman president was Keith Johnson, who had been the manager of Bradman's great '48 side to England, and I can remember him approaching Dad at an Under-12 match and saying, as he looked down at me, "When does he turn ten?" Dad said, "He's not nine yet."

There was a constant push to play me above my age. That's not a bad thing in bigger, more mature boys, but I was still very young, and it worried me a lot. It wasn't that I couldn't handle it, even though the other boys were a lot bigger physically; I simply missed the mateship of the boys my own age, the ones I spent all my time with in my everyday life. I had nothing in common with the older boys, and we didn't even talk much. It got so bad Mum told me I could play tennis if I wanted to. Mosman relented.

Two seasons on, when I was playing Under-16s in the morning, I didn't mind it when I was chosen to play fifth grade against the men in the afternoon. I'd been batting a good while in one fifth grade game when I heard a bloke in the slips say, "We'll never get this little bugger out!" That felt okay.

There was a sense of achievement coming into my game, a determination to prove to my opponent that I was a better player. Muck-around cricket and baseball were out—it had to be the fair dinkum thing. Maybe there's a bit of the perfectionist in me. When I moved to Queensland many years later, Dad was out at Chapel Hill helping me with a fence. I nearly drove him up the wall. He said, "It's straight enough." I said, "It's got to be dead straight—both sides."

Yet, not long after I turned sixteen, my cricket had fallen victim to those wonderful distractions that colour the life of any teenage boy—the beach, girls, and parties. Suddenly I wasn't quite as fair dinkum about my cricket.

With Brett, middle, and Johnno.

GOOD NIGHT, GOOD KNIGHT

Times change. In the 1990s if someone takes his dog for a walk on Balmoral Beach he'll be fined $200. As an old Balmoral Beach 'bum' I can see the irony in that. Because, to get to the beach in the first place the dog owner has to pass by a statue of Mosman's most celebrated dog, 'Billy', who over 17 years was a familiar sight walking alongside his master, a street cleaner.

I changed, too; my priorities took a ride on a roller-coaster.

THE CRICKET: It started to lose a bit of the buzz it had held for me, although many would be surprised to know that this happened when I was promoted to first grade.

Sports writers always seem to be knocking each other down to see who can spot the next "schoolboy champion". They're always on the lookout for the "next Bradman", or the "next Walters". They tagged me "the next Neil Harvey".

Well, I was of compact build, I was a left-hander and I'd made plenty of runs, but the strange thing was when I came into Mosman first grade aged sixteen I was chosen as a left-arm spinner, and I batted at No. 9.

My initiation to first grade cricket wasn't too gentle. When we played Petersham I knew what to expect, because in their team were some of the blokes I played baseball against, and they were notorious for their repartee—sledging—that they hoped would put their opponents off their game, upset their nerve and temperament.

Sure enough, when I walked out to bat and took my guard, I heard a taunting voice float in from the gully region: "Ha, sending a little boy out on a man's errand, eh?"

Then, when I pushed one defensively into the covers the fieldsman picked up the ball and wrung his hands as if they had been stung by the power of my shot. It was just non-stop mocking.

A game or two later Mosman bumped—or, better to say, were bumped by—Jeff Thomson and Len Pascoe, who played with Bankstown.

It wasn't quite a terrifying experience, rather a sobering one. I could see 'Thommo' standing away in the distance at the start of his run, and behind me was the 'keeper, seemingly the length of a couple of cricket pitches back.

At the same moment as Thommo took the first step of his run in I heard Len's throaty voice demanding, "Come on Thommo, knock this kid's head off."

None of that worried me, though. What was getting under my skin was batting so low down the order. If I got a bat I had no time to build an innings, and I just couldn't get a run.

My spin bowling wasn't exactly tying the opposition batsmen in knots, either. I'm still convinced, to this day, that a short spell I bowled to a fellow called Ron

Crippen probably clinched him a spot in the NSW team.

I bowled six overs for 67 runs and Ron made 130 not out. It wasn't long before I was commuting between firsts and seconds. I was just turning up and having a bash, being a general nothing. My cricket had lost its way.

THE BEACH: Balmoral Beach wasn't very far from 'Omaha', about a 20-minute stroll. I'd walk, although when I was very young Mum used to pack us a lunch, then pack us, half a dozen of my mates and me, into the car and down we'd go to have fun in those blow-up rubber tubes.

In my teens I was never a 'surfie'—one of the bleached-blond, bronzed cult figures of that time—but I did like surfing. Out of the water, off my boogie-board, I spent all my time in 'The Oven', a spot at the northern end of Balmoral, where it was easy to create a tan as well as keep a close and critical eye on any worthwhile developments in bikini design.

I began to surf further afield, beaches more to the north such as Avoca and Terrigal. I bought a surfboard, totally useless at Balmoral, but great at another beach, Manly.

But I was a bit of a captive of my new lifestyle. Surfboards and buses didn't go together, so I had to leave mine in my aunt's laundry at Manly. It wasn't even an option for the trips to Avoca and Terrigal.

Clearly I needed 'wheels'.

THE CAR: In those days the main highway west from Sydney was Parramatta Road, with its uneven, split concrete surface and plethora of trucks that inspired bad tempers among drivers. It was Sydney's 'auto alley', because it seemed like every second business was a used-car yard.

I spied what I wanted in a newspaper ad and Dad and I took the Holden and headed over the Harbour Bridge, and out into 'auto alley'. It was one of those small yards, so small we almost missed it. There it was, just like the ad said, a green VW 'beetle', the car every teenager of the day lusted after.

It cost me $600, and went like a dream on the test drive, although later on it did break down a lot. There was a problem with the front brakes, which used to lock on for no apparent good reason, there being no other traffic in the near vicinity. And it was always a good idea to try to leave it on a slight incline, just in case it needed a clutch start. Which it often did.

To pay for it I had a job pulling petrol, the 'work experience' side of the position I'd taken upon leaving school, as a clerk with the BP oil company. Those were the days before self-service, so as well as complying with demands to "Fill it up, young man," because the local population was rather elderly and female, there was plenty of "Check the oil, wipe the windscreen and check the tyres, young man."

I didn't have much idea about tyre pressures, whether it was the big cars that got 28 pounds per square inch, or the little ones, so most of the time I used to just go to each tyre, bend down, and squirt a bit of air into nowhere.

For a bloke who'd been mighty particular about things being just right I'd suddenly got a bit slack.

THE GIRL: Jane Hiscox and I used to chat a bit on school mornings, when she would be on her way to Loreto Convent and I'd be contemplating whether to actually go to North Sydney High School, or meditate under the figs in the park opposite. About that time we were both members of 'The Sexy Six', a group of four boys and two girls who used to help each other out with homework and see a bit of each other socially.

There was no romance then between Jane and I—we were just good friends, as in fact we had been since we were young children. The families Border, Sykes and Hiscox were all involved in Mosman cricket and baseball. John Hiscox, Jane's Dad, had a long stint on the Mosman Cricket Club committee, and so loved the game that his spotlessly clean Daimler car carried the number plate 'HOWZAT'.

My mother assures me I could not have gone as far in cricket as I did had I not had Jane as a partner: "Jane has been around cricket and cricketers all her life. She has even done scoring. She knew about your tardy habits, sitting around after games, having post mortems," she'd say.

She's right, as mothers usually are. But nor would I necessarily have made it without the assistance of Barry Knight, a former England Test allrounder, who had come Down Under to try his luck in the cricket business.

By 1975 my friendship with Jane had blossomed into romance.

CHECK, MATE!

The resuscitation job on my cricket career by Barry Knight turned out to be a classic case of biting the hand that feeds. Barry was the captain-coach of Mosman and I think he'd had a gutful of my attitude. One day he suggested it would be nice if I could bother to turn up at practice—not only so I could learn a bit more about the game, but also to save him having to come down to Balmoral Beach to tell me whether I was in the firsts or the seconds.

Barry ran an indoor cricket centre in a converted old warehouse in the southern part of Sydney, in Kent Street. The nets were up on the second floor, so the action always had a real 'thwack' of the ball on suspended floor, a sort of an echo. The Mosman club had decided to sponsor four coaching scholarships at the centre, and I won one of them.

So, for five weeks, every Thursday after work I caught a train across the Harbour Bridge, then a bus up to the other end of Sydney, and learnt a fair bit more about the game than I ever thought existed. There was a 'human net': you batted and a trio of bowlers tried to sort you out while a video camera recorded your every move. After that 'net' Barry took me aside, replayed the video, and pointed out any weakness I might have had. It was the first time I'd seen a video used that way.

Then he'd take me into the other net where he had one of those old, whirly-gig bowling machines, and he'd set it in such a way as to work on my weakness. Mine was around the off stump—tell me a player who doesn't have a problem there! And when I tried to hit into the covers I opened the face of the bat too much and used to get caught in the slips a bit. The point is that Barry didn't try to change my natural style, he just tried to strengthen it.

It's always hard to tell with technique; some blokes look fantastic, all correct and neat as a button, but they don't produce. Then there are players like Ian Chappell and Doug Walters whose techniques weren't real flash, but they were champions. You never know.

It was the winter of 1975 when I went to Barry Knight's, the baseball season, and I was still very keen on the flat-bat game. In fact, I was showing enough promise for the team management to tell me, "Allan, you can go all the way."

Barry and I had a chat about that. He said, "So what? You're good enough to one day play cricket for your country. Do you know what that means? It means the world is yours. Baseball can't offer you that. You might get a game against the 'also-rans' from Japan and America, but you'll never get a game against any 'All-stars'. In cricket you will."

My father said that wasn't a bad point; and when I thought about it I decided it seemed okay, too. Dad agreed to pay for a few more coaching sessions.

Mosman's first match in the next season, 1975–76, was against our deadly

Hitting out against Balmain at Mosman Oval, a turning point in my career.

rivals, Gordon, a 'next-door' club. Until recent times they were known as 'The Gays', for no other reason than they liked a drink and a good time. But Barry Knight, professional cricketer, had switched from Mosman to Gordon!

I was playing against my coach, the perfect opportunity to find out just how beneficial Barry's advice had been. I made 111, and in the season I hit 600 runs. One of the Gordon bowlers I scored heavily off was a State selector, Dick Guy, who used to bowl loopy leg breaks.

There were a few sixes in that innings and it won me selection in the NSW Colts team to play Queensland, up in Brisbane. I was the twelfth man, but I *was* in the team. The beach and baseball were suddenly a long way from my thoughts.

There is a saying, "Boys will be boys", and I doubt very much if there will ever be an absence of mischief when you put a bunch of blokes together, no matter their ages. Twenty minutes before lunch on the first day of the game one of the local officials shook me on the shoulder and told me, "You'd better see to those lunch orders." I was about to be the victim of a team practical joke.

The NSW boys had 'geed-up' the local to take advantage of the new boy.

So, after asking the obvious question and getting the answer that the caterers needed to know every player's diet, I duly dashed onto the field at the end of an over and said, "Orders please, fellas!"

I ran back and told the caterers, "Six fish, five steaks; and I'll have a steak." When they looked at me blankly I knew why my teammates in the middle had told me to "Piss off!", and why the local official was laughing himself silly.

GETTING HUNGRY

The summer of 1976–77 was near. At the end of the previous summer, for the first time that I could remember, I hadn't announced "Gee, it'll be good to get into the baseball." I played, but I couldn't wait for the next cricket season. I had developed a hate for getting out. We played Balmain, a club steeped in cricket tradition. The great batsman Archie Jackson had played there, and so had that legspinner and great character Arthur Mailey. I made 142 with 25 fours and two sixes. Then I made 139 against Randwick.

It was the summer that Australia played three Tests against Pakistan, then toured New Zealand for two Tests. Because some of those Tests clashed with NSW games, and we had such players as Ian Davis, Alan Turner, Rick McCosker and Doug Walters, I knew in my bones my success had to give me a chance of making the NSW team to play Queensland mid-season.

I waited by the radio, tuned into the ABC sports show that used to come on every evening at 6.30: "The New South Wales team is, D. Colley, captain, A. Border ... " Not bad, two Mosman boys first names out of the hat!

My debut Shield game was at the Sydney Cricket Ground and I only made 36, but we won by an innings, Peter Toohey making a century and David Hourn bamboozling eight Queensland batsmen. I played another three matches, my best being a 68 against Western Australia in the second innings. But it wasn't enough to save us from a defeat. In the first innings I was a Terry Alderman victim—not leg before, but the next worst thing, caught behind!

I had developed an aggressive streak, a bit along the lines of "an eye for an eye"; I used to field in the slips for Mosman, alongside Barry Knight, the first slip. In those days Mosman had an offspin bowler named John MacKenzie, who wore spectacles, and batted at No. 11.

Mosman were playing Bankstown and we were 9/90, even so Jeff Thomson, in those days keen to never let a chance go by to prove he was capable of gaining some lift out of a pitch, almost beheaded MacKenzie.

This prompted Barry Knight to declare the innings closed, and me, standing beside him in the slips when we fielded, to constantly remind him that we'd copped a squillion bouncers, and ask why we weren't reciprocating.

When Thommo came in to bat, Barry grabbed the ball, marked out a run about nine metres longer than normal, called out to Thommo "How are you hooking?" and steamed in.

The all-new run-in caused Barry to lose his stride and he finished up delivering the ball from about 14 metres to an increasingly wide-eyed Thommo.

I was hungry to do well; I'd started a solid training regime. Monday was work only, but Tuesday I practised at the SCG with the State squad, Wednesday was a training run and baseball practice to sharpen my eye reflex, Thursday cricket practice, Friday night baseball, Saturday cricket match, Sunday a match or invitation baseball.

I finished the summer as Mosman's best batsman and Barry said, "Why don't you go play in England in the off-season and polish your game a bit?"

Playing for Metropolitan at the SCG in 1976.

Chapter Two

PASSPORT TO SUCCESS

My improved form meant I could rub shoulders with some 'big names',
Dennis Lillee, Greg Chappell, Rod Marsh and Kim Hughes.

The 'Great Aussie Dream' is often acknowledged in terms of bricks and mortar, owning a home. But when I was growing up there was another priority on just about every young Aussie's wish-list: the overseas trip. Mine was a time of dramatic change in my cricketing fortunes and my life.

A ROUGH PASSAGE

New Year's Eve, January 31, 1974 turned out to be one of those 'dates to remember'. In the first place I received a surprise invitation to the traditional party at the Hiscox residence.

Why was it a surprise? Well, yes, Jane Hiscox and I were mates going back a long way, but she had started to drift away from the cricket and baseball scenes, and had started dating; she and I didn't often bob up at the same place at the same time.

So, how did it come to be that I received what in fact was sort of a 'special request' invitation? During my working stint with BP I had become friendly with a married couple who were also acquaintances of Jane. Jane had invited this couple to her New Year's fling, and because they hadn't seen me for a while they asked Jane if she'd mind inviting Allan Border along, too. "You're good mates from way back, and we'd like to touch base with him."

I saw in the New Year in a tangle of arms and legs, with the wife of the BP couple, on the dance floor—but in the fallen over state, not the strictly ballroom state. I'd had a few drinks, but what the hell, I was 19, single and life was a ball.

Before the night was over, in a more conservative pose than the one I'd assumed at midnight during the singing of 'Auld Lang Syne', my friends from BP took me aside for a bit of chit-chat, and at the end they mentioned, "You know Allan, you and Jane get on so well, you really should go out together a bit."

A lot has happened in the years since that party at Jane's, but every now and again the thought occurs to me that just maybe my friends from BP had been on a match-making expedition that night!

I did ask Jane out, a couple of weeks later. I'd had a long-standing invitation to a mate's wedding, and it turned out to be an unforgettable first date. In fact Jane still mentions it now and again, just to be mischievous, I think.

We arrived at the reception, and you know how it is, you shake a few hands, say a few congratulations, have a few drinks, then you search the tables for your name card. I set off, with Jane beside me … "Here we are—'Allan'," I said to Jane, who was just at my left shoulder. As my gaze shifted across to the next name card I suddenly got that clammy, sinking feeling. I could see Jane reading her place card. It said "Louise". I thought 'Shit a brick!' Jane said, through slightly clenched teeth, "Who's Louise, Allan?" I had forgotten to tell the bride's parents that New Year had been a turning point in my life.

Things blossomed from there, testimony I guess to the adage that true love never runs smooth. It wasn't too long afterwards that I started to seriously think about going to England to play cricket.

I loved the game, there was no doubt about that, and it seemed only sensible that if I could do something I loved and get paid for doing it, then that was the

*Time for a change; in 1977 I decided to quit my job
and head overseas to play cricket.*

way to go. But it was a big decision, and took a lot of weighing up of the opportunities against the disadvantages before I announced to Mum and Dad, "I'm going."

I said to Jane, "How'd you like to come to England with me for a year?" which is a fairly stunning conversation-opener. I think she was a bit taken aback, and maybe not all that keen. She'd never really thought too much about going overseas, especially as a single woman of 20, with a bloke a year older whose only promise was to play as much cricket as he could. But in the end she decided she might as well have a go, and our parents were tremendously supportive. My mum and dad said, "You're doing the right thing—if you don't go you'll die wondering."

So, Jane and I started to watch the pennies; we didn't go to the movies, and any nights out were with The Sexy Six at the pancakes and steak place. Jane did a secretarial course, and together we foot-slogged around Mosman delivering the local paper.

Why it wasn't snowing that bitter day in March 1977 that Jane and I arrived at London's Heathrow airport only God knows, because it was cold enough to freeze a can of XXXX. The good news was that Jane had arranged for an old schoolfriend of hers to meet us, and this schoolfriend was driving her father's Mercedes Benz, in the weather circumstances something as close to heaven as I'm ever likely to experience.

Six months later Jane had done some secretarial work for a pittance, hadn't seen a lot of me, and was frustrated with her lot. We were young, and we didn't foresee the ramifications of the differing expectations we held for our England experience. By the time we came home to Australia our romance was rocky.

But I'd played a lot of cricket and on that side of things I was as happy as a pig in mud. I consider the experience of playing on softer pitches, where the ball comes onto the bat slower, and moves slightly more off the seam, was invaluable and it went a long way towards moulding my future batting style.

THE BARLEY MOW

One of the NSW selectors at the time I made my Sheffield Shield debut was Brian Taber, a former NSW captain and Australia's wicketkeeper during the late 60s. It was about the time of the 1977 Melbourne Centenary Test when I had told 'Tabsy' I was keen to play some cricket in England.

He arranged, during that Test, to look up a friend of his, Frank Twiselton, who was the chairman of Gloucestershire County Cricket Club.

Tabsy said, "I know Frank pretty well and I'm sure if he can help you AB, then he will. Frank is a great bloke, although I have to tell you he is also a very, very funny man." He then told me this story.

When Tabsy had gone to England on Ian Chappell's 1972 tour as second 'keeper to Rod Marsh, he met Frank early in the tour during a few drinks after the Australian's match against Gloucestershire.

Quite a long way into what Tabsy remembers as a very good evening, Frank, after a lot of urging from just about everyone, agreed to do his 'party piece', a performance of a song called 'The Barley Mow'.

There were 19 verses to 'The Barley Mow', plus a chorus that four of Frank's mates attempted to sing; while his mates did the chorus at the end of each verse, Frank had to drink, in stages, a pint glass of beer and a half pint, aiming to finish the beer after the last verse.

Of course, Frank's rate of progress depended not only on his staying power, but on just how fast his chorus sang their lines!

'The Barley Mow' goes like this:

> *Now here's good health to the customers, down at The Barley Mow. Oh, there's Us; the Landlord; Barmaid; Sea; the River; the Pond; the Vat; the Hogshead (54 gals.); the Barrel (36); the Kil (18); the Firk (9); the Pin (4 1/2); the Four Gallon; Two Gallon; Gallon; Half Gallon; the Quart; the Pint; the Half-pint and Iddley, Addley, Aye.*

(It will come as a shock to Frank that I remember the words!)

Then, after each verse—*Oh, there's Us, the landlord*, for example—followed the chorus: *And here's good health, good health, good health to The Barley Mow.*

According to Tabsy, Frank sang—and did his drinking to—'The Barley Mow' whilst standing on a chair.

So impressed was Greg Chappell that he asked Frank for a copy of the words and vowed that by the end of the tour he would not only have memorised 'The Barley Mow', but he'd be able to perform it.

Australia House, in London's Strand, threw the end-of-tour party for that 1972 Australian team, and a confident Greg Chappell invited Frank to join the team afterwards at their hotel, the Waldorf nearby, for a "Barley Mow Challenge".

It was no contest; Frank showed the way, but Chappell and Paul Sheahan, although they tried late into the night, failed. In fact, so late did the challenge go on the Australian manager, Ray Steele, became a little fidgety—there was a game the next day, a one-day finale to the tour.

Steele said to Tabsy, "Hey Brian, this Twiselton fellow … he's not on some sort of sabotage mission on behalf of English cricket is he? He's keeping my boys drinking when they ought to be in bed."

So it wasn't long after that Frank made for home, but no sooner had he got one leg into a waiting London taxi, than Chappell and Sheahan appeared on the team balcony, shouting into the Strand below, "Hey Frank, what comes after the Hogshead?"

Frank Twiselton, right, sets himself for a tilt at 'The Barley Mow'.

Well, naturally Frank paid off the cabbie and came back upstairs, where he wasn't exactly welcomed with open arms by Ray Steele. Chappell and Sheahan though, were clearly delighted to once again be able to discuss the Hogshead.

The next day Australia won the game, Chappell and Sheahan put on a hundred or more together, and Chappell was named the Man Of The Match.

Frank Twiselton came to the match, and while Chappell and Sheahan were thrashing the bowling at will, he confided to Tabsy, "Brian, it occurs to me that if I had been on an Aussie sabotage mission then I certainly haven't done the England cause much good at all!"

When Jane and I arrived in London on that bitterly cold morning I had in my overcoat pocket, courtesy of Brian Taber, Frank Twiselton's telephone number. When I called he answered with, "Yes Allan, welcome to England. Brian Taber has told me all about you. Come on down to Gloucestershire and we'll get you some cricket."

IN THE FOOTSTEPS OF W G GRACE

Frank Twiselton was as good-humoured and as good-natured as Brian Taber had led me to believe. One evening after I'd been at Gloucester a while, Frank and I were sitting, chewing the fat and swapping a few cricket yarns.

He told me about his role as 'safari organiser' the year before, 1976, during the goodwill visit to South Africa by Richie Benaud's Wanderers team. Frank was the assistant manager, and half the team were Aussies, among them Greg Chappell, who still hadn't mastered 'The Barley Mow', and Ashley Mallett.

Frank, and most of the boys, had decided it would be a good idea to go on a drive through the local game park to see first-hand the wildlife, the lions, the elephants and so on. According to the locals the best time for this was first thing in the morning, feeding time. Frank appointed Mallett official cameraman, and one of his first jobs was to videotape Frank and the game park warden perched in the back of a truck, partly caged, driving around hurling out chunks of meat to attract the game.

Frank thought what followed was pretty funny: "Ashley was able to record first-hand, if a little blurred, the exact moment a cheetah leapt into the back of the bloody truck, landed on my foot, grabbed a hunk of meat, and jumped out again." He added, "We had had a few drinks up until dawn, me and the lads."

Frank fixed me up with a spot in the Gloucester Second team, expenses included. In the one game I played with the top team, against Oxford University, I made 15 not out. That was a sort of second-class match and Gloucester's overseas players, Mike Procter, the South African, and Pakistan's Zaheer Abbas, were rested. It was a privilege to get to know 'Proccy' during that season and to watch him play. His bowling was awesome. Kepler Wessels later told me about facing Proccy once in a Currie Cup game.

"I thought all my nightmares had come at once," he lamented. Proccy was such a legend the English fans called Gloucestershire 'Proctershire'. I've bumped into him since a few times, always recognisable by the unbreakable headlock he applies, and the typical, gutteral South African "Guess who?"

There was a lot of cricket tradition at Gloucestershire; the County's two favourite sons were Wally Hammond and W G Grace. In fact, Frank got me games during the summer at Downend, where W G Grace played his young cricket, about four miles outside Bristol. WG's house overlooked the ground, somewhat like 'Omaha' did Mosman Oval. The cricket wasn't too hard for me at Downend, several standards lower than I'd been playing in Sydney, and I scored over 500 runs with a century in my last match, against Long Ashton. But it was great fun and the team spirit was terrific.

Playing such a diverse range of cricket, from County seconds, to Club to Benefit matches, meant a lot of travel, and that meant an exercise in car buying. The owner of the house, where we had the top storey to ourselves, in Bristol, said he knew of a bloke who was keen to sell a good second-hand "motor", as they call a car in England.

It turned out this car was a Hillman Minx, 1959 model, and therefore definitely second-hand; it could have even been fifth-hand, because it broke down just as I was about to turn the corner into our street. I got into a minor flap because I had to head off to a match; Jane wasn't impressed by the breakdown. "I'll fix this," she said, "because there's just no way you can buy a car and it breaks down straightaway. I'll go and see these fellows you got it from."

Our 'landlord' Tom, who had taken me along to do the deal, said, "No, I don't think you really want to do that." Jane said, "Yes I do."

I had to go to the game. When I came back that night the car was out the front of the house. I said to Jane, "Went okay with the car, eh?"

She explained: "Tom dropped me at the top of a laneway"—I remembered it well!—"I went down the laneway and saw the fellows; they were 'backyard boys', Allan, with very large hands"—I remembered them well, too!

She continued: "I said to one of them, 'Excuse me, but that car you sold my boyfriend for seventy-five pounds this morning, it's broken down.' They looked at me, then said, 'Well?'"

Jane had to pay another 15 quid to get it fixed and it went like a beauty for the rest of the time. It lived on oil; in fact it took more oil than it did petrol.

My six months at Gloucester were among the happiest times of my cricketing life. And I still see Frank whenever I go to England. He once said, "You know, I feel very proud to have played a small part in your early cricket, Allan; I only wish you'd been a bloody Englishman!"

I'm the one with the bushy beard, sitting, left. The Downend Cricket Club, 1977.

A WORLD OF DIFFERENCE

I was at Gloucester during the time of the Great Cricket Split, the controversial birth of World Series Cricket, when millionaire businessman Kerry Packer, owner of the Nine television network, signed up about three dozen of the world's top cricketers to take part in his breakaway games, in direct opposition to 'establishment', or official cricket's matches.

When I'd gone to England I'd left behind a tenuous spot in the NSW Sheffield Shield batting order. I was under no illusions about the fact that when I returned home, along with Greg Chappell's 1977 Ashes tourists, I'd be struggling to keep my spot with all the top players in town.

But suddenly, with the announcement of World Series, and rumours about player bans, all that changed. It promised to be a whole new ball game, and not just because the Packer players were talking about white balls and night cricket.

I returned and played a full Sheffield Shield season with NSW. Scoring 617 runs, I was the team's leading run-getter. They were intriguing times. The Cricket Board had lured Bob Simpson back to the game after a ten-year retirement, and he was captain of NSW, and also captained Australia.

As everyone knows 'Simmo' was famous for his running between the wickets, his ability to turn the strike over, and particularly for his taking of the sharpest of short singles.

NSW's first match of the season was in Perth against Western Australia and Simmo and I were trying to turn the ship around, with half the side out for less than a hundred.

He was on strike, when suddenly, tap … he pushed one towards Ric Charlesworth in the covers and gave it the 'running yes'. Ric, as well as being a talented left-hand batsman, was also a fleet-of-foot national hockey player.

Simmo seemed to have forgotten that, and he'd definitely forgotten his own age—41 years. It was a 20-metre nightmare getting home.

The next Australian winter I returned to England, this time as a professional for East Lancashire Club, in the popular Lancashire League. As The Pro I was expected to win every match more or less single-handedly, by scoring the most runs, taking the most wickets, and if a catch went up, no matter where it was, the others would call "Pro's … ".

I scored a record number of runs, but only took about 50 wickets, when I was told the 'norm' was about 100; I think my bowling got me the sack.

When I first arrived I decided to bowl 'Jeff Thomsons'—I was very keen on the old slinging delivery from behind the back. The surprise element soon wore off and it wasn't long before I was copping hidings. I switched to spin, which, when I think about it, I should have done from the very beginning.

In the middle of my stint with East Lancs there were games on successive days one weekend that will give you an idea of why I wasn't the perfect, winning Pro. On the Saturday we played Burnley and made 3/231. I got a hundred by hitting the last ball of the innings for six, generating much joy in the East Lancs camp, which all disappeared when we couldn't dislodge Burnley's last wicket pair, and we lost. On the Sunday I made 179 not out in our massive total of 4/290, but Rawtenstall won by an embarrassing seven-wicket margin.

I received a letter from the then NSW coach, Peter Spence, and was asked to fill in an enclosed questionnaire on my cricket talent. In the space marked "Occupation" I wrote "Professional Cricketer". I imagined the East Lancs management would probably have added, "Yes—but can't bowl."

England was a good learning experience; I was playing just about every day, and in conditions that could vary greatly from one day to the next—weather, pitches, ground size, opposition players. As The Pro there was a lot of pressure on me to do well; every game it was Pro versus Pro—and I was expected to win.

The next season in Australia, 1978–79, I reaped all the benefits of that English experience, playing a tough, uncompromising brand of cricket, concentrating like never before, and scored 775 runs for NSW in the Sheffield Shield, at an average of about 60.

I hit 135 against Western Australia in Perth, a Shield career-high, and my maiden first-class century. Next match, against Victoria on a real 'turner' at the SCG, I made 114, an innings that won me my Test spurs, in the Third Test against Brearley's Englishmen.

World Series Cricket, and the bans on the players, had opened the door for me; my ever-maturing approach to the game had allowed me to stick my foot in the opening.

Whether I could actually knock the door down depended on a couple of things: one, the peace agreement between the Cricket Board and World Series, which allowed the banned players back in the 1979–80 season for the series against the West Indies and England; and two, before that date with destiny I had two tours with Australian sides to prove my worth—the 1979 World Cup in England, and a tour to India.

When the big boys came back there was going to be quite a jostling for positions.

MY SWEET LADY JANE

I decided to walk to my wedding. April in Sydney, autumn, can be the most agreeable time of the year, clear blue skies, breezes that pluck the changing leaves from the trees and also wipe away the humidity—it's hard not to get that 'gee, it's great to be alive' feeling.

I walked to the church, about four or so blocks away from 'Omaha', with my best man and best mate, Marcus Sykes, and my groomsmen, my brother Johnno, and Mick Dodd, who had been one of The Sexy Six. Four young blokes in 'penguin suits' striding it out along the main streets of Mosman on a Saturday afternoon, keen to get to the church on time. There wasn't a cloud in the sky—what a way to go.

Jane and I were married in the Blessed Sacrament Church on April 12, 1980, a date you will recognise as not being in the cricket season.

In fact, I'd not been long back from a tour to Pakistan. What's more, when I think about it, because I was so involved in cricket about that time, Jane had to make all the wedding arrangements. I was in charge of the honeymoon.

The hiccup in our relationship at the end of our Gloucester experience had disappeared pretty quickly once we got back among our Mosman friends on our 'home patch', and Jane and I saw each other constantly.

I confess it was no whirlwind romance; of course, we indulged in all those delightful experiences that young couples who are fond of one another usually indulge in, but I was never conscious of thinking, 'Gee Allan, you'd better get engaged, you've been going out with Jane for a couple years.'

That part of it sort of snuck up on us both. On the eve of the Australian team's departure for England for the 1979 World Cup I had taken Jane to a send-off for one of the team, Andrew Hilditch.

Of course, there were a lot of people there, a lot of young couples, plenty of them married or about to be, plenty of parents, and, there was a fair bit of emotion; the "fond farewell", "good luck", "come home victorious", were the themes of the night. Anyway, afterwards, outside Jane's place, we were sitting in the old VW chatting, and having a kiss and a cuddle, and I popped the question. Out of the blue. Jane said yes.

I think I'd really meant to make a statement, something along the lines of, "… oh well, Jane, here I am off to England again … gee, I'm keen on you, be waiting for me and when I get back maybe we can tie the knot down the line …"

I suppose it was inevitable that we would tie the knot, Jane and I, and not just because we had got along so well together all our lives; Jane and I are perfect subjects for the pursuers of trivia. We were both born at St Moanan's Private Hospital in Mosman, where the midwife tied an unusual knot in the umbilical cords of the new-born. Ours are identical. Howzat!

Jane organised the wedding while I played in the World Cup, came home briefly before going to India, came home briefly before going to Pakistan. We didn't know it then, because my career was still developing, but Jane was already experiencing the absences that created the expression 'cricket widow'. And we weren't even married!

In the middle of this to-ing and fro-ing the dining table at 'Omaha' was, one night, the discussion table where Jane and I finalised the wedding plan. Jane had done a brilliant job.

Jane inquired, "Now, what about your department, the honeymoon?" Ah yes, the honeymoon.

Well, the truth was that cricket had been pretty much on my mind, and nothing else.

We'd been walloped in the World Cup, walloped in India and at home the West Indian quicks, mainly Joel Garner, had made my life a misery. We were about to go to Pakistan—all I knew was that it wasn't going to be any honeymoon, either!

I confessed, "Errr, I haven't done anything about the honeymoon."

Jane could see I had my mind on other things, and thoughtfully suggested a bit of motoring up and down the coast would do. That made me a bit snakey; I wanted our honeymoon to be something special, it was just that I hadn't got around to organising it.

In fact, I'd been selfish and I'd been found out; so I was determined to do something about it. I organised a fortnight in Hawaii, a few days on Maui, a few more on Oahu, the rest in Honolulu, staying in Hyatt luxury. I think Jane had convinced herself it was going to be a motel-up-the-coast affair, because her eyes certainly widened a bit when I said, "We're having the honeymoon in Hawaii."

One of the guests at my wedding was a gentleman named Ron McConnell, a prosperous motor dealer based in Brisbane. Twelve months earlier Ron had made me an offer: "Why don't you come up to Queensland and play your cricket?" It was an offer that prompted a counter-offer from NSW cricket—a job with Tony Greig's Lion Insurance. It was clear from the first day that the insurance industry and I were never going to be the perfect match.

Just before Jane and I left our reception Ron came across to wish us all the best, and added, "When you come back from your honeymoon I'll be in touch. I've got a new offer for you."

Ron was true to his word, and this time there was no haggling, no bartering. "You've got me," I told him.

By September of that year, 1980, Jane and I were travelling north. It was a big, big move. We were leaving a lot behind. Mosman had been our lives. We'd grown up there, our families and friends were all there.

Cricket was my job. I'd played with a great deal of success in Sydney; how would I go at the Gabba? Only time would tell.

Tying the knot with Jane.

Chapter Three

BANANA SKINS ...

Even photos take on an aura of sunshine when you move to Queensland!

Queensland, beautiful one day, perfect the next. That was a successful advertising slogan developed by the local tourism industry in the 80s. But for one reason or another it never applied to Queensland's quest for the Sheffield Shield. Glory has been enticingly within our grasp, then whisked away, sometimes farcically, often cruelly. I've loved every moment of my life in Queensland, but ...

IS THIS THE YEAR, ALLAN?

For as long as I've had anything to do with cricket the home ground of the Queensland Sheffield Shield team has been the Gabba. Which is a lot less of a mouthful than the ground's full name, The Woolloongabba; that was derived from the Aboriginal word 'wulonkoppa', 'wulon' meaning fight talk, 'koppa' meaning gathering place.

When I'm reminded of some of the Test match dramas that have unfolded at the Gabba over 60 or so summers, I'm sure it couldn't have been better named.

It's true that it was an ugly old place to call home: a dilapidated outer, a dog track around it, and grandstands that were classic reminders of the diverse thoughts of architectural community. But it had character, and I loved it for that. There was a real feel about the Gabba on a hot, steamy day, with a full house in, overflowing onto the dog track, wits at work (the crowd once released a pig with 'Botham' printed on one side and 'Eddie', as in Hemmings, on the other) and the old wooden scoreboard.

The Gabba is undergoing a facelift, lights, bigger arena—to cope with the demands of Australian Rules football—and new grandstands. That is long overdue, but cricket authorities seem to be running second to their football counterparts. Cricket may need to guard its leases on grounds a little more closely, or the day may come when ground availability at the start of the summer is limited.

Until hail interrupted play in the First Test between the West Indies and Australia in 1992, it was the famous Brisbane thunderstorm that generally played havoc with Gabba Test matches, because in the early days pitches were left uncovered. Wisden, cricket's 'bible', often started match summaries with "Brisbane provided its customary sticky pitch ..."

So it was when Australia played England in 1950: Australia batted first on a firm, dry pitch and made 228. The second day was a washout and play didn't begin again until 1 p.m. on the third day. England, batting on a thunderstorm-affected pitch, got to 7/68, and their captain, Freddie Brown, declared, forcing Australia to bat on the spiteful pitch.

With just over an hour to go to stumps Australia were 7/32 in their second innings, at which point their captain, Lindsay Hassett, declared.

At stumps England were 6/30. So 20 wickets had fallen after lunch for barely a hundred runs. Fortunately for batsmen pitches are covered these days.

It's good news for administrators, too, because balance sheets no longer go down the same drain as a day's play. It makes you wonder about the commonsense of those over in England who in 1990 were calling for uncovered pitches as a means of introducing excitement into County cricket.

I suppose the idea is to create a result via low scores—that's providing play ever gets underway!

Among the great games the Gabba has seen was the first ever tie in Test cricket, in 1960 between Australia and the West Indies, and Australia's last day battle with the West Indies in 1992 was a beauty, too. But sad to say none of the really great games has been a Sheffield Shield final.

For most Queenslanders that remains a dream, for a few it's a cynical obsession. From a player viewpoint I fear it's become a bit of a nightmare. Since I moved north in 1980 each ensuing summer I seem to hear more and more the question, "Is this the year, Allan?"

As the seasons unfold the 'knockers' come out of the woodwork. If someone happens to drop a catch they're onto it like a shot. And they can be a bit too fickle. If we win we're the greatest, if we get beaten we're rubbished. There doesn't seem to be any such thing any more as applause for being a good competitor. It's pretty cut-throat stuff.

The dream of hosting the final has inspired some mind-boggling forward planning. It has become a bit of a habit for Queensland to jump to a big early lead in the Shield, but fall away at the end.

The Cricketers' Club actually pre-arranged bookings for final functions in the mid-80s when Queensland had looked good early.

In the 1985–86 season Mark Gaskell, a former Queensland opening batsman, now a State selector and a sporting goods business proprietor, considered the 'Banana-benders' over the line. So he bought 10,000 mini-bats for autographs,

The Sheffield Shield. You won't find
any Queensland fingerprints on it.

The fickle Gabba weather turned on a hailstorm in the First Test against the West Indies in 1992.

which he planned to market with the signatures of Queensland's first victorious Sheffield Shield team. Queensland went belly-up and it took him five years to sell them—as he was selling the last few Queensland were once again being touted as Shield champions!

Of course, they are all well-meaning but in the end all it does is build up the pressure on the team to turn in perfect performances, and cricket just isn't the type of sport that allows consistent perfect performance.

The fans that my heart really goes out to are those like Bill Brown, who opened for Queensland and Australia during the Bradman years. Bill is 80, nature's gentleman, always immaculately attired, always smiling and always supportive. And there are other stalwarts who sit in their favourite spots, behind the bowler's arm at the Vulture Street end. I'm sure they live through the same heartache as the players when things go awry.

Like me they hope that one day Queensland will win the Sheffield Shield final. When we do I hope it's at the Gabba because it will be huge, just like the Queensland State Of Origin wins in Rugby League. Probably bigger, come to think of it!

ON THE ROAD, AND POTHOLES

The main reason Queensland jump to an early season lead in the Shield is 'home ground advantage'. It's when the team goes 'on the road'—play away—that the wheels come a bit loose. Early season games are played at the Gabba because the grounds in the southern States, South Australia, Victoria, Tasmania and NSW, are recovering from hard football use.

This is Queensland's record since the 1980 season:

	Played	Won	Lost	Drawn
At Home	64	26	8	30
Away	70	11	24	35

Our 'away' phobia became such a talking point that the team actually took a sports psychologist with them on one tour of the southern States. But it would be wrong to make too much of our lack of success away from the Gabba when discussing our failure to host a Shield final.

For instance, we have had a very high turnover of coaches and captains in recent seasons, a cricketing version of musical chairs. In the last five seasons Queensland have had three coaches—John Bell, Richie Robinson, Jeff Thomson—and five captains—myself, Greg Ritchie, Trevor Hohns, Carl Rackemann and Ian Healy. I suppose I can even add Dirk Wellham in there, seeing he took over from Healy when the 'keeper was on Test duty.

Queensland have had no end of imported players, myself included. They fall into two categories, locals like me and Greg Chappell, and overseas players like Viv Richards, Ian Botham, Kepler Wessels and Graeme Hick.

The make-up of the team has been subject to continual and quite massive change, particularly at the top, and I don't think that has really been a healthy situation.

The team changes seemed to intensify in line with the obsession with winning the Shield. From my point of view I thought it would have been better to replace the desire to "win it this season, or else!" with the more reasonable attitude of "let's build a team that will win down the line, not necessarily at its first attempt". That way we could identify talent in the first couple of seasons, get together the team we believe will do the job, then win the Shield.

Making Ian Healy captain in 1992 was a good move; he's Brisbane-born but played his youth cricket in a tough country men's competition. Some Queensland cricketers have an inferiority complex—is it any wonder?—and I think Healy is the man to rid them of that. He has a real belief in his ability to succeed, he's very tough, a good motivator and I think he'll pull players up to that level.

The other problem confronting Queensland cricket has been its love of turning promising young players into superheroes overnight. Some young bloke comes into the team, does okay in his first match, and next day in mile-high headlines he's being touted for the Test team.

I'd be the first to cheer the next time a young Queensland cricketer makes the Australian team, but until it happens I'd give just as big a cheer to hear someone in charge say, "This is Queensland's plan to win the Sheffield Shield in three years time."

CALLING IAN BOTHAM

When the 1987–88 season rolled around it was Ian Botham's turn to win the Shield for Queensland. Not only was there the general expectation that he would leave Shield challenges in ruins as he had Aussie Ashes challenges, but the Queensland cricket bosses and the sponsor, the Car Phone Group, hoped he'd put a few extra on the gate, too.

He did that—takings at the Gabba doubled.

I was relaxed about Botham joining the team; I'd first bumped him in an England versus NSW match about a decade before, found him tough on the field, but noted that he left it there and at the end of the day he was keen to have a beer and a chat with his opponents. I'd seen a fair bit of him on tours to England after that and we became good mates. His amazing walks for charity that raised huge money for leukaemia victims tended to take the sting out of a few larrikin acts he was accused of off the field.

The Botham that bounced out into the airport lounge at Brisbane in October, 1987, was just what you'd expect—extroverted and self-confident, telling anyone within earshot that he was still the best allrounder in the game and he intended to prove it during his stint with Queensland, which was just what the Queensland public wanted to hear.

But it wasn't long before Botham was feeling exactly the same sort of pressure every other Queensland cricketer has felt in the last few decades. Despite the huge success of the team in the first half of the summer 'Both' hadn't scored one of those vintage centuries full of sixes and slogs, nor had he managed a five-wicket haul.

This led to stories that he was not spending enough time in the nets because he was spending too much time on his favourite relaxation—fishing. And, it was mentioned again by the media that at the start of the season he had preferred to do an ad-promotion rather than go on a pre-season tour to New Zealand.

Someone asked, "Who's running the bloody show, Botham or the Queensland Cricket Association?"

But the team had no complaints and during a Shield match in November they

With Ian Botham during his stint at the Gabba. Cheers turned to 'tears'.

put on a party to celebrate his 32nd birthday. And Both once put on a barbecue for the team at his house and handed out presents—Glenn Trimble got a bat, and next summer hit a six with it in a grade match.

But in the latter part of the season a bit of the larrikin got in the way of team performance—at least that's the way I saw it.

Tasmania beat us outright in Launceston when a Queensland win would have meant we'd have hosted the Shield final for the first time. At the end of that game there was an incident involving Botham, Dennis Lillee, who had made a comeback with Tasmania, and the dreaded drink. That, and the terrible disappointment of the loss and its consequences—we now had to play WA in Perth in the final—provoked me to prohibit the team from drinking.

Maybe my timing was wrong, because we were, until then, a successful and happy-go-lucky team. But we'd gone off the boil.

Both treated the ban as a joke, and took all the steam out of my intended discipline by going on TV and saying, "Already I'm seeing pink spiders climbing the walls."

But that was small beer, pardon the pun, compared to what happened when we flew to Perth to contest the final.

TURBULENCE OVER THE NULLABOR

Queensland have played in six Sheffield Shield finals, all away from the Gabba, and all lost. We have taken on NSW at the SCG four times, and Western Australia in Perth twice.

The second tilt with Western Australia was in 1987–88. I didn't fly out of Brisbane with the team because I had to attend a Cricket Board meeting in Melbourne a day before.

The team flew to Perth via Melbourne and when I caught up with them at Tullamarine they were having a few drinks in the lounge. They seemed in good spirits, and good appetite; I didn't know it then but the pies and pasties that had been ordered to deal with the pangs of hunger were going to be the starting point of one of the lowest moments in my Queensland Shield career.

Apparently some of the blokes had been a bit messy in their eating habits and this had annoyed the Tullamarine staff, who summoned the Federal police. The airport is Commonwealth property, and therefore under Federal rather than State jurisdiction.

I was sitting on the fringe of the group listening to the latest *Twelfth Man* tape, uncensored, and at that stage knew nothing of the pie and pastie incident.

Our flight was duly called, we all filed on board, and Ian Botham, Greg Ritchie and I were seated in one row, Both in the aisle seat. Ritchie and I began discussing Greg's failure to gain a permanent spot in the Australian team. Botham kept interjecting, telling us to "give it a break". This got under my collar a bit, because it was an important conversation—Ritchie's continued omission from the team was creating a lot of comment, particularly in Queensland.

One thing led to another, led to Botham and I raising our voices at each other, led to a passenger turning around and demanding that Botham keep his voice down and his language moderate. That led to Both over-reacting, telling the passenger to mind his own business and physically urging him to keep his eyes straight ahead.

Suddenly things were totally out of hand, yet by the time we landed Botham had apologised to the passenger and I felt it had been accepted. But as we left the plane the Federal police met us—acting on the Tullamarine pie and pasties incident.

Next thing, Botham was being taken away to the Perth City Watchhouse. The rest of the team, stunned, was at the Merlin Hotel, and the Sheffield Shield final was just around the corner.

It was a 'heady' type situation. Botham, charged with assault, has to be bailed. The police ask Greg Ritchie to make a statement; they ask me, too. The team manager, former Queensland opening batsman 'Sugar' Ray Reynolds, raises the $5000 bail for Botham's release, but then he's told, "Sorry sir, bail can only be lodged by a resident of the State."

So, we ring Dennis Lillee. Lillee arrives at the lock-up with a six-pack of beer, and announces, "I thought you blokes might be thirsty."

Things got worse. While I was watching Lillee fill in the official papers for Botham's release on bail, two blokes came through from the lock-up, one of them drunk, the other clearly the 'Good Samaritan' bailing him out.

The drunk grabbed his mate's other arm when he laid eyes on Dennis, then he saw me …

"Jeesh, I've jusht sheen Ian Botham inshide, now here'sh Dennish Lillee—and Allan bloody Border, too! It'sh the greatesht night of my life!"

I'm just sitting there, thinking 'Oh Christ.'

Back at the Merlin we had a team meeting. Botham told me he was sorry, I told him I was sorry. We were all sorry. We resolved to forget everything and set our minds on winning the final.

CRASH LANDING

That ill-fated flight from Melbourne had landed in Perth about 8 o'clock in the evening of Tuesday, March 15, 1988. The Sheffield Shield final was to start on the Friday, and our idea was to give ourselves two full days of hard practice to get the edge on our game.

We practised on the Wednesday morning, but it was very tough getting the players' minds on the job—the media people were swarming, and they weren't too interested in players' form or captain's tactics, they just wanted to know what the latest was on what they had already tagged 'The Botham Incident'.

It was that Wednesday afternoon that the Federal police teed up a meeting with manager Ray Reynolds, Botham and myself in a room at the Merlin. From there we were taken to the Sheraton hotel, where the police had an office, to make our statements. By evening Botham had been charged and it was about 10 p.m. by the time we'd found Lillee and bailed him out.

The next day, our second day of 'hard' practice, Botham had to appear in court, where he faced three charges, his bail was reduced to $3000, and he was bound over for a hearing on the day after the Shield final was scheduled to finish. Ritchie was under investigation for offensive behaviour, and I had been accused of uttering an audible obscenity.

It was a nightmare.

Greg Ritchie was totally distraught. He kept saying, over and over again, "I'm not guilty." He didn't want to play in the final, he just wanted to go back home. I don't think anyone was as emotional about the episode as Ritchie, but then again I don't think anyone was really in the right frame of mind to play a

Sheffield Shield final, either.

So in the circumstances I was amazed we played as well as we did. For instance, during the match, at the breaks in play such as lunch and tea, the Federal police requested that players go to the viewing room to be questioned. This led to a frustrating situation at the end of a day's play; when we'd all be sitting around with a beer and the West Australians would be asking, "Hey, what's the latest? Anyone else been arrested? What's it like in the City Watchhouse ... ha, ha, ha?"

It was total chaos.

We were sent in to bat and made 289, Ritchie 33, Border 66; but at one stage we had been 4/234—ah, what might have been!

And such was the case when we had Western Australia on the ropes at 5/189, but Graeme Wood and Wayne Andrews put on 136 and they finished with 344, a lead of 55 runs. Carl Rackemann's 5/69 off 30 overs was a magnificent, and big-hearted, effort.

At stumps on the third day we had slumped to 4/58, an overall lead of just three runs. You'd have to ask who writes the scripts for Queensland cricket because the two men on whose shoulders rested any hope we had of winning the final, the two not out batsmen, were Ritchie, and—you guessed it—Ian Botham.

Next morning Greg Ritchie padded up to one from Terry Alderman and was leg before without playing a shot for 34, and Botham made his seventh half-century of the summer. We made 216, leaving WA to make 162 to win. At stumps they were 0/71.

First thing on the final morning WA plunged to 3/81 giving us just a sniff of possible victory, a feeling of "Come on fellas, we can still do it!"

But in the end they won by five wickets.

After it was all over their captain Graeme Wood didn't miss us. When he was asked about preparing for a Shield final, he said, "Good discipline. We'd be doing our warm-ups all together, and look across at them and some would be in the nets, some off doing something else."

I thought, 'Yeah Graeme, and you could even have mentioned some of us off being interviewed by the police!'

The day after the final, before we got the noon flight home, Botham appeared in court and was fined $300 for offensive behaviour and $500 for the assault on the passenger. Later the Cricket Board fined him $5000 over the incident on the plane and the fracas in Launceston.

Then Queensland Cricket cut his three-year contract, which was purportedly worth about $200,000.

Of course, the media were hammering on my door wanting to know my feelings about all this. I declined. My cricket season had ended on March 22, and it had been without a doubt my blackest.

ENTER THE PSYCHOLOGIST

The season after the Botham trauma Queensland decided to appoint a new coach. The cynics came leaping out of the woodwork and 'Queensland Coach' jokes took over from 'Irish' jokes; only candidates into self-flagellation need apply, said the cynics.

There were two front-runners for the job, and by a strange coincidence both of them had been wicketkeepers in their careers. They were John Bell and Richie Robinson.

Bell was relatively unknown outside of Queensland, and although he had played a little Sheffield Shield cricket with Queensland, mostly he'd been in the ample shadow of John Maclean, Queensland's 'keeper in the late 70s. Nevertheless, he was highly regarded as a coach because he had guided three different Brisbane A-grade teams to premierships, and he had applied for the Australian coaching job. The word was he got down to the last three.

He was a squat build, like most 'keepers, and had a tough competitive streak; those who had been coached by him regarded him as strong on motivational techniques, intense about discipline, and keen to see fundamentals applied.

Robinson played Sheffield Shield for Victoria and toured England with Australia in 1975 under Ian Chappell and in 1977 under Greg Chappell. Then he played with Kerry Packer's World Series Cricket breakaway. He was unusually tall for a 'keeper, and actually made his reputation more as a batsman. He had been coaching on the Gold Coast with success, and had a reputation as something of a 'clipboard coach'—plenty of statistics and charts to keep abreast of the game.

Robinson had the personal backing of Greg Chappell, and that was seen as a strong boost to his chances given the more or less god-like status Greg enjoyed among Queensland's cricketers.

Apparently that didn't extend to some administrators, because Bell got the nod, despite a recommendation from the Queensland Cricket Association's finance committee that the job should go to Robinson. Whether Greg saw the result as a slap in the face personally I don't know, but not long after that he resigned from all administrative posts in Queensland cricket, and also quit as Queensland's representative on the Australian selection panel.

Talk about drama! And don't forget all this was happening not long after the Botham affair. The word "controversy" was never to be far removed from John Bell's name as the season unfolded.

Chappell revealed his reasons for backing Robinson ahead of Bell: Bell had done good things at club level, but he doubted his capacity to enthuse players at top level, something he was sure Robinson could do. That prompted speculation that Bell would be carrying a bit of lead in his saddlebags, because Chappell's opinions carried so much weight with the players.

One of Bell's first moves as coach was to give me a new vice-captain: Greg Ritchie took over from Robbie Kerr, a move that effectively gave Greg the captaincy, because I was to be away a lot on Australian duty.

Bell quite properly took a tough stance on team discipline, especially in fitness drills. Those who were found guilty of not putting in got the 'treatment', a penalty in the form of extra drills. That sounded okay in theory, but in practice it got the blokes' backs up: making the players do extra laps, often with their arms stretched above their heads, had a feel of the schoolmaster to it, sending the bad boys to the corner.

Bell invited a psychologist, Betty Hedley, to talk to the team about motivation, self-motivation, goal-setting and how to get mentally strong for the season ahead. There was even speculation she had been brought in to counsel players who had been overwhelmed by the Botham incident! The move broke new ground, and there were many in the team who were a bit skeptical about it.

And, of course, the media were feeding on this, having an absolute field day; and they were being helped to no end by disaffected players and rumour. One player had told a writer, "Would you believe Bell's got us practising running between the wickets—it's schoolboy stuff." I know that because the writer came to me looking for a comment! Well, I certainly didn't see anything wrong with refining the fundamentals of our game; you can't beat getting the basics right.

I suppose it was inevitable that on our visit to Perth that summer, almost a year since the Botham incident, there would be some new controversy.

During a tea interval a cricket writer approached me: "Got a minute, AB? I've just had a call from Brisbane to say there's a story doing the rounds that nineteen members of the Sheffield Shield squad have signed a petition demanding Bell be sacked."

I thought, 'This is like a snowball rolling down a bloody mountainside.'

I looked around the room and saw Dirk Tazelaar, Trevor Hohns and Carl Rackemann. I said, "Does anyone here know anything about a list of names on a petition?"

Carl Rackemann said, "Yeah, I know about a list of names. I drew one up a few weeks ago ... to check who'd paid their Gold Lotto."

Incredible though it may seem, through all that we still had a chance to make the Sheffield Shield final when we played NSW in the last match of the summer at the SCG.

Set 270 runs to win in our last innings we went so brilliantly that, with two wickets in hand—one of them Ian Healy—we needed only 21 runs off the last 24 balls.

Maybe we panicked, maybe it was just great bowling from Steve Waugh and Peter Taylor, who thrived in such situations, but the bottom line was we left ourselves in the position of needing a boundary off the last ball.

The loss left us equal second with South Australia, but out of the final on percentages. A win? Well, John Bell probably said it all: "Frankly we consider we were only four runs away from winning the Sheffield Shield in Brisbane."

Bell's heart was definitely in the right place, although I sometimes doubted the wisdom of some of his methods. But let's face it, no two coaches are alike. A couple of months later, almost a year to the day that he got the coaching job, John Bell lost it.

And, in yet another of those strange twists for which Queensland cricket has become famous, his replacement was Richie Robinson.

PUNCTURES AND BLOWOUTS

Fast bowler Carl Rackemann is one of Queensland cricket's favourite sons, a gentle giant. But physically he's a half-and-half—you look him over and think wow! then uh-oh! From the waist up he's magnificently built, strong in the shoulders and torso, thick arms. From the waist down he's skinny, totally out of sync with the upper part of his body; chicken legs.

For Carl, that physique, and his violently twisting bowling action, has meant a lot of injuries over his career. When he delivers the ball, his left foot, the front one, points down the pitch towards first slip; his right foot twists backwards, pointing at mid-on—an angle at the groin of about 120 degrees. Try it for yourself, slowly, and see how much stress is imparted to the groin, knees and ankles. Once, before he pulled out of a game, Carl announced to me, "I've had a blowout, AB." I'd never heard the expression before, but it certainly sounded serious.

Generally when Carl had fitness problems they were monitored by Errol Alcott, the Australian team physio. Errol would ask, "Tell me Carl, how does the pain feel on a scale of one to ten … a seven, a five …?"

Carl would stretch and wince, before saying, "I don't know that I can give you a scale, Errol; it feels … well, like a harpoon going in."

The next day, after treatment, Errol would look for improvement still on the scale of one to ten: "How does it feel, Carl?" And Carl would smile, "Like a tack going in, Errol."

I don't think there's much doubt that Carl's susceptibility to injury cast doubt into the minds of the Australian selectors, who probably had visions of a 'blowout' occurring in the middle of a series-deciding Test match.

OPPOSITE: Fun on the job. After cricket a career with the brewery industry beckons.

They should have been there on the last gut-wrenching day of the 1985 Shield final when Queensland were trying to stop NSW winning the trophy for the 38th time.

I still get a bit of a shiver when I think back on the astonishing spell of bowling Carl turned in that day. NSW needed 220 runs to win, and started the day at 3/63. The SCG pitch didn't have so much as a breath of life in it, the weather was hot and humid. There were times that day when Carl seemed to have bowled us into a winning position: NSW were 5/100, later they were 8/175.

Through it all, especially in the last two sessions, I called on Carl for a superhuman effort, and he never once shirked it. He bowled for two and a half hours straight and in the spell took 4/34; his dehydration was such that he twice developed severe headaches and had to stop for tablets and water. But he wouldn't hear of giving up the ball.

He was near exhaustion when the NSW No. 11 batsman, Dave Gilbert, took the winning runs off the second ball of his 31st over of the innings. He finished with 6/54, an incredible performance, and I haven't seen too many better ones.

THE BOYS IN BLUE

At the end of November 1989, just a couple of months after all the Ashes euphoria, Ian Healy, Carl Rackemann and myself were loading our cricket gear bags and suit bags into a station wagon at Sydney airport.

We had jetted in from Perth, where we should have won the First Test against New Zealand to add to our euphoria, but instead had to settle for a draw when the Kiwis held on in their second innings for about two days.

We were on our way to the NSW steel town of Newcastle, north of Sydney, to play our oldest Sheffield Shield enemies, NSW. Rather than take a small commuter jet, we decided to drive, and I was at the wheel. We travelled the freeway, which whilst not offering scenery as spectacular as the old coastal Pacific Highway, has been brilliantly carved out of sandstone hills, and around Brooklyn the water views are sensational.

I have to admit, what with the water view and the inquest into our failure to skittle the Kiwis, I wasn't concentrating a hundred per cent on my driving.

Until we went past a radar speed trap. You know when you're in trouble because as you go past the guy operating it sort of points at you. I looked down and saw the needle was on 150 k/ph when it should have been on 110 k/ph. Stupid me.

Further along two police from a car parked off the road flagged us in, and approached. I was thinking, 'Oh, Christ, I'm gone here.'

They looked at me, then at the others, and one said to the other, "Oh, it's

Happy with my move to the Gabba.

Allan Border and the boys." His mate said, "Going a bit fast, AB."

I said, "Yes, I'm very sorry. We're going to Newcastle for a Shield game and I was pushing it a bit too hard. I am sorry."

They looked at one another then one said, "Just a minute, I think I'd better have a word with the 'Sarge' down on the machine," and went back to his two-way radio.

We overheard the conversation, loud, and very clear:

Policeman: Hey 'Sarge', you know that white Ford station wagon you just pulled over … ?

'Sarge' (voice crackling): Yeah, yeah—they were doing one fifty.

Policeman: Uhhh well, it's the Australian cricket captain Allan Border and two other Aussie cricketers. They're heading for a game in Newcastle. What would you like us to do?

'Sarge': I don't give a f— who it is. Book 'em.

Our arrival at the ground, and the subsequent re-telling of the story, prompted plenty of opinions about my lack of brainpower when I had a steering wheel in my hand. And a lone opinion, from a superstitious type, that it was just another example of the hex NSW had on Queensland cricketers.

I have to say I'm not an avid reader of cricket history, although I do stick my head into a Wisden now and again. But I was fascinated, in view of our misfortune against NSW in Sheffield Shield finals, to discover that Queensland's very first game in the Shield was against NSW.

Until Queensland wins a Shield final at the Gabba, the biggest day in the State's cricket history will remain May 7, 1926, the day Queensland was officially admitted into Shield ranks.

In that first match against NSW, over five days, Queensland had to score 400 in the last innings to win. At stumps on the third evening they were 1/13. And at stumps on the fourth evening they were 8/378.

So, with two wickets in hand they needed just 21 runs to win—sounds familiar!

On the last morning the ninth wicket fell at 381, then with nine runs needed the last wicket fell, to a run out.

Any cricket seer present that morning might have held his head in his hands and muttered, "I see similar black times ahead." We appeared to have fallen on our own sword, and there are plenty of cricket fans Australia-wide who maintain we still are doing just that.

Queensland's desire to win the Sheffield Shield was a strong influence on my thoughts about moving north from NSW. I had always had an 'edge' to my game—to do well personally—and I figured if I could maintain strong personal performance it would be to Queensland's advantage.

Moving to Queensland also gave me the chance to play alongside the great

Greg Chappell. One of the characteristics of cricket is that the players who make it to the top have very little between them technically. What distinguishes the champions from the also-rans is temperament. Players with strong temperaments know how to handle a crisis—every time one comes along, not just occasionally.

So, playing in the same team as a bloke like Greg, who by the time I moved north had been on the Test scene for a decade, was the icing on the cake for me. It was more than just practising together; there were hours spent in dressing rooms, having a quiet beer or two after games, when we'd talk about experiences on tours, incidents in certain matches, the dramas, the laughs. For me, it was a big part in my coming of age in the game. And, of course, if my form was good enough then the odds were I was going to spend a lot of time standing up the other end of the pitch watching him first-hand, running with him, and learning how to read a game as it unfolded.

My first Shield game with Queensland was a few weeks after I moved up from Sydney—and yes, it was against NSW! There were a few butterflies at the Gabba that day, all of them inside my stomach. I naturally wanted to show that the faith a lot of Queenslanders had shown in me wasn't misplaced. It was a challenge. It's not that I mind a challenge, but playing first up against the team that I had been accused, by some, of "deserting", well it was certainly a stern test of my temperament.

As you would expect, the home crowd was right on my side: "Good on yer, Al," and "You beauty, Al," and plenty of cheerful support. I got some special attention from my old NSW teammates, too. It was strange walking out to bat against blokes who, up until then, you'd spent all your career playing alongside.

Len Pascoe was at his peak about then. Len had a flying mane of jet black hair, had a run to the wicket like a bull that can see a china shop in the near distance, and loved bowling short.

It was different from facing him in the nets as a teammate, that's for sure.

I made 13. Naturally, I got a send-off from my old NSW teammates, which was totally expected. What stunned me a bit was the send-off the crowd gave me: "Go home, Border." Talk about fickle—when I scored a century in the second innings they gave me a standing ovation.

It took NSW fans a longer time to accept that I'd gone, and the viciousness of some of the remarks strained my relations with people off the field. It reached rock-bottom in a McDonald's Cup game when SCG fans tagged me a "traitor" and a "turncoat", embellished with no shortage of adjectives. It was rough stuff, nasty, and I didn't think I deserved it. At the end of the match I told the NSW players, when they came over to our room for a drink and a chat, "You can stick your bloody beer!"

Yes, an over-reaction, but I do have a habit of wearing the heart on the sleeve, as they say.

THE JAWS OF VICTORY

Jack Gibson was a Sydney rugby league coach in the 80s whose methods won him more than a few premierships, and plenty of accolades over a stack of Australian winters. Jack had a theory that you could learn the most about people when they were thrown out of gear, when they were under a bit of pressure. That gets back to the sporting saying about winners and losers separating themselves along narrow lines: one has the presence to walk tall, the other finds the banana skin.

And the most frustrating point to it all is that Queensland seem to find a totally different way of finding the banana skin, season upon season. In 1989–90 we knew if we beat Victoria outright in the second last game then we would host the final at the Gabba; our target to achieve that was 200 runs off 49 overs.

Came the last over and we needed seven runs, but eight wickets were down. Off the second last ball, our best hope of victory, Craig McDermott—he'd swiped 33 runs off 36 balls—was run out, making us 9/195.

So, we only needed five runs to win—a silly thought, because clearly it had to be a six off the last ball, or nothing. It was nothing. Under captain Greg Ritchie's orders last man Dirk Tazelaar opted for discretion ahead of valour, and blocked it.

Six-hits off the last ball of a match are pretty rare—I can only remember two, both in limited-overs, the first by West Indian Wayne Daniel at VFL Park off Mick Malone during the Packer World Series, and most recently when Steve Waugh went for six in a World Series match against Pakistan in Hobart.

Hitting out in the interstate one-day series.

*FAI Cup winners, 1989, but it would be nicer
holding the Sheffield Shield.*

Our miss meant we finished level on points with NSW, but they got the final because they had more outright wins. The great irony in our failure to host the final was that while we were being thrashed in Sydney, it rained cats and dogs at the Gabba—Queensland would have been assured of winning the Shield!

In the very next season, 1990–91, with our stocks boosted by our import Graeme Hick, the comeback by Trevor Hohns to captain the team, and a new coach in Jeff Thomson, the Victorian match at the end of the season brought us down yet again.

We had been set 192 to win outright. We made 79, and it was a case of 'From Gabba to Third'.

The 1991–92 season was the one where we set South Australia, not exactly the strongest team in the Shield that summer, 506 in their fourth innings to win—and they got them with six wickets down.

When these things happen someone will always say to me: "Hey AB, has it ever occurred to you that if you hadn't decided to leave New South Wales in 1980 by now you'd have played in four Shield-winning teams?"

I say, "Yes, but has it occurred to you that there are any number of New South Wales cricketers who can lay claim to that? No Queenslander can, yet. And I want to be there when it happens for the first time."

Chapter Four

JOB AT THE TOP

Captaincy, and one of its beautiful moments.

My first few years as captain of Australia were very tough going for a range of reasons, not the least of which was the controversial way in which I got the job. Now, after nine years at the top I can say the highs outweighed the lows by about ten to one. The captaincy was something I really enjoyed doing.

THE KIM HUGHES RESIGNATION

I played under three Test captains, Greg Chappell, Graham Yallop and Kim Hughes, and always tried to be supportive. I failed to do so only once, when I was the vice-captain to Kim on the Australian tour to Pakistan in 1982.

It was not a successful tour; we were whitewashed, beaten three-nil in the Tests and beaten two-nil in the one-day series, the final match of which was abandoned in clouds of tear gas when the crowd rioted and rained bottles and rocks onto the Karachi stadium.

My negative attitude on the tour had nothing at all to do with Kim, or his captaincy, but was provoked by my total lack of form—I scored a pathetic 84 runs in the Tests. Such a poor personal performance left me in no doubt that I was letting the side down, a situation that has always rested more uncomfortably with me than it might others. My moods were mostly black, I lost my sense of humour, and I regret to say I was not a good vice-captain.

Kim and I played some tough campaigns together, that Pakistan one being squeezed in between the 1981 Ashes debacle and the 1984 Caribbean blitzkrieg, none of them a place for faint hearts.

When Kim and I joined forces in the middle it often led to big partnerships, one of 222 against India in Madras, and I know we shared about five other century stands. Cricket gave us a chance to become really good mates, a friendship that blossomed about the time of the game's great split, establishment versus Packer cricket.

If the Packer World Series breakaway brought temporary instability to the game as everyone knew it, then the peace brought controversy, not just about which establishment players would join the World Series players in the new Test team, but also about the prospective captain.

The conjecture was the captain and vice-captain would come from three players, Greg Chappell, who had been Australian captain before Packer signed him, Kim Hughes, or Rod Marsh. Chappell got the nod, and Hughes.

It was the summer of 1979–80, and by the time Kim was finally dropped from the Australian side in the 1984–85 summer his career had seen plenty of highs and lows. I saw it all.

The captaincy question was to prove a fairly destabilising factor in the team during this period, mainly because there was a touch of 'musical chairs' about it. Greg missed the England 1981 and Pakistan 1982 tours because of personal and business reasons and Kim took over; suddenly the captaincy debate was reignited by claims that some of the senior players in the team didn't want Kim as captain. This produced a divided dressing room, with all sorts of undercurrents and dramas.

Kim's relationship with Dennis Lillee seemed to border on Cold War status.

At the time I couldn't really understand how that ill feeling had developed, but all these years on I've often thought it might have had something to do with Kim being made WA captain in the 1980–81 season over Rod Marsh, Dennis Lillee's great mate.

The tension got so bad that when Kim batted in the net at practice he'd cop the 'full catastrophe' from the bowlers, especially Dennis. I suppose it was a great contest, bat versus ball, but none of the rest of us had to cop it.

Of course, Kim saw it as a great challenge, this sort of Test match atmosphere in the nets; he's a cocky, confident bloke. I have no doubt he coveted the Australian captaincy, and wanted it because he was sure he could handle it. That confidence shone through in his batting in the middle.

Anybody who was at Lord's for the Centenary Test in 1980 would not soon forget his two outstanding innings of 117 and 84, but my memory of his best dig was an unbeaten, even century against the might of the West Indies in 1981, a magnificent lone hand.

Kim was what I call an 'adrenalin player'—when he got into the groove he'd go for it. Not quite a case of thinking the bowlers couldn't bowl, but sometimes he was inclined to play too many of the big shots at the wrong time. A lot of people thought there was too much adrenalin in his captaincy, too, that he should have been prepared to gamble less and think tactics through a bit more. Think to himself 'What if ...?' more.

Pakistan visited Australia in the summer of 1983–84 and before the season began Greg Chappell announced he was standing down as captain, because it was to be his last season as a player. The Cricket Board decided on Hughes as his successor but the word went around that the choice was not unanimous, a strange qualification which only intensified the controversy.

Kim, despite his self-confidence, couldn't have felt all that comfortable. Yet I'm sure he must have been relieved to have finally got the opportunity to show what he could do as a captain on his home ground, and with a team that was at full strength with the Big Three, Chappell, Lillee and Marsh.

Australia won the five-Test series two-nil, and on the way Greg Chappell passed Sir Donald Bradman's run-getting record in Tests, and Dennis Lillee and Rod Marsh each got their 350th Test victim. Marsh spent a lot of time up on the table that summer leading us in 'Underneath the Southern Cross I Stand', the team victory song.

Bradman's record was 6996 runs in 52 Tests; at the end of the Pakistan series I had scored 3968 Test runs in 56 Tests. It was to take me another 36 Tests to pass the great man. It had been a good series for me, with two centuries, an aggregate of 429, second to Graham Yallop's 554, and an average of 85.80.

Immediately after that series we left for the West Indies, but any confidence that might have been inspired by the Pakistan series win was discounted by the

At the Gabba in 1982 during the Ashes series. We weren't talking about the captaincy, but as it turned out we were all chances. From the left, Kim Hughes, me, Kepler Wessels, Rodney Marsh.

retirement of Chappell and Lillee, and the unavailability of Marsh and Yallop.

That was a bad starting point and the West Indies were waiting for us; a case of the lame rabbit blinded in the glare of the spotlight, and the hunter with both barrels cocked.

We copped the lot: Kepler Wessels came home early with a knee problem and his replacement, Graeme Wood, had a finger broken; it was the tour where the first whispers surfaced of a Rebel Australian tour to South Africa; we were beaten in the Tests three-nil, and three-one in the one-dayers.

The Caribbean certainly hadn't 'killed Kim with kindness'—on his previous tour, 1978, he'd been operated on for appendicitis. Now, in the face of this onslaught in 1984, we wondered over a beer one night if maybe there wasn't a little doll-like figure of him, with pins sticking out of it, lying around in some Caribbean hut.

On the eve of the Second Test, Australia, led by Kim, played a three-day match against Trinidad at a place called Guaracara Park, in the shadows of an oil refinery at Point-a-Pierre. It turned out to be a perfect venue, as you could say an explosive situation developed.

On the last day, Kim, eager for a batting challenge before the Test, suggested to his opposite that a declaration would be a good idea.

His opposite thought not, and Trinidad's last second innings wicket didn't fall until half an hour after tea, leaving Australia to get 189, and leaving Kim very bloody annoyed. His response was to open the batting, pat back long hops, full tosses and half volleys, and generally refuse to take even the easiest of runs. His batting partner, Wayne Phillips, at one stage sat on the ground while the bowler was delivering a ball to Kim. In the final over Phillips took his pads off and held them under his arm.

To Kim it was a protest, to the local authorities it was an insult. Team management fined Kim about $300.

That was a 'snap'. There's any number of sporting experts who'll tell you it shouldn't happen, but it does. The pressure can get to you. It got to Kim Hughes that afternoon, and it was to get to him again a few months later, only then with a tragic finality.

It seemed like we'd only been back in Australia five minutes before we were strapping on the pads and facing up to Clive Lloyd's 'flame-throwers' yet again. In fact the Fifth Test against them had finished in Jamaica in May, now we were playing the First Test of a new series in Perth in November. Talk about punishment! Jamaica had been a loss by ten wickets. Perth was a thrashing by an innings and 112 runs.

The Second Test, at the Gabba, finished in defeat—our fifth in succession against the West Indies. It was November 26. Kim Hughes, the captain, and Allan Border, the vice-captain, had been dismissed the evening before, Kim to one that kept low.

That final morning all either of us could do was sweat it out on the benches outside the dressing room and watch our team get nailed. At lunch we were in a hopeless position, still five runs behind overall and only two wickets standing.

As I rose to head off for the 'last supper', Kim said, "AB, like to talk to you for a minute ..."

He handed me a piece of paper, and said, "I'd like you to read this and tell me what you think."

It was his resignation as captain of Australia. I couldn't believe it. I told him I thought he was over-reacting. "It's not your fault ... the team is playing badly ... there's no problem with your captaincy ... the West Indies are a great team."

He went ahead anyway. "The constant speculation, criticism and innuendo from former players and sections of the media over the last four or five years have finally taken their toll," he said.

I had been there in 1979 when Kim first captained Australia, replacing Graham Yallop who was injured. Ironically, Kim spent most of the game off the field after treading on a ball at practice and spraining his ankle.

Five years on that must have seemed like a terrible omen. It was against that backdrop that I was to become the 38th captain of Australia.

With the captaincy came a new, bushier look.

TOP BANANA

In the months leading up to the arrival of Pakistan for the Test series in 1983–84 there were a lot of stories doing the rounds that Greg Chappell might step down as Australian captain. The most common theory advanced was that his on-again-off-again attitude to the captaincy was a disruptive force in the Australian team's performance. It was felt he should either be available all the time or hand over to someone who was.

Naturally such stories led to conjecture about just who that 'someone' should be; Rod Marsh's name popped up again, but was just as quickly discounted on the grounds that he'd have got the captaincy long ago if the Cricket Board had wanted him.

David Hookes was mentioned, but he'd been in hot water and fined over some public criticism he'd made of Kim Hughes as a captain. And there was Kim Hughes, the most logical successor, given the Board had used him as the stand-in for Chappell.

Then, in August, just before the season began, it was announced that Greg had decided to stand down as Queensland captain, and that I would take over.

It was not the cut-and-dried succession that many imagined. Kepler Wessels, who'd been vice-captain to Greg the previous summer, also had his hat in the ring for the job.

The "Border Queensland Captain" headline was followed not long after by Greg Chappell's decision to stand down as Australian captain; suddenly my name was added to the list of possible candidates for that job. I immediately thought to myself, 'Paper talk. Just not on.' Think about it: my only previous experience as a captain was at junior level, high school, when you don't do much more than write down the bowling order the night before the game and dream it will all work the next day. And my short stint as vice-captain of Australia in Pakistan was hardly the sort of reference to make the Australian selectors shout with glee, "Get AB on the phone!"

That's not to say someone didn't think I had leadership qualities—I had been a prefect throughout a fair bit of my schooling; or, did I get the prefect's job only because I was captain of the cricket team?

With the benefit of hindsight, a healthy respect for Greg Chappell's far-sighted thought processes on the game, and perhaps just a trace of rubbery mathematics (putting two and two together and coming up with five), I think maybe the talk in that Queensland selection room had been along the lines of, "What are the chances of the man we make Queensland captain one day being the captain of Australia?"

The choice was between Wessels and me. Chappell may have taken the attitude that I, the dinky-di Aussie, would have a better chance of getting the nod than Kepler Wessels, a South African who had adopted Australia so he could play Test cricket. And my form, apart from the disaster in Pakistan in 1982, had been remarkably consistent—heading for 4000 Test runs at an average of 40, so on the grounds of holding my spot in the team I was okay.

But, of course, the bottom line was I had to show some form as a captain, and the fact that I would have Greg looking over my shoulder when I took over the Queensland job was seen as a problem by some.

I wasn't worried, and I certainly didn't feel inhibited. Nor did I subscribe to the theory that Greg was a hard act to follow. I can't recall a time during the season when I looked sidelong at Greg and thought, "I wonder what he'd be doing now." And nor did Greg ever come up to me and say, "What about trying so-and-so …?"

Of course I bounced ideas off him—how silly would I have been not to? But there was nothing new in a captain doing that. Even now, after all the years in the job, I'm prepared to seek out another opinion. It's not the sort of thing you do every over or confusion is king. It's just making sure there's not a better assessment of the state of the game around.

Queensland had a big summer, winning enough games outright to play WA in the final at Perth, where Greg Chappell was captain because I was in the Caribbean with Kim Hughes's team. Along with me were a few other 'top bananas'.

A newspaper clipping arrived in the West Indies after the Shield final. It was of a photo taken during the game. It showed a sheet hanging on the fence at the WACA, and written on it was "No Rackemann, No Wessels, No Maguire, No Border, No Ritchie, No Hope Bananabenders."

We lost by just four wickets. It wasn't the first time I was going to think 'If only …' during my career as the captain of either Queensland, or Australia.

AN EVENING WITH SIR DONALD

While Kim Hughes was reading out his resignation as captain it dawned on me that I was 'Australian captain-elect', if for no other reason than I was the vice-captain. In the days following the phone was rarely quiet; the most popular question was, "What happened?" followed by the prophecy, "Well, you're the obvious choice, AB—you'll have to do it."

Well, with everyone from total strangers to best mates thinking that way, it was soon firmly fixed in my mind that 'this is going to happen'. It was a strange feeling, day after day, waiting for the official announcement. On the one hand I was excited, but on the other hand I was starting to think 'Oh no!' I reasoned, 'Maybe this is not the time to cop this job, Allan … two down in the series, we've just lost the skipper, and the media are using words like 'Australian rabble!' ' I'd seen Kim Hughes's demise. I thought, 'That's not for me. I'm really happy just playing. Very happy. I don't need that sort of drama.'

A few days after Kim's abdication Queensland were playing Tasmania in a Sheffield Shield match at Launceston. Greg Chappell was there in his new role in Australian cricket, a national selector, just one season after he'd retired as a player. He pulled me to one side and told me the Cricket Board had accepted the selectors' proposal that I become the new captain of Australia.

How did I feel? Well, I have been known to raise a fist in victory, but I guess I only gave a grin of satisfaction. It topped a few good 'days at the office'—I'd led Queensland to victory by an innings and 105 runs and I'd hit an unbeaten 114.

To tell you the truth I still had a few doubts about my new role in Australian cricket, which I suppose is an insight into my character, or at least the way I see myself.

It has never been in my personality to be overly forceful or overbearing with other people. That's not to say I lack determination, and I'd back myself to grit my teeth harder than the next bloke. But I like to be 'one of the boys'. That trait in my character was obvious as I made my way through the various stages of my cricket development. I had the idea that the captain was a tough guy, a Mr Big who had to be mean to get his message across. I wasn't like that and I worried that the blokes mightn't see me as a 'captain type', and therefore might not respond to my methods.

The media caught up with me at Melbourne's Tullamarine as I headed for Adelaide, and the questions came thick and fast.

"How will you change the direction of Australian cricket, Allan?"

"Where do you think Australian cricket is headed, Allan—and how fast?"

Some of them were casting doubt on our courage and I can remember making one point to them: "Look, if you put a baggy green cap on an Australian cricketer I can tell you he'll be giving a hundred per cent."

What I didn't bother to tell them was that I had a broken finger. During the Tasmania game a rising ball from a bowler named Brown had snapped the little finger on my right hand clean through. I may have had all those edgy thoughts about my debut as captain of Australia, but I sure wasn't going to miss it because of a sore little finger.

Like a good many people I get a little uncomfortable if I have to get to my feet at a large gathering and speak. Oratory is not one of my talents. So I was just a bit nervous about the team meeting on the eve of the Adelaide Test, and there were two reasons for that.

Naturally I would be expected to generate a bit of new feeling into my troops, a bit of steel into their souls. The other reason was that in the 'audience' would be a special guest, Sir Donald Bradman. We'd had a special guest at each of our team meetings—it was all kept pretty quiet, but was supposed to add that little extra edge. It just happened that Sir Don was invited to my first team meeting.

I was brief, and to the point: "We're in a helluva fix, the best way out of it is to pull together as a team." I just didn't feel right about making some long, motivational type speech—there was definitely a good 'feel' about the team, a strong resolve to do well.

Then Sir Donald rose to speak. There was an air of expectation among the players, one because it was such a unique occurrence, and two because we were all probably hoping for a few tips from the greatest batsman of all on just how to cope with the relentless West Indian pace attack.

He chose not to 'coach' us, rather he compared the 1980s tactics of the West Indies fastmen to the Bodyline Australia faced in the 1932–33 series against England. He acknowledged the difficulty of facing the West Indies—they

Talking cricket with Sir Donald.

My first challenge as captain was the toughest of all—head-to-head with the West Indies.

weren't bowling directly at the body, but their pace was more relentless. He offered encouragement only, which I thought was fair enough, after all what might have worked for Bradman's freakish 'eye' and reflexes might not have worked for us mere mortals.

Once the official part of the evening ended we had the opportunity to chat with Sir Donald, and naturally everyone was keen to get his ear.

Our opening batsmen for the Test were Graeme Wood and John Dyson. Dyson was very fastidious when it came to looking after his bat. You could always find him in a corner of the dressing room with the fine sandpaper, the scraper and an oily rag.

Bats were the subject Dyson chose to broach with Sir Donald: "What was the weight of the bat you used, Sir Donald?"

Sir Donald replied that he used bats weighing 2 lb 2 oz—incredibly light when compared to those used in modern times when most bats are as heavy as 2 lb 10 oz, even more.

Dyson: "Oh, and how long would a bat last you, Sir Donald?"

Sir Donald: "About one thousand, maybe fifteen hundred runs."

Dyson: "Oh, only a couple of weeks then …"

HEADS, TAILS AND HEADLINES

It would have been completely naive of me to have expected some sort of 'honeymoon period', one free of controversy or drama, when I took over as captain. But I was just a bit surprised that what I regarded as little things turned into big headlines.

I won my first toss in a Test at the Adelaide Oval on December 7, 1984, but we lost the Test; where I went wrong according to all the experts was that I sent the West Indies in to bat, then lost. Running through the opinions was more than a hint that it was a negative move on my part, that I was scared of another batting collapse.

Not true. I'd given it a lot of careful thought. The Adelaide pitch can give bowlers help on the first day and hadn't our bowlers had the early West Indies order on the ropes in the first two Tests?

Yes. In Perth they were 5/104, then recovered, and at the Gabba they were 5/184, then recovered. Why not see if we could go all the way this time?

As it was, even though we were never going to win the Test, we could have saved it—until between lunch and tea on the final day when we lost our last seven wickets for just 84 runs. I didn't know it then but batting crashes like that were going to haunt me to the point of nearly throwing in the captaincy, and not all that many Tests down the line.

There quickly followed a short, sharp education in the side of captaincy the public rarely sees—diplomacy. Feelings between the West Indies and Australian players had been running high for most of the summer.

Bit like a bushfire jumping a road; Geoff Lawson and Dessie Haynes had words at the Gabba, Kepler Wessels and Viv Richards and Jeff Dujon got a bit snarly in Adelaide, then in the Fourth Test at the Melbourne Cricket Ground Lawson and Gordon Greenidge locked horns.

Basically what happened was Lawson got Greenidge leg before then gave him a send-off, shooing him off like a park ranger might a kid who's disobeyed a 'Keep off the Grass' sign. The old point-to-the-pavilion trick, but with a lot more feeling. The upshot was Lawson was fined $2000, but $1500 was in the form of a good behaviour bond, so the actual fine was only $500.

I thought it was ridiculous, simply on the grounds that fast bowlers get carried away. I then made two mistakes: one, I said I thought team manager Bob Merriman's decision to fine Lawson was wrong, and two, I announced that the rest of the team would help 'Henry' pay his fine.

The team was not very happy—that was my third mistake, I hadn't asked them first if they'd like to reach into their 'kicks' and donate $40 to my 'Help Henry Fund'.

Even my first win as Australian captain, the Fifth Test of the series at the

SCG, seemed to have a certain hollowness about it. Not that it wasn't a wonderful victory, it's just that forces were at work to try to taint it.

Australia took the field with two new faces, Murray Bennett and Bob Holland, the NSW spin twins. Between them they took 15 of the 20 West Indies wickets to fall, and we won by an innings and 55 runs. It was Australia's first win over the West Indies in four years, and their first defeat by an innings for 17 years.

I was over the moon until the knockers got to work and started suggesting we'd fixed the pitch. Well, I've played on the SCG since I was in my late teens, and I've never known it not to take spin. In fact, three years on, it took enough spin for me to grab match figures of 11/96 in another Australian win. It's not the fact that the dry, brown SCG pitch spins that causes batsmen the trouble. It's the variation in that spin. One season it might be sharp spin, with bounce, other times it can be slow and low spin. In 1985 it was the former, in 1988, the latter.

A good few weeks later I was back at the SCG with Queensland for the Sheffield Shield final against NSW. I was filthy. I'd just come back to my hotel room after practice to find a thief had snitched my wallet.

The phone rang, and a jovial voice said, "Congratulations AB—another 'ton' up, mate."

It was a journalist wanting to talk about my first 100 days as Australian captain. Well, I'd been robbed ...

Certainly the results hadn't been anything to write home about, but I did feel there were some positive signs, that the players were showing a willingness to support me, and a fighting spirit.

But my lasting impression of those early days was that I, Allan Border, who a few months before had been just another Test cricketer, was now, as captain, being asked to go everywhere and had become everybody's best mate.

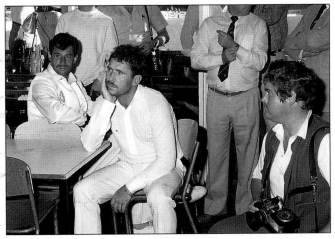

Not all that happy after being beaten by the Kiwis in 1985.
They were rough times.

PRINCESS DI AND THE MAHARAJAH

One of the thought-provoking sides of being the Australian cricket captain is being able to walk down a Brisbane street and have a total stranger come up to me and say "G'day", and six months later find myself shaking the hand of the Queen at Lord's. A couple of times I've even said "Good afternoon, ma'am," to Her Majesty over a cuppa at Buckingham Palace.

In Canberra, I have said "Cheers" over a beer with a prime minister, Bob Hawke, and in India I have burned the candle at both ends with a Maharajah.

When I'm relaxing white wine is not my favourite alcohol, beer is, and to be precise, XXXX beer. In India in 1986 there was no XXXX beer, and when I was offered a sample of the local brew I have to confess that I did say "No thanks." As I looked at it the thought crossed my mind that it could probably start a tractor.

On that tour we played a game at a place called Gwalior and after a day's play the team coach, Bob Simpson, the manager Alan Crompton, and myself, were invited out to the Maharajah of Gwalior's palace for dinner. The Maharajah was more a politician than a prince, in fact he was the minister for railways.

As palaces go this one wasn't only big in size, it was big on preservation of the tradition and lifestyle of bygone eras. Walking into the ballroom was like walking into a goldmine, so extensive was all the intricate gold leafing up in the ceilings and around the windows and doors. The place was thick with tiger skins. "Never shot a tiger in my life," said our host, noticing our interest. He explained they were all the work of his father and grandfather.

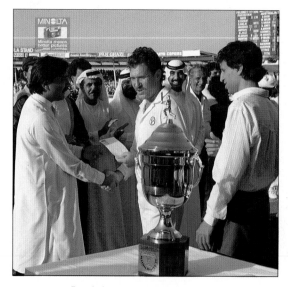

Receiving a testimonial cheque, Sharjah, 1990.

With Prime Minister Bob Hawke at the 1989 Ashes victory dinner.

Meeting the Queen, Lord's, 1981;
a great moment for any cricketer.

When it gonged dinner time we moved into the dining hall and sat at a table big enough and long enough to seat 40, let alone four. As you might expect from a minister for railways, there was a mini-railway track circling the table. Running along it was an engine pulling a number of carriages, each of which carried a cargo with a sign … "Scotch", "Gin", "Vodka" and so on. As it passed in front of me I picked up the decanter marked "White wine", and the train stopped. Once I had poured my drink and replaced the decanter, off it went again.

This happened several times, and I had worked up quite a head of steam by the time the magnificent old clock in the dining room struck three in the morning. Naturally there was a lot of conversation, and near the end of the 'night' I assumed we must all have been talking shorthand, because I thought I heard the Maharajah say, "Let's go for a sulky ride!"

But, that's exactly what he did say, and what's more I was driving the sulky, with Simmo, Crompton and the Maharajah in the back.

Following along behind us, running, was a squad of the toughest looking security men you could imagine. Even to this day I wonder if they were there to protect the Maharajah from assassins, or to protect him from me on my debut as a sulky driver. I was pretty relaxed, I can tell you.

I have been less relaxed on some other occasions, those when I have had to spend a good deal of time with people you might call VIPs.

My first major tour as Australian captain was to England in 1985, and one of my major moments was in Bristol where we were to play Gloucestershire, because I had played there in 1977.

But it was also special because Gloucestershire were to induct a new patron, Lady Diana, Princess of Wales. It occurred to me that no cricket club had ever had a better looking patron.

How did Gloucestershire swing it? The previous patron had passed away and an eagle eye in the club recalled reading a newspaper item in which Lady Diana's father said he hoped his grandson might one day play County cricket.

So, up went the cry, Prince Harry for Gloucester, and out went a letter to the Palace asking the Princess of Wales if she would kindly consider becoming the club patron.

The induction was a fifty pounds a head, glittering affair that among the smoked salmon and champagne called upon me to introduce my team to Lady Diana. That's not normally a big deal, just a case of walking along the line with the Princess and saying, "… and this is David Boon, ma'am …"

Gloucestershire captain David Graveney and I were also expected to spend a fair bit of time chatting idly to the Princess before making a grand entrance with her to the formal part of the evening.

That made me nervous, but as it turned out, that was the easy part. The Princess, looking absolutely stunning in a full-length gown, and perfectly relaxed, put me at ease with a very knowledgeable discussion about the game.

The worries began when I started introducing the players—and that was supposed to be the easy part.

The day before this gala evening there had been a lot of speculation in the press about the Princess's health. One newspaper had published a photo of her, scarf around her head, almost unrecognisable, leaving a shopping centre. The shop in the direct background carried the sign "Mothercraft"—the clear inference was that the Princess was expecting.

I walked along the line of my players. Everything was going smoothly, when I saw before me the grinning faces of the team 'wags', Greg 'Fat Cat' Ritchie and Wayne 'Flipper' Phillips. Flipper shook Lady Diana's hand. "Saw your photo in the paper yesterday, Your Highness. I didn't think the scarf suited you," he said.

The Princess displayed an admirable sense of tolerance. "Yes," she replied, "It is difficult to go about unnoticed."

Ritchie was next in the line and I fixed him with pleading eyes, 'Please don't terrorise your beloved captain any more.'

But his expression was a worry. He shook the Princess's hand, and then said, "Were you really coming out of that Mothercraft shop?"

Without so much as a pregnant pause Lady Diana smiled, and just moved right along.

Wayne Phillips, left, and Greg Ritchie test the Princess of Wales's sense of humour. I'm in the background, forcing a smile!

BIRTH OF THE BLUES

It had been a long, hot summer, the one of 1984–85, when I'd taken over as Australian captain, and at the end of it I opted for a battery re-charge. Jane and I, and Dene, who was only just nearing his first birthday, headed up to Noosa with my best friend, Marcus Sykes, and his family.

Lazy rivers, golden beaches, rainforests … Noosa might just be the most relaxing place on earth. That changed on the morning of April 12, 1985.

We'd had breakfast, and while our wives pottered Marcus and I had our feet up on the balcony making the tough decision for the day—what time to head for the beach. The gentle background music on the radio was interrupted by the news flash that there was going to be an Australian cricket tour of South Africa, an unofficial one. Australian Rebel tours to South Africa were organised to heighten the profile of cricket in the Republic after its rigid stance on apartheid led to it being banned from world competition by cricket's ruling body, the ICC.

The odds were that seven members of the Australian team I was about to lead to England for the 1985 Ashes tour were now going to go to South Africa instead.

"Just great! Another drama," I said to Marcus. "Still, the good news is I'm here at Noosa and nobody will be able to pester me." The seven defectors from the Ashes team were named as Wayne Phillips, Graeme Wood, Terry Alderman, Rod McCurdy, Murray Bennett, Dirk Wellham and Steve Rixon. I was sort of dumbstruck.

We stayed on at Noosa for another couple of days but the magic was vanishing from my family holiday. My mind was churning: What would this all mean as far as the Ashes tour was concerned? What would it mean as far as Australian cricket was concerned? I felt really let down.

Then, in the weeks before the Ashes side was due to leave, four of the South Africa tourists changed their minds—Phillips, Wood, Wellham and Bennett.

It sort of became a monumental shit fight.

A few questions were being asked, the main one "Why?" It turned out some players had taken up new employment opportunities. Phillips had joined a radio station in Adelaide, Wood had joined one in Perth, and Wellham had secured a job with PBL Marketing. The common thread in all this was that the radio stations and PBL were all in some way linked financially to Kerry Packer. This caused a bitter reaction among members of the Ashes team, just how bitter probably captured by Kepler Wessels's comment, "Since when has Kerry Packer been an Australian selector?"

I was a very unhappy captain, and I clearly had a very unhappy team on my hands. I decided, for the sake of morale, that I had to find out just how this controversy was likely to affect our Ashes challenge. But how to do it?

I decided on a meeting at which they would have to answer questions from the rest of the team. How loyal were they? How committed to the Ashes challenge? Was there any truth in the rumour that they had been guaranteed the amount of their South African contracts to stay with the establishment?

I was accused of running a 'kangaroo court'; I should have taken each player aside and sought his commitment, I was told. No, what I wanted was everything out in the open, all cards on the table. This wasn't like a captain taking a player aside for having a late night.

Those three weeks were some of the most harrowing in my cricket life, certainly the most harrowing of my 20-week reign as captain of Australia. The sort of crisis that makes you wonder, 'What have I done to deserve this?' You even wonder about the Chinese meal you had a week before and try to remember if you'd run over a Chinaman—or even a family of them!—on your way home.

A few months, and about a dozen Test matches, after the South African controversy, I knew I'd run over the family.

By then we'd lost the Ashes three-one, and the Kiwis had come to Australia and Richard Hadlee had bowled them to an historic two-one series win. That was the 1985–86 summer.

There were six Tests that summer, the three against the Kiwis and three against India. The first two Tests in the Indian series had been draws, the third was to be decided in the early days of the new year.

Then, Jane was pregnant again, and because I'd been in the West Indies for the birth of Dene, I was determined not to miss the birth of my second child. Arranging that was definitely more difficult than doing a batting order! The Test was to be played at the SCG from January 2 to 6. The baby was due on January 20, but after the Test we were to start the hectic schedule of World Series matches. We had a World Series game in Melbourne on January 9 and another in Brisbane on January 11. Jane and I decided that if the baby could be induced on January 7, I could be there.

One of the great attractions of Test cricket is its ebb and flow, but there are times when a spectator needs the patience of a label sticker to get the full advantage of it. The Third Test against India had one great day in five—and that was the fifth.

We dropped five catches on day one, India reached 4/600 on day two, we were 0/169 on day three—the beginning of 'Boon and Marsh'—and at the end of day four, 4/347.

When the morning of the final day dawned the only thing running through my mind was that the Test was going to finish in a very boring draw. The follow-on hadn't crossed my mind, nor had the baby.

India's captain Kapil Dev knew that to have any chance in the game he needed to take half a dozen wickets before we reached 400, the follow-on, so he

Jane with Dene and Nicole. I missed both births because of cricket duty.

attacked with his spinners. The SCG pitch was turning, as usual.

Even though I'd reached 70 I wasn't middling the ball, and in fact I was bogged down. I thought, 'I'll whack one over the top and spread the field a bit to take off the pressure.'

Admirable plan, poor execution—I simply skied it miles in the air and one of their blokes took a good catch running back, never easy when they're swirling a bit. When I got out we needed just 31 more runs to avoid the follow-on.

Back in the dressing room it seemed that I'd no sooner got the pads off than I received a phone call from Jane: "Something's happening! The baby might be on the way."

I sat down and started to think, 'Well, we've advanced to 5/387 so when we get to 400 and save the follow-on, I can take off, get on a plane to Brisbane, be with Jane and hopefully be there for the birth of the baby.'

Being the batting team that we were in those days we got bowled out just before lunch for just less than 400!

We had to bat again, but only for two sessions, to save the game. I thought, 'Once the game is basically saved I can shoot through and try to get to Brisbane in time for the birth. Maybe she'll be in labour for a long time.'

Not too long before tea Geoff Marsh and David Boon had reached 50, by tea we were 3/61. I hadn't batted. I was down the list, hoping I wouldn't be needed. Wishful thinking.

The dressing room phone rang. It was Gracie, a nurse from Brisbane's Mater Mothers hospital. "Congratulations," she said. "It's a girl, the baby and Jane are both well."

'Terrific,' I thought, 'I missed the birth; but Jane's okay, fantastic.'

We lost another wicket and I had to go in. There was still about an hour to go and we looked like we could do the impossible—lose the game.

As I walked in a message flashed onto the electronic scoreboard: "Congratulations on the birth of your baby." I was out straightaway, just sort of played one straight to gully. Greg Ritchie saved the game for us, batting about two hours in all for just 17 runs.

Jane's Dad was at the game, waiting at the dressing room door the moment the game finished. We tore off in his car to the airport, got me on the plane home, and I went to visit Jane in hospital. She looked fantastic.

Then they brought Nicole in; she was the first new-born baby I'd seen, small, wrapped in a blanket, reddish, wrinkled face peeping out. I was surprised because I suppose I expected to see her all creamy and smooth and beautiful. I looked at her and thought, 'Oh, you poor little thing. I'll have to pay someone to marry you.'

It had been that sort of a day.

A MAGIC INTERLUDE

My changed family status, and the Test team's ordinary day, inspired one newspaper headline writer: "Border Left Holding The Baby."

But in those days there wasn't much time to wallow in self-pity about the Test disappointments—six played, two lost, four drawn. Because straightaway the World Series Cup started up, India and New Zealand the other two teams.

It turned out to be an extraordinary, and fascinating, contest. We were so dominant we lost only three of our preliminary matches, yet in the middle of all those triumphs New Zealand scored a massive 276 against us, then rissoled us for 70! Kiwi captain Jeremy Coney joked to me, "Allan, I think I will send you in for the outright."

From memory it was Australia's lowest ever World Series score. What went wrong? Simple, I decided to experiment with the batting order—and it's an experience I've never forgotten in later years when the critics are calling for massive change in the make-up of our one-day teams.

There was an absolute outcry all around Australia over our poor performance, because the day that I'd chosen for my experiment was none other than—Australia Day!

So much for the extraordinary. The fascinating aspect of that season's Cup

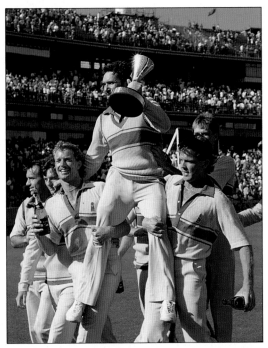

*No doubt , 1986 was a rough
summer until we won the World
Series Cup, and celebrated with a
lap of honour of the MCG.*

Not out 152 against the Kiwis at the Gabba—but we lost the Test.

Opposite: *Triumph in a summer of stress.
After beating India in the World Series finals, 1986.*

were some personal performances, and how they were to have a fairly lasting influence on Australian cricket in the years ahead.

Dean Jones returned a batting strike rate of 83 runs per 100 balls, Bruce Reid took a hat-trick, only the second in limited-overs history, and the new opening batting pair of David Boon and Geoff Marsh had great success. Another new face, Stephen Waugh, won two Man Of The Match awards.

And when Wayne Phillips, the wicketkeeper, was hurt, I found myself donning the gloves.

But the best thing by far about that Cup was that we won it. We beat India two-nil, the clincher at the MCG.

There were 72,000 fans at the MCG that day, and after we'd won I don't think there were too many of them keen to budge. There had been few wins to cheer in recent times, and now they clearly wanted to be part of this celebration. The cheering came in waves, roars that reached a crescendo, then rolled away.

After I'd been presented with the Cup I moved back among the team until I was alongside the manager, Bob Merriman, who nudged me hard with his elbow, and shouted over the roar of the crowd, "Why don't you do a lap of honour?"

I thought, 'No, they'll think that's corny for sure; they'll think the cricketers are stealing the football boys' thunder.' But Merriman, a Victorian, knew his crowd. He pressed me to do the lap of honour with the team. And the rest of the boys were keen, urging "Come on AB, let's do it."

So, off we jogged. It was a moment of glory. McDermott and Davis lifted me onto their shoulders and I raised the Cup to the crowd.

It was heady stuff. With a short tour of New Zealand around the corner it was just the tonic Australia's cricketers and their fans needed.

EVERY CLOUD HAS A SILVER LINING

Legend has it that when the Maoris first set eyes upon New Zealand they were so fascinated by the expanse of cloud hovering over the land they called it "Aotearoa"—Maori for "land of the long white cloud".

We arrived in the middle of February, 1986, for a three-Test series and, from memory, four one-day matches. When we left at the end of March, beaten in the Tests and all-square in the one-dayers, I felt like one of those blokes you sometimes see in comic strips—the bloke who you guess is down on his luck because a little black cloud, with rain, has been drawn above his head.

Mind you, our early tour form had been pretty good. We had transferred our World Series confidence to Tests, drawing the first two, even contests both of them, although in the first we once again showed our alarming inclination to collapse, losing our last five wickets for 31 in 40 minutes.

Even so, we went to Auckland for the final Test confident that we could win, and thus win back the Trans-Tasman Trophy which had been lost in Australia just a few months before. Certainly I didn't want to lose, because I'd been reminded by some prophet of gloom that to lose this series would give the Kiwis the title of being the only team to beat Australia in two Test rubbers in the one season.

So, you can probably imagine how I felt when our total reached 1/193— definitely not cock-a-hoop, not being that type, but certainly I'd allowed myself a smile of satisfaction.

And even though we made only 314 from that terrific foundation it wasn't 'alarm bells'—we bowled New Zealand out for 258, a good lead, and what's more the pitch was starting to throw up puffs of dust.

It was the sort of situation a captain dreams about; he's won the toss, the team's got a handy lead, the opposition has to bat last on a dicey pitch.

I reasoned if we scored 200–plus in our second innings the Test would be ours; instead we scored only 103. Geoff Marsh, who made a century in the first innings, his maiden Test hundred, was out for a first ball duck. Bizarre. Boon batted right through the innings for 58 not out. In 40 minutes on the fourth morning we lost 5/12.

Yet, although the Kiwis only needed 160 runs in about nine hours to win, I maintained the odds on winning were still in our favour.

Crazy? Not really, after all why couldn't our spinners, Greg Matthews and Ray Bright, do exactly what their spinner John Bracewell had done—take six wickets?

The Kiwis got the runs in a cakewalk, with only two wickets lost.

This was a devastating loss for me; six months earlier the Kiwis had come to Australia having never beaten us in a Test series, now they'd beaten us in two in a row. It bloody hurt. It hurt because we'd gone to New Zealand full of hope. We were a promising and emerging young side, we'd worked damned hard and we'd played good cricket most of the time. But we'd lost again.

This generated a long AB soul-search session in which I began, for the first time seriously, to ask myself: Am I the right man to captain Australia? Maybe I was being too expectant of the young guys; some of them, Craig McDermott and Steve Waugh, were barely into their 20s.

Or, maybe they simply weren't responding to my style of captaincy. That worried me a lot, because although I'd put everything I knew into the job we were still succumbing to pressure, still basically doing the same things wrong. I'm no outspoken motivator of men, one of those guys who jumps up and down with all the power-talk. I try to do the right thing tactically, and I expect the guys to give a hundred per cent when they're out there. Maybe this young bunch needed a hot-gospeller to crank them up to the hundred per cent limit?

Two days after we lost that Test we played a one-day game, containing New Zealand to 6/186 off 50 overs, a winning performance—except we rolled over for 156 in 47 overs. It deepened my depression.

The next one-dayer was in Christchurch, three days later; our match-eve practice was disgraceful. We were slack, our drills were haphazard, all the classic symptoms of a team in defeat mode.

I said what I was thinking: "Well, here we are, playing cricket for Australia, the ultimate, and there's no ticker in the side. If you can't win, you just don't roll over and lose, but that's what you're doing." I was starting to suspect there were a few in the team who didn't regard playing for their country as the ultimate sporting honour. I had a total dose of the shits.

The press conference after practice was typical of the ones about that time: "The team promises but never delivers," ... "How much longer do fans have to put up with it?" ... "How much longer can you as captain put up with it?"

Above & Opposite: Two faces of captaincy. The celebration was at Lord's, 1985.

Well, as you know, I'd been mulling that last question over in my mind since the end of the Third Test; I'd decided that when I got back home I'd have a chat to Jane about it all. But instead of answering in that fashion I let the 'needle' in the questions get to me. I lost it, and poured out my feelings.

My ultimatum to the team (via the media)—"win or I quit"—was wrong, of course, and would have been far better discussed behind closed doors. What it was, was a frustrated cry for a better effort from the team.

I had always subscribed to the theory that a captain's only as good as the players he has at his disposal. You can be a terrific captain, but if your players aren't performing well or near to their potential, or you haven't got the right players, then I don't think it matters what the captain does.

In the 15 months I'd had the job there was no doubt I'd shaken hands with a few players—28 I think, from memory. That must have been some sort of a selection record, even allowing for the South African breakaway. The constant chopping and changing meant the team was always struggling to find harmony. Blokes started worrying about being dropped, instead of thinking about the team performance as a whole.

In all my time as captain all I seemed to have been thinking was, "How in hell's name am I going to save this game?"

The remarkable side of this black period in my career was that in team adversity my own batting flourished. In 15 Tests I scored 1464 runs with six centuries.

Against England there were 597 runs at 66, including 196 at Lord's, and 146 not out, with a broken finger, at Old Trafford that helped us save the match.

Against New Zealand at home there were 279 runs at 55, including 152 not out at the Gabba, but we lost the Test.

Against India there were 298 runs at 59, and my 163 at the MCG helped us force a draw.

Against New Zealand in New Zealand there were 290 runs at 72, with twin centuries, 140 and 114 not out, in the Second Test at Christchurch.

Only one, the 196 at Lord's in 1985, was good enough to help us force a win.

IN THE FRONT LINE

The captaincy changed my approach to my batting; I lost a certain freedom about my strokeplay, probably cramped a bit by my determination to lead from the front.

As the captain, I was even more conscious not to play some loose, swashbuckling shot, some dumb swipe that might have set the rest of the team thinking, 'Ha, have a look at that, he's into us about trying harder and look what he goes and does!' When I was a player only, 'one of the boys', I confess I found it difficult to watch every ball bowled in a match. I'd watch for a while, but then I would more than likely go out the back and read a little bit, or even do a few not-too-strenuous sit-ups. But once I took over the captaincy I began to 'ride' every ball; it was as if everything I'd done before, watching occasionally, had intensified ten times. At the end of the day, if we'd been batting, I was more mentally drained than I had been at any time in my career. I just had to know exactly what was happening out in the middle. I tried to relax, tried to duck out the back, tried to read, but at the first roar of the crowd I'd be up.

As a player only, the state or result of the game is important, but the tendency is always to worry first about your own result. As a captain it is quite another matter; suddenly I was worried about players dropping catches, or bowlers losing their length and line and concentration.

As a player only, I was the master of my own destiny, just another batsman versus the bowlers; as the captain my destiny was in the hands of others. If I'd been dismissed I would watch, and suddenly realise I was wishing I could go back out there again to do something personally about our situation. I'd have to say to myself, 'Stop being an idiot, you're not allowed to bat twice.' I reached the stage where I saw every bad day, every poor result, every hiccup, as a reflection upon me personally.

My captaincy style was savaged by the media. I won't ever forget the way they called for my head—I'd been in the job the proverbial five minutes, I'd copped the West Indies speed machine, the South African split, the team had seen more changes than in a game of gridiron, and the 'experts' were into me:

Keith Miller (1986): "Look at Border, sleeves rolled down, scruffy beard, hand on the chin; he looks more like an escapee from a Ned Kelly gang movie. He stands in the slips, scratching his beard or his bottom, and offers the players little encouragement."

Even later on there was some sharp stuff written:

Ian Chappell (1988): "When things go wrong Border withdraws into his shell like a beleaguered tortoise."

Neil Harvey (1992): "Quit."

Well, they were all flamboyant cricketers; I just happen to have a different personality from all of them. And I have my own style of captaincy.

I like to think that once the team became settled, from 1988 onwards, my style has been successful. Of course, I would've loved to have won every Test and one-day series we played. It grates that we didn't, but it has been a source of great pleasure to me that we did become one of Australia's most successful outfits, ever.

To say that we'd have been more successful if I'd had a personality transplant is to draw a mighty long bow.

Chapter Five

THERE'LL ALWAYS BE AN ENGLAND

Lord's has a magic about it that no other ground in the world can match.

Strange to say, the common thread in many of my cricketing milestones has been England. Lord's remains my favourite cricket ground, and games I have played against England, with one notable exception, among the most enjoyable.

SEASON'S GREETINGS

There was a lot of joy at 'Omaha' when I was chosen for my first Test; it was the Third Test played between England and Australia at the MCG, over five days from December 29, 1978—an Ashes Test, the ultimate.

The bad news was England, captained by Mike Brearley, were already two-up in the series.

The phone rang incessantly, telegrams kept arriving and Mum said to Dad, "I never knew so many people were interested in Allan's cricket."

One phone call was from a Mosman family who had moved to Melbourne. They thought it only right and proper that Mum and Dad should travel down to watch their son's big moment and offered some accommodation at a friend's place, and my elder brother Mark shouted Mum and Dad the air fares. So my first Test was definitely a family affair, which I thought was a nice touch given the way they'd all been involved in my development.

When you're playing for Australia the greatest place for crowd reaction is the MCG. Going in to bat it's a long, long walk from the dressing room to the gate, downhill and between what seems like a hundred rows of seats. My mind wasn't blank, more hazy from nerves. I have a memory of a sort of dull roar from the crowd as they welcomed the new boy. I had a strange thought: 'I'm from New South Wales, and all these Victorians are cheering me.' I was No. 6 and our score was 4/189.

Brearley crowded me with close fielders. In the next few years I was to learn he was a very smart captain, one who never seemed to lose control of the game. And, a captain who tried things.

It was the first time he'd seen me and he tried spin, then the second new ball, they slanted the ball across me and bowled bumpers. But at stumps I was still there on 25 not out, with Graeme Wood, who was 100 not out.

We were 4/243, but next morning went out and lost our last six wickets for 15 runs! Yet, we still won the Test because Rodney Hogg—very quick, very straight and a very good bowler—took 10/66 in the match. They've been bad figures for England ever since Hastings!

So, we were back in the hunt for the Ashes, quite an initiation for me, and I'd got my first big pay cheque as a professional cricketer—$800, the fee for a Test in those days. It didn't worry me at the time, but it was clear to anyone who looked at the match attendance—128,758—and the gate receipts—$279,158—why some players had 'split' to Packer's World Series.

Unemployment, of a kind, was just around the corner for me. In the second innings I was facing spin and Brearley had crowded me again. I hadn't scored, and it being my first Test, I was more eager than I might otherwise have been to get off the mark.

My first catch in Test cricket, Gooch, c Border, b Dymock.

I swept one quite sweetly and thought, 'I'm off it here ...' Mike Hendrick, at backward short leg, stuck out his right hand and not only stopped it, but threw it! I thought, 'Whoa there Allan ...' Too late! Run out, 0.

Next Test, on a real turner at the SCG, England couldn't get me out in either innings, but my 60 not out and my 45 not out couldn't stave off the defeat that once again widened the gap between the teams.

I'm not sure why the crisis brought out the best in me, nor why that has been the case over the years. Something just seems to happen inside me. I know I have to dig deeper and somehow it works. I don't feel that I'm batting any differently.

I only made 11 and one in the Fifth Test—another loss—and the selectors dropped me for the Sixth Test. I thought it was a pretty strange decision, because the Test was to be played at the SCG where, in the scorebook at least, I had done damned well just a couple of digs ago. The word was I didn't fit the selectors' philosophy for that game, which was apparently 'attack, attack, attack'.

We were down 4-1 in the series so I suppose they were entitled to do something. But I was on top of the averages, and my aggregate compared favourably with the blokes who'd played all series.

It taught me a valuable lesson—never feel too comfortable about your spot in a Test cricket team.

Another record bites the dust. I catch Ratnayake, my 123rd Test catch, beating Greg Chappell.

WAS MY FACE RED!

England were back in town the very next summer, which was unusual because they normally only tour every four years. This timetable change had come about because the Cricket Board was keen to maximise income following the outbreak of peace with Packer's World Series.

But England, who had the Ashes after giving us a hiding the previous summer, now refused to put them on the line against an Australian team strengthened by the return of the World Series players. They maintained it wasn't a fair dinkum series because only three Tests were to be played. The other three Tests of the summer were against the West Indies, whom we played first at the Gabba.

I failed badly and went on to the First Test against England in Perth fearful that my spot in the team was once again under threat, and as a result I confess I didn't play my natural game. That's always a mistake. Instead I poked and prodded my way to an inglorious four runs before I was given out leg before to Botham.

So, I started the long walk back, very out of sorts, and thinking dark, negative thoughts, 'Well, that's it for me. I've blown my place in this team.' My mind was absolutely racing.

In those days there was an old yellow picket fence around the WACA; I prodded the gate open with my bat, then started up the path and steps to the players' balcony, home team to the left, visiting team to the right.

This was my Test debut at the WACA; before I'd only been there with the NSW team, a visitor. The dressing room door was slightly ajar and I shoulder-chested it open. I was so dirty at my stupidity in changing my natural game, and worse, falling to Botham. I tossed my bat towards the locker, ripped off my gloves and threw them after the bat, then called everyone, including Poms, for everything.

I had just exhausted my entire vocabulary of expletives and looked up—to see I was standing in the England dressing room, and not very far away from a wide-eyed England manager!

It turned out to be that sort of a Test series. In the second innings I made my maiden Ashes century, but not without some pain. I missed a short, fast one from Graham Dilley which didn't miss my head and I had to retire hurt at 109.

Not very long before lunch on the fourth day of that Test, we were 7/225 in our second innings, and with a first innings lead of only 16 runs, we were looking down the barrel. I was then about 60 not out, and striding towards me was the formidable form of Dennis Lillee, swinging a wooden bat.

Dennis was still pretty twitchy because he'd had an aluminium bat taken off him in the first innings, after a protest from England. Dennis had named his

Sharing a light moment with Dennis Lillee. Check out those flared trousers!

revolutionary, hi-tech aluminium blade 'The Combat'.

I think Dennis fancied his chances of making a few dollars once the environmental push really took hold and less willow trees were cut down for cricket bats, meaning bat makers would need a substitute material. I had actually used The Combat a few years before in the nets at Barry Knight's. Dennis had brought one across for a promotion. When I hit the ball there was a sort of hollow 'clonk' noise.

"What do you think, Allan?" he asked.

I was a bit in awe of Dennis at that stage, so I said, "Yeah, not bad." But I had a tingling in the hands that told me the willow people wouldn't be losing too much sleep.

In fact, Dennis had used The Combat in the First Test against the West Indies, the week before the Perth Test against England, without any protest from the West Indies—which was only to be expected, because he made a duck. But when he batted with it against the Poms and 'clonked' a cover drive for three runs—it would have been four if he'd been using a wooden bat, and less noisy—play came to an abrupt halt.

There was a lot of chin-stroking, lip-tugging and beard-scratching while Brearley and Co made out a case for the illegality of aluminium cricket bats. The damning evidence appeared to be a scuff mark on the ball that hadn't been there before Dennis's cover drive, so the umpires told Dennis his luck was out: "You'll have to change the bat for a wooden one."

There wasn't exactly steam coming from under Dennis's white helmet by the time Greg Chappell arrived with the replacement bat, but Dennis was clearly unhappy about the situation.

After a short, sharp chat with Greg, his captain, he hurled The Combat about 18 metres back towards the pavilion.

So, in the second innings, with us in crisis, Dennis Lillee looked pretty damned determined, and batted accordingly. Together we put on 71, before Dennis was out—Lillee, caught Willey, bowled Dilley—and I don't think it's stretching things too much to say those runs probably played a big part in our winning the Test.

One of Sydney's big wets turned the Second Test pitch at the SCG into a batsman's nightmare; England made 123 and Australia's legspinner, Jim Higgs, bowled only one over. Greg Chappell could see the irony in that on a pitch where spinners usually got the ball after a few overs.

He sympathised with 'Higgsy': "Bad luck 'Gladdy',"—Higgs used to carry some of his cricket gear in an old Gladstone bag— "but why would I want to bowl a legspinner who could turn the ball a foot, when the fast bowlers could cut it exactly as far but at eighty miles an hour?"

To give you an idea of just how tough it was batting, I spent half an hour on eight, my 15 runs took me 80 minutes and I didn't hit one boundary. It was tough.

England were back in again an hour before stumps on the second day, and out again about that long before stumps on the third day, leaving us to get 216 to win, a task made so much easier, as in those days we had a rest day, and the sun shone like it hadn't for quite a while, drying the pitch out into a batsman's dream.

We won the series two-nil, but it was frustrating that the Ashes hadn't been on the line. A year later, 1981, they were when we toured England. But after the Headingley Test on that tour I was in total desolation.

ALL BETS OFF

It seems contradictory to describe one of the lowest points in my cricketing life as a milestone; a millstone seems more appropriate. It took me many years to come to grips with what happened to the pride of Australian cricket at Headingley in 1981. When the nightmare finally faded in our Ashes glory of 1989 it's easy to understand why our celebration of the occasion was so long, and filled with laughter.

Headingley, Leeds, is not an attractive cricket ground; the skies are often slate-grey atop the rows of chimney stacks in the near distance, reinforcing the feeling of, "What are we doing here?" that can sometimes overwhelm you.

When we reached Headingley for the Third Test in 1981 we were already one-up—Terry Alderman's 9/130 had clinched the First Test, and the Second was drawn, a state of affairs so depressing for England that they decided to replace Ian Botham as captain, and recalled Mike Brearley.

At the end of day one the pitch had been so unpredictable that Brearley announced, "If all went well you could bowl a side out for ninety on that pitch." Which made our 3/210 look pretty good.

At the end of day two, when we'd made 401, Australia's captain Kim Hughes—Greg Chappell had missed the tour for family reasons—announced, "I reckon our four hundred is worth about a thousand on that pitch." I made eight, leg before to Botham.

I was one of his six victims. As an interesting sidelight it was the first time Botham had done anything in the series, lending weight to the theory that the captaincy had weighed down his personal performance.

There was a suggestion his success had come hard on the heels of some clever psychology from Brearley, who had started calling him the 'Side-step Queen'. In an effort to gain more swing in early games Botham had opted for a quick sideways movement just before the delivery, but Brearley thought it had taken away some of his zip, and wanted him to revert to his old action. To encourage him he teased 'Guy the Gorilla', as Botham was known, with something a good deal less masculine.

However, our fast bowlers needed no more inspiration than the sight of the pitch, and Lillee, Alderman and Lawson rolled England for 174—a score which, in the minds of some England players, was so far short of our 401 they booked out of their hotel on the fourth morning of the game!

About tea that day England were 7/135 in their second innings, still 92 runs away from avoiding defeat, and Brearley had packed his bags! We were in high spirits, heading for a two-nil lead in the series, and three Tests to play. We could 'smell' the Ashes.

Several things then happened that changed the course of the game, the series, and the lives of a few cricketers.

The Headingley ground authorities had installed a new electronic scoreboard, and while we were sipping on our tea the latest betting on the game was flashed onto the screen: 1–4 Australia, 5–2 draw, 500–1 England.

Now there are punters, and there are mug punters; punters say "Odds-on, look on." Mug punters dream about backing winners at 500–1. Dennis Lillee, as it turned out, is one of the latter. He thought it would be a great lark to put fifty quid of our team fund money on the Poms.

A joke. We might never have heard another thing about it but we did go on just a little bit too long about Dennis being stupid, so Dennis being Dennis, the original rebel with "I'll show you blokes" tattooed on his personality, he gave the team bus driver £10 to put on England.

And Rodney Marsh, being Dennis's best mate in mischief, decided to have a fiver on the Poms.

By stumps England had reached 9/351, Botham had passed his century in 87 balls and belted us all around the park, and out of it, to the tune of 145 not out. England's lead was 124 and Brearley had to unpack his bag, and hotel rooms had to be re-booked.

We were a bit stunned, but hardly demoralised. Logic suggested England's last pair couldn't put on many on the last morning, so our final target wasn't going to be all that huge. In fact, it turned out to be 130, and the theory abounded that if Botham could get 149 then a whole team of us wouldn't have any trouble with 130. Which was good, positive thinking.

Little targets can sometimes cause the most problems because batsmen are tempted to depart from their natural game. We reached 1/56 then snatched defeat from the jaws of victory. We lost 9/55, and 35 of those were scored by Lillee and Ray Bright, two tailenders.

It was about a week before the wedding of Prince Charles and Lady Diana and we'd managed to give the whole of England some invaluable practice at waving the Union Jack.

Ian Botham. He was a handful off the field, too.

Easing the pain. Old Trafford, 1981, when my 123 not out, Australia's then slowest Test century, wasn't enough to save the Ashes. I batted with a broken bone in my left hand.

A traumatic team collapse like Headingley can often be repeated straightaway; it was. Next Test we needed only 151 for victory, but collapsed from 4/105 to 121 all out when Botham took 5/1 in 28 balls. More heartbreak.

I had come to the crease at 1/2; it was the fourth day, about ten overs to stumps, never an easy time to bat, simply because you don't want to. You'd much rather the openers hang on, or a nightwatchman does your 'dirty work' for you.

I hung on grimly, which is precisely how I felt next morning, when I woke up with a severe case of 'Birmingham Belly' from dinner the night before. I was so crook I was hesitant about batting, but reasoned that that option might throw the whole team out. Kim Hughes saw Brearley with a suggestion that if I was caught short would England mind waiting for me to return to the field. Brearley smiled, but I don't think he was amused, really.

I was the fifth man out, for 40, at 105, caught in close on the legside from a freakish ball from the offspinner Emburey that bounced, thudded into my glove and flew to Gatting.

We lost that series three-one; we should have won it three-nil. And on the way down we created the legend of Botham The Bogeyman.

ASHES AND GNASHES

The Ashes changed hands quite a bit through the 80s; we lost them in 1981, won them back under Greg Chappell in 1982–83 in Australia, lost them in 1985 and 1986–87, then won them back in 1989.

That's one of the good things about playing for a trophy like the Ashes, it can accentuate the ebb and flow of cricket which is so essential to the survival of the Test game.

I captained the 1985 team to England—me, 'Defender of The Urn'. It was a young and inexperienced team, as the selection process had been upset by the defections of some players to the Rebel tour of South Africa.

Normally when an Australian team arrives in England it is referred to as "the weakest ever"; my team in 1985 was only called "Australia's Second XI". Yet for all but the last two three weeks of the tour we gave England, at full strength, a mighty run for the money.

Matters money raised their head early in the piece. I had started out the tour with three consecutive centuries against County sides, 106, 135, 125, and if I could hit a fourth then I would become the first player to open a season in that way. The fourth match was against Derbyshire and my teammate Wayne Phillips took a stroll to the Ladbrokes' betting tent, and returned to announce he'd bet against me reaching the milestone.

I hadn't really thought anything about the hundred up until then, but now I decided on a course of action. "Flipper," I said, "I'm going to make you suffer for this, you unpatriotic bastard." At lunch I was 20 not out. I leaned over to Flipper and reminded him, "Fifth of the way there, mate. How's your money looking?"

Between lunch and tea I advanced to 90, then edged my way to 99—I looked up at our balcony and there was Flipper out waving a white hankie! I pushed the single that gave me a neat hundred, said a little prayer hoping the scorers weren't one run out, then hit a lollipop catch. I thought Flipper looked a bit poorly when I got back to the rooms.

Early days in the tour were good; we were keen and sharp, which I suppose you could put down to youthful exuberance. We won the one-day series, lost the First Test at Headingley—fast developing a reputation as a graveyard for Australia—won the next at Lord's, then drew the next two.

With two Tests still to play we weren't in bad shape to hang onto the Ashes, except there were some worrying signs that we were going off the boil.

After the series finished Sir Len Hutton, the former England captain, described our bowling attack as one of the worst to reach English shores. I'll concede he had a point—of the main Test bowlers McDermott and Lawson took 52 wickets between them, but the others, O'Donnell, Thomson and Holland, only took 15 between them.

Our plight was never more evident than in the final two Tests when we bowled aimlessly and allowed England to run up scores of 595 in the Fifth, and 464 in the Sixth, when they were 3/376 after the first day!

We just lacked that hard edge and depth of experience which might have allowed us to survive, and therefore hold the Ashes.

David Gower, my opposite, seized on that in the Fifth Test. It was a run-athon; we made 335, England declared at 5/595 an hour and a half before the end of the fourth day. We weren't a rabble, but we were rooted.

It was one of those sweltering English summer days that just drag the energy out of you, and sap you mentally as well. Gower went for the throat, our challenge was to see if we could keep the start of our second innings intact.

As so often happens in those circumstances, even to teams more experienced than our 1985 outfit, there was an almighty collapse.

With 25 minutes to stumps we looked solid enough, then Wessels went; I opted to send in a nightwatchman, Bob Holland, rather than myself, figuring I'd be wise to save myself up in case we needed any back-to-the-wall stuff on the last day.

Bob Holland got out first ball and I had to go in, not quite what I had in mind. Three runs later Graeme Wood was out, one run later I was out, and at stumps we were 5/37.

We might have saved this Test if Lady Luck had embraced us, rather than only allowing us just a touch.

When I peeled back the curtains the next morning I saw a most beautiful sight—rain, and lots of it. I thought, 'If this keeps up and we can get away with a draw we might just be able to re-group in the week before the Sixth Test and save the series.'

When play started up again Wayne Phillips and Greg Ritchie were in charge of the rescue mission—they had to bat for the time left in the match, two hours plus 20 overs. They managed the two hours, then Flipper, facing up to the spinner Phil Edmonds, laid back on a short one, and hit it like a rocket, aiming for cover point.

Allan Lamb was fielding at short cover point, about one metre from the bat. As Flipper drew back Lamb knew instinctively what was coming. He raised his hands to protect his face, half-turned his body and jumped in the air.

The ball hit Lamb's right foot and ballooned into the air, and into the hands of Gower fielding nearby. There was an appeal, and to my amazement, after the umpires consulted, Phillips was given out caught. Their opinion was that the ball had reached Lamb's foot on the full.

Well, eight years before some cricket countries started using a third umpire with a slow motion replay, I went and watched television playbacks of the incident and I couldn't really tell if the ball did, or didn't reach Lamb's boot on the full. I think my eyesight is okay, so if I couldn't be sure on a slow motion replay, how could the umpires be sure with the naked eye? Surely it had to be a case where the batsman was afforded the benefit of any reasonable doubt. I was bagged as a whinger by the English media, who felt I was in some way detracting from the merit of Gower's victory.

I've got only one thought on that: suppose the umpires had given Phillips the benefit of the doubt, he'd held the England bowlers at bay for the next 20 overs, and forced the draw that would have meant England had to win the Sixth Test to win back the Ashes?

I know who would have had a few words to say about doubtful catches then!

KICKING TURF WITH THE GNOME

I made two trips to England to play County cricket, each time with Essex. Times had been tough in the couple of years since I'd been handed the job of captaining Australia. I was playing well myself but the team just wasn't gelling. Our cricket was mostly bad. So when, during that 1985 Ashes tour, I was approached by Essex with an offer to join them the following season, I jumped at it. I saw it as a chance for me to be just a player again, a chance to get back to simply enjoying the game. Like turning the cold shower tap full on your head

The incredible sequence of events that probably cost us a Test match, maybe even the Ashes, in 1985. Phillips cuts into Lamb's foot. But, did it bounce?

when you've got a hangover.

And what made it really good was that I took Jane, Dene and Nicole with me. It was a far cry from the days when I hauled Jane off to Gloucester. In 1988 we lived in a delightful little cottage in the village of Ingatestone, made some lasting friendships—and I didn't have to visit any backyards hunting up a car! Essex gave me a plush, white Audi Quatro. Life was great.

I thought I'd score millions, because both my tours, 1981 and 1985, had been successful, but County groundsmen had been primed to prepare 'result wickets'. So you'd arrive at grounds and you wouldn't be able to tell the pitch from the outfield it was so green and grassy. And the seam on the balls was big, so anyone could run in and move the ball around; he didn't necessarily have to be a bowler. I made 1200 runs at 50.

In 1988, being a batsman was hard yakka, too; I got sliced, and concussed when I missed a bouncer, and even though I hit six hundreds my final aggregate of 1300 runs at 59 will give you a hint that I had too many low scores for my liking.

My captain was Graham Gooch, but because he was on Test duty the captain most of the time was Keith Fletcher, 'The Gnome'. Fletcher is short in stature and he carries himself in a way that suggests he's a bit timid, even insipid. I remember Australian fans used to give him a razz when he was in England's middle-order against Lillee and Thomson in the 1975 series. But take it from me, The Gnome is as tough as anyone.

There were quite a few West Indian quicks in the County sides in 1986, and given the uneven, sub-standard state of some of the pitches, whenever we were due to face a bit of Caribbean 'music', some of the blokes in our side were a bit

England revisited. Essex in 1986 was a lot more fun for Jane than our first trip had been in 1977.

My first County match for Essex, scoring 34 against Warwickshire.

An unusual moment: the 1992 World Cup "Essex Connection"–from left, Salim Malik (Pak.), Graham Gooch, Derek Pringle (Eng.), Mark Waugh, Border (Aust.), Don Topley (Zimb.).

psyched out. They used to put padding over just about every part of their bodies.

But not The Gnome. He was 42 years old then, yet he never got armoured up like some of the young blokes.

It was in the mind area that I benefited most from my association with Fletcher. As a captain he wasn't a raver and a ranter, but a shrewd man manager. If he wanted to make a point with a certain player he'd do it singly; sometimes you'd see him walking to the middle with his arm around some bloke, encouraging him, or 'giving him the message'.

He was always hustling and bustling, trying things to give Essex the edge; he'd built up a vast knowledge of opposing players, so when a particular player came in to bat the field would be changed accordingly, and The Gnome would be up at the bowler's side reminding him of the game plan.

I got a lot out of The Gnome. If things happened to be not going all that well he had a habit of kicking the turf with the toe of his boot, roughing it up. The clear message to the team was 'Fletch has got the shits.' We all have our own way of letting on we're not happy. My trademark is 'The Teapot'. Hands on hips means harassed.

PETER WHO?

The early Tests in the 1986–87 Ashes series in Australia saw a fair few 'teapots' from me; England, who had sacked Gower for Mike Gatting, had done poorly enough in the tour openers to be rated "Can't bat, can't bowl, can't field," by one of the English commentators with the team.

I knew that was bullshit because I'd spent the Australian winter with Essex playing against most of them. All that assessment did was raise unrealistically the expectations of an Australian victory—though we had done well on a short tour to India before the series, tying one Test and drawing the other two.

The fate of the Ashes was decided by the Fourth Test, and again our problem was the bowlers' inability to maintain a good line and build up any sort of pressure on the England batsmen, and so give any game plan we had a fair chance of working.

The last Test was at the SCG, and the selectors made a change that led not only to me throwing a wobbly, but to one of Test cricket's true fairy tale endings.

In fact, they made three changes, dropping David Boon and bringing in Dirk Wellham and Greg Ritchie, but it was the name of the extra spinner they chose that wrinkled a few brows—Peter Taylor.

A spectacular attempt at a catch against England in Adelaide, 1986.
Note how I've braced my left wrist.

Nobody knew much about Peter Taylor. "Who's Peter Taylor?" was the question on the lips of every player in the team—we were over in Perth for a limited-overs series called The Challenge—and the media ran the headline, "Peter Who?"

I knew him because I'd played schoolboy cricket with him. As I ran my eye down the list I'd been handed by a Cricket Board official, I could hardly believe my eyes. The list contained only one opening batsman, Geoff Marsh.

I said to the official, "Who's going to open the batting?" To this day those selectors have never given me an answer to that question.

No-one ever came to me as captain of the team, and explained, "We've picked the side like this because … you could open with Wellham … we think that's the best balanced side … we picked Peter Taylor because it's at the SCG …"

In the days before the Test the question of who would open developed into a toss-of-the-coin job, until Greg Ritchie came to me and said, "Oh well, I guess I'll do it then."

There has been a lot of conjecture since that Greg Chappell was a strong advocate for Taylor, that he'd been impressed by his performance in the 1986 Sheffield Shield final, match bowling of 5/109 and a fighting second innings 42 that probably saved NSW's bacon.

To me the whole thing smacked of a mistake—they were so keen on getting Peter Taylor in they forgot about the opening batting. I don't think they picked the wrong Taylor, as was the common theory at the time. Certainly Mark Taylor was among the runs, but it's stretching credibility to the limit to suggest the panel mixed up two such dissimilar players.

This raises the question of whether the captain should be a selector, and despite the problems over that team I don't think he should.

He should be consulted, yes, but to have the captain in on the final selection would, in my view, open up a can of worms. It would completely change how players reacted in the dressing room situation.

Troubled players need a captain's ear, and vice-versa, and there would be a certain reluctance to confess if the player feared it might damage his selection prospects.

That's why I don't think the coach should be a selector, either. Consultant yes, because there has to be feedback on team direction. But I think on the whole to have a captain or a coach on the selection panel leaves the process too open to compromise, and that would be a weakness when the really tough decisions have to be made.

OPPOSITE: *The sweetest victory of all, Ashes Glory 1989.*

When you've played in more Test matches than anyone there's bound to be a classic or two among them. The Fifth Test between England and Australia at the SCG in January, 1987—Peter Taylor's debut Test—was one of the classics:

- Dean Jones, batting at No. 3, made 184 not out in our first innings of 343;
- Our bowlers found the bullseye for the first time in the series, rolling England for 275, Taylor 6/78, including Botham;
- At 7/145 in our second innings, a lead of just 213, we looked like being whitewashed in the series, then Steve Waugh and Taylor added 98 priceless runs;
- England, chasing 320 for victory, suffered from a freakish double-wicket doldrums syndrome—losing two wickets at the same score three times, 91, 102 and 257;
- One of those wickets was Gower, bowled Border, my first Test wicket for about four years;
- Pessimism swamped us when Gatting's gallant 96 got England into a winning position, 90 runs needed off the last 20 overs;
- Optimism took over when we needed four wickets off ten overs, and England an improbable 64 runs for victory;
- Peter Sleep bowled the second last over of the match, and with the last ball, dead straight, flat, and going on with the arm, he bowled England's last man, Emburey.

Our win ended Australia's longest spell of Test losses, 14 in a row. A reporter asked me how I felt. I said, "Until now it was a bit of a drag getting out of bed in the mornings." And I wasn't kidding!

Coping with a WACA heatwave in 1991 when we completed a three-nil series win over England.

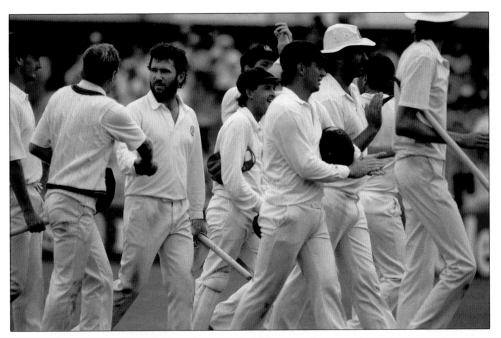

Leaving the SCG after beating England in the Fifth Test, 1987.

*Beating England is always a good feeling, but that SCG win in 1987
lifted a great weight from my shoulders.*

Chapter Six

CURRIES, AND CRACKERS

Fireworks at Madras after Australia's 1987 World Cup win.

Boyhood cricketing dreams are about scoring centuries at the Sydney Cricket Ground, or at Lord's, not in India or against Pakistan. But that's what happened to me at the start of my Test career, and in circumstances so spiced with controversy that contests between us thereafter rarely failed to make a headline.

BREAD AND WATER

I'd only just had my first birthday party when an Australian cricket team made their first tour to India and Pakistan in 1956. And I had just celebrated my 24th birthday when the Australians made their fifth tour—and I was on it, 12 weeks of complete cricket culture shock.

That experience was extended barely three months later when, after a short time back in Australia, I was chosen for a four week tour to Pakistan, the first by Australia in 15 years.

The time back in Australia was home, sweet home for me—I passed a thousand runs in Test cricket, the quickest among Australian batsmen to that milestone. Certainly I was in good touch, but I was also aware of the huge amount of cricket that I'd been lucky enough to play in a short time.

Australia played six Tests against India, three each against England and the West Indies, and three against Pakistan. Cricket tours of India have a certain stamp to them; jokes and stories are all about food and illness or the birth credentials and credibility of the local umpires.

Cricketers all know the timeless Fred Trueman joke ... the one that sees Fred running in for the first ball after a spicy curry lunch, past the umpire, past the startled batsman on strike, past his 'keeper, past the man at fine leg on the fence, up the pavilion stairs ... and the last thing his teammates out on the field hear is the slamming of a small door and a loud sigh of relief.

And the one about the umpire who took a few seconds short of a minute to give out caught behind an Indian batsman, and when asked by the bowler, Australian spinner John Gleeson, why it had taken so long, announced the wind had been gusting away from him, thus delaying the arrival of 'the snick'.

So you go to India, if not paranoid, then certainly pessimistic. But of course, as with most things in life, time and experience are great educators, and maturity has allowed me to be much more sympathetic towards the subcontinent.

On that first tour in 1979 I struggled. I wasn't a big curry fan; I liked only traditional Western dishes, so I found myself surviving on naan bread, rice, and bananas with a boiled water chaser. For a 'home body' used to thick steaks and crisp green salads all his life it came as a shock to the system. I lost so much weight on that trip it was ridiculous.

Kim Hughes, the captain of the team, had no such problems. He subscribed to The Roman Theory—when in Wherever eat Whatever the Whoevers are eating. Peter Sleep, the legspinner, was so impressed by Kim's good health he decided it was just what the doctor ordered for his largish appetite.

We were at one of those typical welcoming cocktail parties and Peter was wading into the savouries as if there was no tomorrow. Another dish was whisked before him and Peter surveyed it, then reached out for the red caviar on a tiny square of dried toast. Up to the mouth it went, a delicate snap of the teeth, and half was gone.

Peter grimaced a bit, then looked around the room and headed off to a pot plant, where he deposited the other half. Then he came bustling back over to me and whispered, "Hey mate, like spread it around, the old strawberry jam tastes a bit fishy."

India can be a very complex sort of place, especially on your first visit; but now that I've been back a few times I've learned to appreciate their way of life, their culture, their habits, their religious beliefs and their food.

These days I enjoy the local dishes, and I've got quite an appetite for curries—even though it was acquired during my stint with Essex in England!

The cricket was a new experience, too; it wasn't the first time I had had to face spinning ball after spinning ball on a crumbling, dry pitch. I'd done that plenty of times on Sydney's underprepared grade pitches, but in India I was facing Test bowlers with fieldsmen breathing down my neck, discussing my technique in a foreign language, with their hands outstretched waiting for a bat-pad catch.

My twin tours to India and Pakistan in the 1979–80 season were the foundation for some of the most daunting moments in my cricket career.

On my first birthday, with my grandparents, and Australia
were heading for India for the first time.

HEAT IN THE KITCHEN

Peace might have broken out between Kerry Packer's World Series Cricket and the Cricket Board in May of 1979, but Kim Hughes's Australian team that toured India later in that year was under some mild threat of having to come back home because of a 'war' of sorts.

A group called the Kammu Kashmir Liberation Front started to make noises about disputed territory between India and Pakistan, and there was a suggestion we may have been in some danger.

As it turned out a youthfully exuberant, naive, and in hindsight stupidly immature, Allan Border was the only Australian cricketer to go close to being shot at.

Our first game was at Srinigar, up in the north, in the cool, peaceful shadows of the Himalayas ... at first glance all you'd dreamed Shangri-la to be. At second glance our hotel had fortifications around it, there were soldiers everywhere, and at our game most of the crowd were soldiers ... we were in the middle of the trouble spot.

Our hotel was a multi-storeyed affair, my room was on the fourth floor and it had a nice balcony. It was possible for me to reach Kim Hughes's room, next door, via a narrow catwalk that ran between the balconies. Naturally, my preferred method of visiting Kim was to leave my room by the door into the corridor, walk to the right and knock on Kim's door.

But the practical joker in me leapt to the surface one night and, fortified by a beer or three, I took it upon myself to walk the plank between my balcony and skipper Kim's.

I was halfway along the plank, when—spotlight on sport!

From far below the plank the Indian soldiers had fixed me with a searchlight and were bellowing commands like "Halt" and "Surrender". They say never to look down when you're four storeys up, but I did, and in the wash of the searchlight I could see a marksman pointing something at me. It was probably an automatic rifle but it could have been a napalm thrower or a missile launcher it looked so bloody big.

I knew exactly what to do. I didn't move a muscle and in a voice strangled with fear I managed to choke out "Aussie cricketer, Aussie cricketer ..."

The morning after was even more sobering for me when the team manager Bob Merriman issued the official dressing down, but believe me, it was the chilling reminder from local officials of what could have been that left me a much wiser 24-year-old on his first cricket tour abroad.

The cricket was less life-threatening, but had more than a dash of frustration and controversy. The practice balls were as hard as ball-bearings and played hell with the soft willow of our new bats; in Srinigar I experienced changing in a dressing-tent for the first time; when the crowd threw pieces of fruit at Rodney Hogg in Hyderabad, he threw them back, and from then on any of us who chased a ball to the boundary copped the fruit treatment; in Nagpur the driver of the team bus announced the key had gone missing, but when we found the key the driver was missing.

Short tests of a cricketer's temperament which, in the circumstances we were in, mightn't have been such a bad thing.

Despite the peace there were no World Series Cricket players in our team— the selection process wasn't scheduled to be 'full on' until we returned, when the team to play England was to be chosen. So we were on trial in India to see who would eventually play alongside the Chappells, Lillee and Marsh etc.

The First Test was at Madras, where later in my career I would enjoy some of my most memorable moments as the captain of Australia.

At stumps we had reached 2/244 and I was unbeaten on 129; the next day I went on to reach 162, at which point I was run out. A Graham Yallop straight drive ricocheted onto the stumps off bowler Doshi's hand. Unlucky! Later I was told another run would have made my 163 the equal of Norm O'Neill's, a record in Tests between Australia and India.

Kim Hughes and I had put on 222, which was just 14 short of the Bradman and Barnes record stand against India in 1947 at Adelaide. My staying power at the crease all seemed a long, long way from the slash-and-nick days at Mosman Oval when I was just a kid.

The team though was having less good fortune; in the Second Test at Bangalore an umpire named Ramaswam no-balled Rodney Hogg, I think four times in the one over, which prompted Rodney to vent his anger by kicking the middle stump out of the ground.

By the middle of the Third Test Rodney had delivered a century of no-balls on the tour, which was probably as much a reflection of the front-foot no-ball rule as it was Hoggy's long final stride.

We crashed for 125 in the fourth innings of the Third Test on a pitch at Kanpur that was a horror for Australian batsmen because it was playing at heights between the knee and the ankle.

The loss niggled because for most of the Test we'd been in command; it meant we were one down, and we knew if we couldn't come back strongly we'd be the first Australian team to lose a Test series in India. Suddenly there was a lot more pressure around.

The Indian cricket followers' fascination with us didn't really help; even though we had lost the Test they continued to follow us back to our hotel each night, where they would stand around for hours, some blowing whistles, most ringing bicycle bells.

In the Fourth Test at Delhi a disputed run out decision against India's captain,

Sunil 'Sunny' Gavaskar, brought the issue of umpiring close to the boil. Sunny was not many at the time and went on to make his 21st Test century in India's 510, obviously a total that shut us out of the game.

But, after being out for 298 and following-on, we showed terrific character to make 413 in our last innings and force the draw. It was very uplifting.

There are a million theories about how to play cricket and win, and Kim Hughes decided the time had come to try a couple of them before the Fifth Test. The game between Tests was at Cuttack against East Zone, one of the weaker provincial teams.

Because the conditions at Cuttack were a bit ordinary Kim struck upon a theory to intensify our Fifth Test build-up. His theory was that we would beat East Zone in two days, instead of the scheduled three, and arrive in Calcutta a day early for the Test, which would allow us to maintain our winning impetus as well as take advantage of better practice conditions.

Current Australian coach Bob Simpson, himself a former Australian captain, tells a story about one player's assessment of some of Richie Benaud's captaincy gambles. A Benaud gamble that had no right to succeed had succeeded, prompting the player to remark, "Fair dinkum 'Benords' if you put your head in a bucket of pig slops you'd come up with a mouthful of diamonds!"

For Kim, it was 'diamonds' at the end of day one; we'd declared and rolled East Zone, gaining a lead of 34 runs. The news on day two wasn't so hot.

We declared again, leaving East Zone 153 to win on a pitch that was looking very dicey indeed. All the signs suggested they couldn't survive, particularly as we'd gone easy and used nine bowlers to get them out in the first innings. But survive they did! Not only that, they batted into the third day and went on to win the game.

It was one of those 'what if ... ' situations: pull off a gamble like that and you're a hero, blow it and you're a chump. You can't win.

Winning was the No. 1 priority in the Fifth Test, clearly our last chance to salvage a series win; Kim decided to risk his hand again, this time declaring closed our second innings at 6/151, of which he made a personal contribution of 64. It was a bold move, and it so very nearly came off.

After three days this was the state of play: Australia 442, India 2/214, the third day being memorable because only one wicket fell—caught Border, later to be Australian captain, bowled Jim Higgs, later to be an Australian selector.

The Hughes declaration on the last day left India to score 247 to win from about 70 overs, which, when you think about it, is leaving the door a bit ajar. When India were 4/130 I started to think 'We can pull this off,' but we put a catch down and that sparked what is best described, in terms of a Test match in India, as the 'fireworks'.

The crowd went berserk when Yashpal Sharma started hitting out for victory, clubbing 85; there were bells ringing and fireworks exploding, and the acrid smell of gunpowder drifted across the Calcutta outfield. I'd never seen anything like it before, and my eyes must have been wide with amazement.

With three and bit overs to go they still needed 47 runs to win, but they had six wickets left and Sharma was going like a fire in an oil refinery. Calcutta the 'City of Joy' was certainly that for thousands of Indian cricket fans at that moment.

Then we agreed with the umpires that the light was too bad to continue and all hell broke loose. Instead of lighting fireworks the fans lit the stands in protest.

I can look back on it now, push my tongue firmly into my cheek, manage a wry smile, and tell you there was 'a whiff of controversy' in that finish, but at the time I couldn't believe the chaos.

So, we crossed the breadth of India to Bombay for the final Test, with just two days to regroup. We were a young side on a tough tour—and doing it tough.

India's strength hadn't been decimated by World Series Cricket as had Australia's. Players like Gavaskar, Viswanath, Vengsarkar, Kapil Dev, Kirmani and Amarnath had the edge on us in experience, as well as 'home' conditions.

For all that, we were still only one down in the series; it had become clear to our batsmen that our batting survival techniques needed to be improved, because at the beginning of the Bombay Test the leg before count stood at Australia 20, India 8.

The frustration of that 'death toll' boiled over on the second day of this Test that we had to win. The first day was a bit of a nightmare, because Gavaskar and Chauhan put on 192 for the first wicket and at stumps India were 3/231 and looked like they could bat for all five days.

Not long into the second day we had turned it all around; Rodney Hogg was on the boil, and India were 6/281, when we went up for what we knew in our hearts should have been our ninth successful leg before appeal of the series—Kapil Dev caught in front to Hogg.

Of course, umpiring is all a matter of opinion, and in this instance our opinion was contrary to the umpire's. 'Hoggy' got frustrated and booted the ball away, Hughes came in and confronted the umpire, India made 400 runs, we made less than 200 in each innings and went home two-nil losers.

Gavaskar made 123, his 22nd Test century, before Kim Hughes caught him off my bowling. I didn't know what number Test wicket it was, and I certainly didn't know, as I celebrated, that 14 years on I'd be challenging Gavaskar for the title of champion Test run-getter. But I did know this trip to India had been the first true test of my character as a cricketer.

OPPOSITE: Cricket in India—where crowds can sometimes become a little over excited, and pitches can be frustratingly different—is a true test of character.

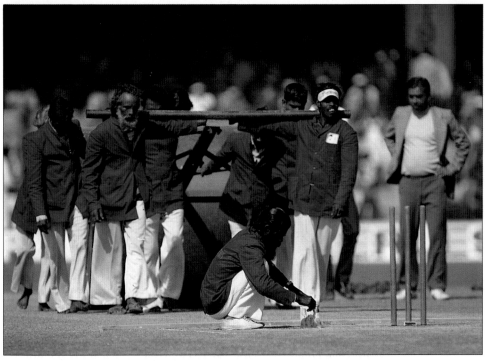

THE OTHER TEN THOUSAND RUN MAN

Diamonds seem to be synonymous with cricket success in India; the World Cup trophy we brought home in 1987 had a diamond-studded top.

But I first came across the tradition in 1986 when I made my second tour of India, on which I was captain.

India had had a change of captain too when Sunny Gavaskar made way for Kapil Dev. Hughes wasn't in our team—he'd gone to South Africa to try his luck—but Gavaskar was clearly still a very important part of the Indian line-up. In the Third Test, in his home town of Bombay, Sunny scored his 33rd Test hundred, but it was an achievement that caused a mild panic among Indian cricket officials, because it created a small, and expensive dilemma.

For quite a while the officials had been planning to honour the little master batsman with a special presentation, and to that end they had commissioned a jeweller in Bangalore to fashion a large silver salver engraved with a map of the cricket world.

The budget for the project, late in 1985, had been set at the equivalent of about 12,000 Australian dollars. You might say Sunny's appetite for centuries created a slight budget over-run.

The original proposal was that the jeweller would fix 30 diamonds on the map, each diamond denoting a century and the Test venue at which it was scored.

But no sooner had work begun than Sunny, on a tour to Australia, scored hundreds in Adelaide and Melbourne, which raised the diamond count to 32. And hit the silver salver budget! There had to be further discussions about the cut, size and clarity of the diamonds.

Finally, all was in readiness, and the presentation to Sunny was arranged for a dinner during the Third Test at Bombay, on our 1986 tour—and out he comes and knocks us around for that 33rd Test century, 103!

"Get another diamond," pleaded someone, but the 33rd diamond never made it. Sunny, tagged by Indian fans 'The Maharajah of Bombay', had scored so many Test centuries in his home town that there was just no room for another diamond anyway.

I saw a lot of Sunny in the middle, mostly with a bat in his hands, the white sunhat as much his trademark as the brilliantly tight technique.

In many ways our batting was similar. I had the edge in physique, because he was only a bit of a school ruler over five feet—and I'm a left-hander, always a plus! But we were both able to maintain concentration at the crease over very long periods, and we both had a lot of shots, but also the ability to accumulate big scores.

OPPOSITE: The style of Gavaskar.

He quit the game when he was 38 years old and when he had passed the magical 10,000 run mark. He was so determined to leave the game the way he wanted to that he delayed his announcement of retirement so that he could play in the MCC Bicentenary match at Lord's in 1987.

I was captain of The Rest Of The World and saw him make 188, a terrific free-flowing innings that a lot of people didn't think Sunny could play. It was as good a hundred as any I've ever seen.

In the second innings he was bowled for a duck, thus leaving the world cricket stage in exactly the same statistical way as had Bradman, whose run-making record Sunny had long passed. It was quite a coincidence.

TO THE BRIDE AND GROOM...

I still can't explain it, but there was something about arriving in India or Pakistan that brought out the very worst of the Guy Fawkes spirit in Australian cricketers. Perhaps it was because fireworks—as in bungers and skyrockets—were virtually outlawed back home.

I look back now, and most of the crazy things that happened to us in India and Pakistan seem to have arisen from a lunatic compulsion to blow each other up. Greg Ritchie, 'Fat Cat' to his friends, was one who was obsessed with fireworks.

On our 1986 tour to India Fat Cat managed to make a nervous wreck of cricket writer Allan Shiell, who was covering the tour for an Adelaide newspaper. Allan used to keep pretty late nights, so his nerves weren't always a thousand per cent anyway. We'd be sitting around the hotel courtyard in the evening, discussing the day's play, and Fat Cat would edge his way around behind 'Sheffield'—as Shiell was known—and put a lighted cracker under his chair. The thing would go off and poor Allan would be airborne, then hit the deck like a shot duck.

It got to the stage where one of us only had to make a hissing noise and Allan would bolt for safety; or, if someone lit a cigarette and threw the match in Allan's direction he'd take off. By the end of the tour he was shell-shocked.

I had experienced fireworks mania on my first trip to Pakistan in 1980, and then when I returned two years later I joined some of the other boys on a shopping expedition in Lahore, seeking out the biggest and best crackers we could find. The staff at our hotel directed us to the Old Lahore market, an area of the city seething with humanity and livestock mainly in the form of donkeys, carts and masters. When, eventually, we found the shop, the owner turned out to be a cricket fanatic, who in return for our autographs, gave us most of his stock at very discounted prices.

That night there was a big Muslim wedding held on the lawns and paving around our hotel pool, and as we stood on our balconies, sipping beer and watching the celebrations below, Fat Cat decided this was the perfect moment for the perfect gesture—a contribution by us to the friendly atmosphere of the proceedings.

It was decided we would fire a rocket into the sky over the wedding assembly, our biggest and best rocket in keeping with the enormity of the moment.

As a launching pad for the rocket, Greg chose an empty, medium-sized Coke bottle, which a few of us argued looked a bit inadequate. We suggested something more substantial might be in order, as the rocket stem was about the size of a garden stake, and the explosive head looked like it weighed at least a kilogram.

"No," said Fat Cat, the self-proclaimed explosives expert, "the Coke bottle will do nicely, but thanks very much for your concern, anyway."

So, Fat Cat calculated the trajectory, set the stem in the bottle, moistened his right forefinger, checked the wind direction, and lit the wick.

On ignition, the Coke bottle trembled; on take-off it toppled over and launched the rocket horizontally, like a guided missile.

We watched helplessly as the rocket cleared the bridal party and guests by very little, and exploded in smoke, masses of sparks and brilliant colours into a wall behind.

"Holy shit 'Cat', hit the deck!" was our cry, and amidst much hilarity, sobered somewhat by our guilt at what might have been, we all crawled away, commando-style, and split up to confuse the posse that would surely be on the perpetrator's trail.

SPIN OUT AT FAISALABAD

Greg Chappell's 1980 team was the first from Australia to visit Pakistan for 15 years. As part of the preparation for what was clearly an important tour for both countries, the man who was to manage the Australian team, Fred Bennett, visited Pakistan about six months beforehand.

They say a day is a long time in politics, but take it from me six months is a long time in the cricket business.

On his pre-tour fact finding mission on conditions, cricket and accommodation, Fred had been pleased to note there was grass on the pitches. When he returned with the team he stood with the groundsman at Karachi, asking, "What has happened to the grass?"

The Pakistan Board had appointed the former opening batsman, Hanif Mohammad, to the position of Director of Cricket Pitch Preparation, and the groundsman explained that Hanif wasn't quite as keen on grassy pitches as he had been.

Karachi was the venue for the First Test. We lost, the Pakistan spinners Tauseef and Qasim taking 18 of the 20 Australian wickets that fell.

This was only a three-Test series, and Pakistan, one up, soon showed they were keen to keep it that way, at the same time revealing how the competitiveness can be stifled in a 'quickie' tour, which this was.

The Second Test was to be played in Faisalabad, a city teeming with people, in the fertile Punjab, commercially strong in wheat and cotton, but not accommodation. We stayed in a guesthouse, the kitchen of which, according to Dennis Lillee who visited it, may not have been cleaned since Fred Bennett's pre-tour reconnaissance.

Originally Faisalabad had been called Lyallpur, after Sir Alfred Lyall, an early British governor; remarkably part of the city's street system has been laid out along the lines of the Union Jack. I'm not sure it did anything to reduce traffic chaos, which together with our accommodation hassles, our First Test mishap, and the weather, was proving to be frustrating.

These were still the days when Test cricket allowed for a rest day, but when the first day of this Second Test was washed out Greg Chappell hit upon the idea of using the rest day as a play day, thus ensuring the Test was played over five days. And, of course, he reasoned we had a better chance of winning the Test in five days, rather than four.

But Pakistan, one up in the series, saw no benefits in Greg's suggestion and that angered Greg.

He won the toss and batted, but before you could say "Faisalabad" we were one out for next to zilch. Greg was sitting with the pads on, scheduled to go in at No. 4, when a Pakistani poked his head around the corner and asked Greg if he'd like to re-open the discussion about playing on the rest day. Cheeky so-and-so had a huge grin!

Greg was not amused. He came in at lunch, not out and in absolutely menacing touch. He immediately called a team meeting, and told us, "I want us to bat for four days."

So, he went out and got 235, Yallop got 172, Hughes got 88, Marsh got 71—and I got run out for bugger all! We made 617, but because we only batted for two and a half days, Greg was as dirty as I've ever seen anyone.

We had to spend a day and a half fielding and bowling in the hot sun. So Greg gave everyone a bowl—even Rodney Marsh, the wicketkeeper, bowled ten overs. A little bit of Greg venting his spleen, maybe.

The Third Test in Lahore offered us our last chance to square the series, but it also offered us the strangest sight. Two pitches had been prepared for the Test—one with grass, one without. Fred Bennett was ropable, demanding, "Where's that bloody Hanif?"—but he was told that Hanif was too ill for Fred to see him.

It was crazy; no-one could tell us which pitch we'd be playing the Test on! We hatched a plan in the hope it would force them to show their hand. More than that, we hoped it would make them decide to play on the grassed pitch.

We spread the rumour that we were flying in offspinner Ashley Mallett to take advantage of the bare, spinning pitches. At the same time, it was decided Dennis Lillee, who clearly would have appreciated a pitch with anything on it resembling a blade of grass, would fake an injury. We wanted Pakistan to think, "Oh, Lillee's not playing and we've got Imran and Sarfraz, let's take them on with our fast bowlers."

So, at practice Lillee ran in, buckled at the knees, screamed in pain as he clutched his knee, and groaned, "I think I've done my back again." We carried him off.

The next day we started the Test on the bare, flat pitch. Naturally Dennis played, and took his only three wickets of the tour. I made 150 not out in the first innings and 153 in the second innings, which turned out to be something of a milestone, and one not without coincidence.

It made me the only batsman to have scored 150 in each innings of a Test in Pakistan. The coincidence is that one batsman had scored a century in each innings before—none other than the man who was to become Australian coach, Bob Simpson!

In the second innings I was out stumped, by the Pakistan captain Javed Miandad. So what, you say? Well, it just so happened Javed, Greg Chappell's opposite number, had taken over the 'keeping duties so he could call up his wicketkeeper, Taslim, to have a bowl. Exactly what Greg Chappell had done in the Second Test.

Maybe, just maybe, it was Javed's way of getting a bit further under our skins.

THE OLD 'GET-SQUARE'

The hangover from Australia's 1980 tour to Pakistan, after which we made some pointed references to pitch doctoring, plus the odd 'bushfire' in Test series between us since, has been something of a running sore for both players and administrators.

These controversies haven't been confined to series with Australia; when the allegations over ball doctoring hit the headlines during Pakistan's 1992 series against England, a mate of mine remarked, "Isn't it funny how when there's trouble the Pakistanis seem to bob up more than most?"

That's one way of looking at it, but a Pakistani cricketer probably takes the view that the Aussies and Englishmen rate high on the pain-in-the-neck scale. Some cricket commentators are convinced the root of the trouble lies with a 'master and pupil' syndrome—that 'the colonials', Australia and England, the oldest Test playing countries, just can't accept new boy Pakistan's rise to prominence. They say Pakistan regard this attitude as 'born to rule', and that has made them all the more determined to win. I can see a bit of 'get-square' in all this, the Old Testament eye-for-an-eye theory.

Pakistan's cricketers are volatile, there is no doubt about that, just as there is no doubt Australia's cricketers retain a tough, competitive streak. England's cricketers are a little harder to judge, but there is an air of we're-better-than-you about them.

When all those personalities are brought together, seeking world cricket supremacy and the massive prize money on offer these days, the mix can be as explosive as a Greg Ritchie rocket at a Lahore wedding!

Cricket's tradition is that of a game for gentlemen, but in truth it has a revenge factor just like any other sport. After all, that is the nature of any Test series—lose one, try to win the next. And if one team thinks they've had a rough deal from the other, they'll be sweating it out to even things up next time they meet.

I soon became aware of that, and very early in my career, in fact in only my second Test series and only my fifth Test match. We were playing Pakistan at the MCG in 1979.

Rodney Hogg, Australia's No. 10, was batting, and fielding close in was Javed Miandad, about whom I knew nothing at that stage. But I decided pretty quickly that he was a competitive bugger.

Rodney blocked one and then, determined to indulge in what batsmen call a 'spot of gardening'—repairs to the pitch surface by tapping the bat on it—walked out of his crease. Javed swooped on the ball, ran to the stumps, whipped off the bails and appealed for run out.

The umpire, 'Mick' Harvey, gave Rodney out, much to Rodney's surprise, because as he told Mick, as far as he was concerned the ball was 'dead'. Pakistan's captain, Mushtaq Mohammad, apparently agreed, because after calling a team meeting he decided to call Rodney back, a sort of 'Sorry Rod, come back, we didn't mean it.'

Well, Rodney had no sooner returned to his crease than umpire Harvey had a meeting with his fellow umpire, Robin Bailhache, and they decided, no, Rodney had to go.

Which is when Rodney, with a mighty swish of his bat reminiscent of King Arthur swinging Excalibur, left only one stump standing.

It was very funny—but it wasn't, if you know what I mean. Hogg was probably out by the strictest interpretation of the rules, but even now, 14 years on, I still feel the umpires could have been more tolerant in the circumstances, given that Mushtaq had withdrawn the appeal.

I regarded Javed's action as unsporting, because Hogg was clearly not trying to take a run; I thought Javed could have shown a bit more feeling for the spirit of the game. Bit naive of me probably, but I had just come into the Test scene.

There were only two Tests in that series, and we went to Perth one down. One down in more ways than one, if we counted the Javed incident. On the last morning of the Second Test, we had worked ourselves into a strong winning position. Pakistan were 9/263, but because we had a 50-run lead they were in fact only 213.

With the best part of the day to play, and only one Pakistan wicket to be taken, we were confident of a win. But the Pakistan last pair, No. 6 Asif Iqbal, a century-plus and batting like a genius, and No. 11 Sikhander, frustrated us.

Asif clearly didn't rate Sikhander as a batsman because at every opportunity he'd 'farm' the strike from him. We just couldn't get a crack at the 'bunny', Sikhander. Asif would be on strike, the end of an over would come around, and 'donk'—off they'd hare for a single. New over, four to Asif, then 'donk'—single, end of the over. And so on, until drinks had to be taken. Time was starting to slip away from us.

At drinks we had a team meeting, during which the point was made that Sikhander was 'fudging' when he backed up at the bowler's end, clearly a big help when it came to Asif's tactic of taking short singles at the end of overs. Alan Hurst, who had to bowl the first over after the break, was under instructions: "When you run in and see Sikhander has backed up too far, stop, and warn him that if he doesn't stop cheating we'll run him out."

So Hurst ran in, and stopped … and there was Sikhander, out of the blocks faster than Carl Lewis, well down the pitch. Hurst gave him the London Bobby look—the one that says, 'Well, what's going on 'ere then?' Then Hurst knocked the bails off and appealed for run out.

We all thought 'Oh no!' Asif was filthy and belted into his stumps with his bat. As we started filing off we asked Hurst, "What happened to the warning?" and he explained that he'd got so steamed up when he saw Sikhander so far down the pitch he'd just thought 'Bugger him' and decided to run him out.

By the time we'd reached the fence we'd talked ourselves into believing we'd done the right thing. "Serves him right for bloody well cheating," sort of thing. But it was a mistake.

There was, to put it mildly, a fair bit of tension around when we started our second innings run chase for victory. We had reached 87, which for cricketers is some sort of devil's number, being 13 from 100, when Rick Darling, facing Sarfraz, played one down to Sikhander at mid-off.

Sikhander tossed the ball back to Sarfraz, but it ended up instead at the feet of the non-striking batsman, Andrew Hilditch, who bent down, picked it up and lobbed it to Sarfraz, who instead of catching it and rewarding the Good Samaritan Andrew with a word of thanks, appealed for 'handled the ball'.

I was batting No. 3 in those days and had to pass Andrew coming out as I went in; his face was not a pretty sight. It was a battle for me to achieve maximum concentration, not just because of Andrew's plight, but because there was still plenty of jabbering in the middle when I arrived to take guard.

As it turned out we got the 236 we needed to win and lost only three wickets, two run outs, and a handled the ball—so no Pakistan bowler got a wicket! I was unbeaten on 66 at the end—most satisfying. And we levelled the series.

At the end of the Tests I wondered if the umpires could have taken a different stance on not just the Hogg decision, but Sikhander and Hilditch, too. Wouldn't it have been better to have just said "Come off it, fellas!" But I suppose the problem is that you can't have umpires getting user-friendly with the rules of the game, or you'd have chaos. When it comes right down to it, the players are probably the ones who have to protect the spirit of the game.

HUNDREDS AND THOUSAND

Not only did I make my Test debut at the MCG in December 1978, but coincidentally, I made my first Test century there a few months later, during the same Test in which Javed Miandad ran out Rodney Hogg.

My clearest memory of batting in that Test is of being surprised at the pace Imran Khan generated. He was faster than any other bowler I'd faced up until then. My first innings was a nightmare; he kept hitting me in the back because I just couldn't pick up his line properly, nor the length, and I finished up sort of turning my back to the ball, taking my eye off it.

Not only that, I was bamboozled by the movement he got. Imran liked to get out wide on the crease, and because I was a left-hander my cricket brain triggered the reaction, 'The ball will spear across me towards the slips', which it did. But occasionally, and unexpectedly with his wide-of-the-crease delivery, Imran made one come back in.

So, as well as being bruised about the back, my mind finished up a little battered too, because I let a ball go that came back and toppled the off stump. That was it for me, 20 runs.

When we batted again it was at the invitation of Pakistan captain Mushtaq, who had declared their second innings between lunch and tea on the fourth day, and set us 382 to win. That's a tough target at any time.

But Mushtaq had left the door slightly open, by allowing us 540 minutes, probably because they had their Packer World Series Cricket players in their team, and we didn't.

The 'spell' Imran had cast over my batting in the first innings had got me thinking, 'How can I come to grips with his bowling style?' About the tea break on the final day I was a pretty happy batsman. I had coped well with the intricacies and speed of Imran, I was unbeaten and had scored a century, my first in Tests.

What was better was Australia's score was 300 and we'd only lost three wickets. Kim Hughes and I had put on 177 together, and now we had a full session to make just a few runs over 80 and victory was ours.

But after tea the old ball suddenly started to swing around—swinging 'Irish' as cricketers call it, where the bowler loads up one side of the ball with sweat and keeps the other side rough. Sarfraz swung one into me, hitting me on the inside of the front pad, and from there it ricocheted into my stumps. And so ended my maiden Test century.

By the time I'd walked off, up that long, long path to the dressing room, acknowledged the other blokes in the viewing room, walked down into the changing basement, taken my pads off, and started the self-inquest into why I'd missed the ball—yes, no celebration!—it was complete mayhem in the middle.

Sarfraz took seven wickets for one run and we lost seven wickets for five runs.

It sort of took the edge off my maiden Test century. That was March, 1979. In December of that year I made another century, my first against England, during which I went past the magical 1000 runs in Tests.

The statisticians announced it had taken me 354 days, making me the Australian batsman quickest to that target.

*Matching it with 'Sunny'. On the occasion of my 125th Test, Sunny's milestone,
I received a watch. Coincidentally it was India versus Australia, and Sunny, right,
just happened to be there.*

Chapter Seven

ASHES GLORY

Another England batsman bites the dust in 1989, and we take another few steps into the record books.

The Ashes have been the symbol of cricket supremacy between Australia and England for longer than a century. To lose them is hell, to win them heaven. In 1989 Australia won them back on English soil, a feat that hadn't been achieved since 1934.

DON'T TELL THE TRADITIONALISTS

Mentioning favourably limited-overs cricket—or 'the white ball game', or 'pyjama cricket', call it what you will—in the same sentence as Test cricket can bring the odd crease to the forehead in cricket's traditional kingdoms, like the Lord's Long Room.

But I have to say it: the limited-overs game created the positive mood that enveloped the Australian team at a vital time during our Ashes challenge of 1989.

To put you in the picture I must first tell you about a War With The Windies, the one that took place during the 1988–89 Australian summer, just a few months before we went to England. That summer the World Series white ball matches fell between the Third Test in Melbourne—we were annihilated—and the Fourth Test in Sydney.

If we'd been racehorses we'd have been swabbed, or whatever they do to racehorses guilty of miraculous form reversals. What triggered our turnaround was an incident during the best-of-three final matches in the World Series.

The series-decider was the third final, played on a dry, bare SCG pitch. During the game the parched SCG had to cope with two downpours that would have done justice to anything Brisbane can turn on in the thunderstorm department.

The first downpour dropped buckets when we were batting; the second came during the West Indies innings, and effectively swamped any hopes we had of winning the game, and the Cup.

We were 2/83 off 24 overs when it first rained, but when we started up again the match referee had made it a 38-over contest.

In our 14 remaining overs Dean Jones and Steve Waugh belted the pick-handles out of the West Indian fast bowlers to the tune of an absolutely astonishing 143 runs. It meant that the West Indies had to make 226 off their 38 overs, and 226 runs can be a pretty big ask even in a 50-over game.

In the first over of the West Indian innings Terry Alderman picked up two great wickets, Greenidge and Richardson, and the West Indies were two out for four runs.

The rain came back when the batsmen, Haynes and Richards, had taken the score to 47 off six overs and four balls. But when we finally went back on, the win equation for the West Indies had been even further reduced; they needed to score only 108 runs off 18 overs for victory.

So in effect all they had to score was 61 runs in 11 overs and two balls, which was a waltz for a couple of 'Master Blasters' like Dessie and Viv. Especially as the ball we were using was like a piece of soap that's been on the shower floor for a couple of days.

It was this 'mis-match', if you like, that led to the change in the rain rule

Limited-overs. At times it can inspire a revitalised approach to Test cricket.

calculations in the following season; the West Indies win on this occasion left us, and the fans, with the niggling feeling that 'we wuz robbed'.

But I also sensed a new feeling in the team, one of 'we can beat these blokes'. And we did just that—we won the Fourth Test very handsomely.

England's equivalent of Australia's World Series is the Texaco Trophy, but the overs are limited to 55, it is a best-of-three only series, and it is completed before the Tests start. Whilst I thought winning the Texaco could be a handy plus psychologically, I wasn't going to be too disappointed if we got beaten. The Test matches were the real business, and Headingley, venue for the First Test, June 8, 1989 was, as coach Bob Simpson put it, our "date with destiny".

In the first Texaco match at Old Trafford England blitzed us, 231 to 136—our worst one-day effort in years—the headlines the length and breadth of the country shouted "We told you so, they are the worst Aussie team ever."

The second match in the series, at Trent Bridge, ended in a tie and with me absolutely ropable over what became known as 'The Ben Johnson Incident'.

In our mad helter skelter for runs at the end, when we needed something like a run a ball off the last two overs, Ian Healy twisted a knee and called for a runner. We decided to send out Dean Jones, the team 'greyhound'. Jones had been in the middle hardly a ball when Healy slashed one down to third man—and started running!

There were guys running everywhere, and Healy actually outpaced Jones. If the pressure hadn't been so great I suppose I'd have laughed, but I could only think out loud, "What the f—'s going on out there?" England captain David Gower protested to umpire Dickie Bird, who decided Healy wasn't hurt badly enough to need a runner.

Jones came back into the rooms and joked, "I've been sent off." It sounded funny, but I was filthy, and even filthier after the match when Gower made some wisecrack about Healy "running faster than Ben Johnson".

The fact of the matter was that Healy was so bad when he came off at the end of the game team physio Errol Alcott feared he might miss the rest of the tour. Naturally he was out of the third match at Lord's, and because our reserve 'keeper Tim Zoehrer was also injured, Mike Veletta had to take the gloves. When I went out to toss with Gower I told him our team, "… and the 'keeper is Veletta. The steroids have stuffed up Healy's knee so badly he can't play." David gave me a wry smile—I think he knew I wasn't all that happy about his 'Johnson' jibe at Trent Bridge.

Lord's was a full house, 24,000 people, all of them in short sleeves, packed in on a hot summer's day—it was a sight to inspire any cricketer. The sight of a pretty, young woman streaking across the ground was inspiring, too.

We were set 280, which in a limited-overs game is a bit like chasing 400 to win on the last day of a Test match. But Lord's is an unusual shape—long at the corners and short at the sides, and what appears to be a large target there is more achievable than elsewhere because it can be hard for the fielding captain to defend.

At the 45th over we still needed to score about eight runs an over to win, but we had seven wickets in hand, one of whom was Geoff 'Swampy' Marsh, playing the sheet anchor role to perfection. He was still there on 111 when 'Long Tom' Moody belted the winning run, with three balls to spare.

We joked about the likelihood of the next day's newspaper headlines reading "Aussies not worst team ever." Three hours later we were still in the rooms celebrating when the Lord's groundsman knocked on the door to announce he'd had enough. "Five minutes to get out, or stay the night," was his ultimatum.

Seemed a helluva way to stop the party. There was a time when we used to worry that we couldn't convert our successes in limited-overs to success in Tests, but that third World Series final against the West Indies a few months before had changed all that.

MIND GAMES

Ian Chappell once told me, "I can handle you losing to the West Indies, India and Pakistan, but for God's sake don't lose to the Poms!"

Australia's two Ashes tours prior to 1989 probably had given 'Chappelli' brief bouts of apoplexy, and after the 1985 loss to Gower's team he accused me, as captain, of being too 'chummy' with the Poms. He was referring to my obvious good relationship with some of the England players; he was particularly annoyed by my on-field friendliness towards them. He felt England was 'the enemy' and as such there should be no fraternisation on the field, because it would have a negative effect on the rest of my team. He said to me after the '85 tour, "AB, those blokes were belting the hell out of you but you were out there being their best mate for Christ's sake!"

So in 1989 I thought, 'Okay, this time I'll be a lot tougher.' I decided not to talk to the England players on the field, unless I really had to. In fact, I decided I'd be aggressive towards them. And I was, so much so that David Gower was to make a pointed reference to my changed character in his autobiography.

He recalled inviting Geoff Marsh, Geoff Lawson and me to his home for a barbecue, where I'd made my thoughts quite clear. I told him, "David, the last time we came here I was a nice guy who came last. I've been through all sorts of ups and downs with my team, but this time we had a bloody good chance to win. I was prepared to be as ruthless as I could be to stuff you up."

There was an incident in the Second Test at Lord's, when Neil Foster was bowling and served me up the weirdest ball I've ever faced.

Either his hand brushed his leg, or the umpire, or he just forgot to let the ball go, because it bounced once near his feet, then bobbled along the wicket, outside my legs. I thought 'God, where's that gone?' then 'It's gonna be a free hit ... I can belt this!' then 'Be careful, Al, because you'll look a real dope if you bash it straight to someone ... or miss it.'

In the end I missed it and looked a real goog. I tossed my bat away in disgust; the Poms were laughing, "Nice effort to hit that one, AB," and in 1985 I'd have probably laughed with them.

The 1989 Ashes tour was the high of my highs as a captain, better than the wins over the very strong West Indies teams at the SCG in 1985 and 1989, which came in the middle of otherwise bleak summers. And bigger than the 1986 tied Test in Madras.

It was satisfying not just because success finally came my way, but because of the great achievements of the team. Cricket is all about enjoying the game, and comradeship. My team was strong in both those areas. I had what is called 'a good dressing room'.

And, I'll be honest, I discovered that whoever said "winners are grinners" was

My friendship with David Gower, England's captain in 1985,
raised the hackles of Ian Chappell.

dead right. The bloke nicknamed 'Grumpy' over a couple of early-career, slightly dark, displays of sourness in the face of misfortune, the bloke who was later tagged 'Captain Cranky', laughed along with the rest when his Sixth Test blooper was revealed.

I'd gone out to bat and as I was marking my guard I thought, 'These spikes seem a bit flat,' and when I had a look I discovered I'd put on odd boots, one with a spiked sole, the other just rubber.

When I came back in I told Swampy Marsh, quietly, that I'd made a late run for Dill Of The Year. That night I was copping it from the whole team. Swampy's huge grin said it all—he had blabbed.

Nevertheless, after the tour I got the impression that David Gower thought I might have taken the 'ruthless' bit a touch far. That he thought I didn't mind upsetting anyone at all as long as I got the right result.

That's not quite right, but it was an opinion that may have been strengthened by my views about players' wives and girlfriends coming on the tour.

In 1981 the women weren't allowed to stay with the players in the team hotel, so most of the players stayed outside. I thought that had an adverse effect on team morale and performance. In 1985 they stayed in the team hotel. This wasn't ideal either, as some had very young children with them, which I don't think did a great deal for either sleep patterns or team timetables.

So in 1989 I tried to convince the players that their families should not join the tour until it was well underway. And the hard and fast rule was: no women in the team hotel during Test matches.

Well, in this day of the liberated woman it went over like a lead balloon. Of course the media got it wrong: "Allan Border says Wives Can't go on Tour!" I would have loved to have had my family, Jane, Nicole and Dene, over with me, but I sacrificed just as I had asked the other players to sacrifice. I know Jane didn't like staying at home any more than any other wife, but she understood my stance. "If you think it's important, then it must be," she said.

Whenever the matter came up in discussion with a wife on the tour, my point was simply this: When you think about it the only reason you are in England is because your husband is playing cricket for Australia. That has to come first.

POMS ON THE MENU

Team dinners are generally very relaxed affairs; the only nerves around might be among the Test debutants, or there can be a general air of tension before the first Test in a series.

Our dinner before the First Test at Headingley suffered an immediate hiccup—the Social Committee of Tom Moody, Ian Healy and Merv Hughes had

had a bit of a get-together and decided the ideal venue for our dinner was a club down the road from the team hotel. When they went down to make the booking they discovered the club had been booked for England for their team dinner!

The purpose of any team dinner is to discuss your opponents, and assess their strengths and weaknesses. The input at our meeting was very good, because some of us could speak from previous English experience. Terry Alderman had toured before in 1981, Geoff Lawson and I had been in 1981 and 1985, and David Boon had been in 1985. There were some in the team who had played County cricket, too.

We talked about the England opening pair first, Gooch and Broad. During my two seasons with Essex, Gooch's County team, I noticed he scored a lot of runs through mid-wicket. Often the ball went for a short way in the air, so we decided we'd place a man there rather than have the more conventional bat-pad fielder.

The idea was to cut Gooch's run flow and frustrate him into playing an unnatural game. As things turned out Alderman executed the plan perfectly. The headlines said it all: "Gooch Alderman's 'Bunny' ". From memory I think he got him four times in nine digs.

A beautiful sight in 1989, Gooch leg before to Terry Alderman.

Broad had had outstanding form in Australia when England won the Ashes in the 1986–87 season, scoring three centuries. Then he got another in the Bicentennial Test, so we'd had an eyeful of him—and a gutful! Stupidly, in those Tests we'd bowled at his pads. His legside play had been so murderous I can remember thinking, 'I wish this was Rugby Union—fifteen men would be handy out here!' So, nothing on Broad's legs was the plan.

Sometimes in a team meeting there comes a flash of inspiration; at this Headingley meeting it was Geoff Lawson who 'flicked the lightswitch'. Elephants are supposed to have long memories, but Henry would give any elephant a run for the money.

When we got to Gower, Henry said, "If you don't mind AB, and the circumstances are right, I'm just going to throw the odd ball down the legside." He went on to explain that when England were in Australia in 1982—yes, seven years before!—Gower had been out caught down the legside three times. In fact, Henry had got him once caught by Kepler Wessels at leg slip.

I was just a bit sceptical about the idea for the simple reason that in a Test match you just don't believe, 'Yeah, we'll bowl it leg stump and he'll fall for the three-card trick and get out caught at leg slip.' It seemed sort of unreal.

But in the second innings of the Headingley Test we placed a leg slip to Geoff's bowling and Gower was caught down the legside by the 'keeper Ian Healy. It was a mirror-image of Gower's dismissal in the second innings of the Second Test at the Gabba in 1982, when he was caught down the legside by Rod Marsh off Jeff Thomson.

We laid our plans well, but importantly we stuck to them so well they invariably worked to our advantage.

I'll admit it now, I was probably more nervous than anyone at that Headingley team dinner. I had no fond memories of the place where Botham had gone berserk against us in 1981, reducing us to a rabble; it had been at that time the lowest point in my cricketing life. And, of course, my future as captain was almost certainly on the line. So, after winning the Ashes I naturally felt good about the captaincy, and very satisfied that I had survived the job's darker moments.

On the way back to Australia it crossed my mind that if I were to lose the captaincy down the line I'd have to say, "I'll miss being the head of the family."

OPPOSITE: *The end of the nightmare.*
We enjoy victory at Headingley in 1989.

END OF THE NIGHTMARE

On June 13, 1989 Australia beat England by 210 runs in the First Test and finally laid to rest the Headingley bogey that had haunted us since 1981.

The winning feeling was better than it had been when we'd won the World Cup in 1987—even though this was only the first in a six-Test series.

Terry Alderman, named Man Of The Match for his 10/151 haul, made sure we kept the win in the right perspective: his £500 went into the team kitty—but so did a magnum of champagne. Terry said, "Put it on ice until we win the Ashes."

Terry is superstitious. He'd given me a bollicking before the Test over the dramatically altered state of my face. On Test eve I was trimming my beard when I thought, 'Why not do something completely different for this Test?' So I shaved off my beard. It was half gone when I thought, 'Terry Alderman won't be happy about this—the team's playing great cricket with the beard on, why risk it all for a shave?'

Superstition got totally out of hand in the Second Test at Lord's. To win we needed to score 119 on the last day, but crumbled to 4/67.

That's when I started to smoke a few of the team Benson and Hedges, and in the end, unable to sit and watch so intense was the fight for runs, I opted for a long shower. I thought, 'I won't go back into the room until we're almost home. While I'm in here nobody's getting out.' When I finally dried off and went back into the room, Terry Alderman leapt up and ordered me back into the shower. "Never change a winning situation," he shouted.

So, back into the shower I went. When I couldn't stand the water any longer— my skin had wrinkled and I looked like a white prune—I had a shave.

Finally they let me back into the room when we needed ten runs to win. We went two up after two Tests and Bradman's great '48 side was the last to be in that situation.

To hold the Ashes England also needed a Bradman-like effort: his 1936–37 team was the only one to win a rubber from two down.

The Third Test was a draw, but significant because England played Ian Botham, whose inclusion prompted the media to yet again regurgitate all the stuff about Botham blitzing the Aussies eight years before. How he was the big, bad bogeyman. He took on Merv Hughes, and lost. We had to keep it that way next Test.

We had now reached the most vital part of the tour. Previously, in 1981 and 1985, our Ashes campaigns had gone badly adrift about Fourth Test time. Now, every day before the Old Trafford Test, where a win would clinch the Ashes, we reminded ourselves: stay on the boil.

Mid-afternoon on the first day legspinner Trevor Hohns came on to bowl to David Gower, and in his loosening up period gave him a rank long-hop, the ball that pitches halfway down and sits up, saying, 'Hit me!'

Gower didn't, but he certainly thought about it, because he got himself into position for the shot over the top to the mid-wicket fence, but then pulled out.

Strange, really. And I wondered why, because he does like to play that shot, and plays it well. Was it pressure? He'd come under extraordinary attack from the media over his captaincy in the first two Tests. Or was it another symptom of the shoulder injury that was giving him such hell in the field?

Gower stared ruefully in the direction of the fence where he might have hit it, and I could almost read his mind: 'Trevor my boy, if you bowl another one of those that's where I'm going to whack it.'

I thought, 'Okay, I can't go setting fields for long-hops, leave it as it is.'

Next over 'Cracker' Hohns produced 'the flipper', a ball which pitches halfway down too, just like a long-hop. But it doesn't sit up and say 'Hit me!' It just looks like a long-hop, but what it does is skid through low and fast.

Gower went back to belt it over mid-wicket but his bat was hardly even into

ABOVE: *Oops ... actually I had it under control all the time! Smith caught off Lawson for a duck in the Headingley Test.*

Terry Alderman's Man Of The Match award—"Keep it on ice," he told me.

the downswing when the ball rapped him on the pads. Out—leg before, and you bloody beauty, Cracker had one for none.

Botham was the new batsman. Trevor Hohns hasn't always been known as 'Cracker'. When Botham was doing his stint with Queensland in the Sheffield Shield, Hohns became known as 'Step-and-Fetch-it'. Botham liked to play 'kill the bowler' at net practice, which meant he liked to smash the ball straight, and far. Hohns, being a spinner, used to have to bear the brunt of Botham's fun more than most. He'd bowl, Both would take a step, hit the ball a mile, and Hohns would have to fetch it.

At Old Trafford I didn't set an outfield for Botham, but had in place pressure fielders, the bat-pads. Botham, therefore, more or less had a licence to slog.

He played a couple back defensively to Cracker, then—woof! He tried to hit one out of the park and was bowled. As Botham walked off, past Cracker, he'd have to have overheard his spirited reaction: "Hey, Step-and-Fetch-it has struck!"

By the end of the Test the Australian team rated by the English media as "the weakest ever" had won the Ashes.

Suitably embarrassed by their total lack of judgment they chose to ignore our remarkable performance and instead opted for headlines about "England's Rebel Tour To South Africa", or "Gower Must Go", or, in what must be the ultimate about-face, "Weakest England Team Ever".

I think we deserved better than that.

THE VICTORY

It's a big bit of cricket history: Old Trafford, Manchester, Fourth Test, last day, August 1, 1989; the winning run hit by David Boon, a sweep to leg off the fifth ball of England spinner Nick Cook's fifth over. The time was 5.40 p.m.

Australia had regained the Ashes in England for the first time since 1934. I was ecstatic.

Four years before I'd been a loser. England's captain then had been my friend David Gower, and he was captain in 1989. I went to see David not long after we'd won. He was in the Captain's Room, one of those quaint traditions that remain in English cricket, even as we move towards the year 2000. The idea is that the captain can pop along there and do his own thing without being pestered by the other players—strange idea.

Gower wasn't alone; the new chairman of selectors, Ted Dexter, was with him for a short time. When Dexter left David was very good about our victory, very congratulatory. "If we had to lose then I'm happy we lost to you," was his sentiment. But he was very down. We chatted on a bit but what seemed like

*The welcoming party in
the rooms at Old
Trafford after we'd
won the Ashes back.*

Wet, inside and out.

every few seconds there'd be a bang on the door, and Swampy Marsh, wearing his baggy green Aussie cap, would stick his head in and say, "You coming, AB?" Finally I had to say, "Okay, okay …"

I went back to our dressing room and as I went through the door Swampy shouted out, "Three cheers for AB!" and they did sound great—but with the three cheers came about 25 cans of frothing XXXX beer and the contents of five bottles of champagne, all freezing, and all poured over my head.

I thought I'd drown. That cold champagne just took my breath away.

Then I saw David Boon. Even in the milling throng it was hard to miss him, because he was on the table and wearing only a jock strap, an Aussie jumper, and like his great mate Swampy, the baggy green Aussie cap.

He started to sing our victory song, "Underneath the Southern Cross I stand, a sprig of wattle in my hand …" and it was only then that I thought to myself, 'Hey, we've won the Ashes—that's one helluva performance.'

Maybe the enormity of what we'd done took some time to sink in because it had taken us a lot longer to wrap up the Fourth Test win than we'd hoped.

Just after lunch on the fourth day we had England 6/59 in their second innings, still 128 short of avoiding an innings defeat. It was a scoreline that screamed, "Victory today!"

But gutsy little wicketkeeper 'Jack' Russell scampered runs and John Emburey stayed with him. Then it rained. Worse still the next day they avoided the follow-on. I found myself clenching my teeth in frustration.

Here we were about to set foot on the summit of cricket's Mt Everest, and we couldn't find the flag!

At lunch on the final day Russell and Emburey were still together. I told my blokes, "Look, I don't want to leave here with two Tests up and two to play, with England having a sniff of levelling the series and holding the bloody Ashes."

After lunch there was more 'edge' to our game; I could see our batsmen were making a mental note of the equation: runs to score, time to go, overs to be bowled. That spurred the bowlers on to greater efforts. Our complacency evaporated.

Terry Alderman got Emburey with the second new ball and the rest went pretty quickly, the target to win 78 runs in 80 minutes, plus 20 overs.

Swampy Marsh was out when we were just 16 runs short of victory. Up on the balcony there was a groan of sympathy for Swampy—I think everyone in the side would have loved to have seen him hit the winning run because he'd done so much for the team during the tough times.

Boon was next in. I knew he'd been thinking of the winning run, too, because as Marsh and Taylor advanced towards the target he said to me, "AB, why don't you go and put the pads on mate, then if a wicket falls you can go out and be there when the winning run's hit."

Soaking up the glory. On the balcony at The Oval, after the last Test in the series.

I didn't think that was necessary. I was quite happy for Boon to have that honour. He'd been at No. 3 in the batting order throughout the series, and more than that, in 1985 some of the Poms hadn't thought Boon could play much, and let him know.

So, it was a tremendous thing for Boon to be able to look back and say, "I hit the winning run when we regained the Ashes in 1989."

Merv Hughes led the beer and champagne 'squirt charge'.

After our Second Test victory at Lord's Merv's style had been a little cramped by 'The Colonel'—team manager Laurie Sawle. As Merv made his fifth trip in as many minutes to the icebox for $50 bottles of champagne, which he then pointed and sprayed like a fireman dousing the Towering Inferno, The Colonel had said to the Lord's room attendant, "For heaven's sake hide the rest or there'll be none left to drink!"

This prompted Merv to take a different tack—holding full opened cans of XXXX at arm's length, one in each hand, squeezing the contents over anyone within range. We thought it could have been a hangover from his days as a fullback with Werribee in the VFA.

It was in the middle of this tumult of laughter, shouting, popping corks and cans and Cold Chisel tapes blaring, that the Ashes arrived in the room.

I just couldn't believe it, and I offered the bloke holding them, David Frith from Wisden, a thousand quid for them, then and there. My offer was a shade generous—understandable in the rather euphoric circumstances!—because they weren't actually the real Ashes, but a perfect replica, of which there are only three in existence.

I was allowed to hold them, my smile as wide as Brisbane's Gateway Bridge. Merv Hughes asked, "How about letting the fast bowler have a nurse, AB?" But Frith, having seen Merv making mayhem, discreetly suggested a mere touch for the rest of the boys would be in order.

It was a great moment. I didn't know it then, but incredibly there would later be an even greater moment—the ticker-tape welcome home.

MILESTONES

When people talk about the 1989 Ashes tour, the first point they usually make is that we were the first Australian team in 55 years to regain the Ashes in England.

I understand that, but it was a record only made possible by marvellous team spirit and team work, the basis of which was freakish individual performance.

Some observers were prepared to compare our undefeated 1989 Test performance with that of Bradman's famous '48 team, but I would discourage that, except to say a champion in one era would almost certainly be a champion in any other era. Teams, though, are a different matter; there are just too many variables.

Just for the record, it is worth noting some of the highlights of the 1989 team's performance.

THE FIRST TEST
- Australia totalled 7/601 declared, which was the highest innings total at Leeds by any nation.
- Mark Taylor, 135, became the 16th Australian to score a century on debut in a Test against England.
- Steve Waugh scored his first Test century, and his highest Test score, 177 not out.
- Steve Waugh and Merv Hughes added 147 for the 7th wicket, an Australian Test record for any Test against England in England.
- Terry Alderman took ten wickets in a Test for the first time in his career.
- Allan Border, 7957 runs in Tests, moved past Viv Richards, 7849.
- Mark Taylor and Allan Border added 117 for the 3rd wicket, the 39th time Border had been associated in a century stand, a record for an Australian.

THE SECOND TEST
- Australia defeated England for the 11th time in Tests at Lord's.
- The Test was Allan Border's 100th consecutive Test.
- Terry Alderman took his 100th Test wicket, Gooch.
- Steve Waugh and Geoff Lawson added 130 for the 9th wicket, an Australian record at Lord's.

THE THIRD TEST

- Dean Jones became only the second Australian to score a Test century at Birmingham. His 157 surpassed the previous highest, 114 by Neil Harvey in 1961.
- Steve Waugh's Test aggregate reached 393 before he was dismissed, a record.
- Allan Border passed 8000 runs in his 105th Test.

THE FOURTH TEST

- Australia regained the Ashes in England for the first time since 1934.
- Australia recorded their first Test win at Old Trafford since 1968.
- Australia's victory was their 100th in Tests against England, and their 200th in all Tests.

THE FIFTH TEST

- Australia's victory margin by an innings and 180 runs was their biggest in England and their 7th biggest in all Tests.
- Allan Border, 8081 runs, passed Gary Sobers, 8032, to move to third on the all-time Test run-getters list.
- Geoff Marsh and Mark Taylor added 329 for the 1st wicket, the highest opening partnership on English soil, and the second highest opening partnership for Australia. They became the first openers to bat through a complete day's play in a Test in England.
- Geoff Marsh's 138 was his highest Test score, Mark Taylor's 219 the fourth highest among Australian openers.

THE SIXTH TEST

- Australia scored 468 in their first innings, establishing a Test record of totalling 400 or more in their first innings in eight consecutive Tests.
- Australia's victory gave them a four-nil winning margin in the series, equalling the 1921 and 1948 teams.
- Steve Waugh became the third player to average more than 100 in an Ashes series.
- Terry Alderman took 41 wickets in the series, the only player in Test history to take 40 or more wickets twice in a series.
- Three Australians, Mark Taylor (839 runs), Dean Jones (566) and Steve Waugh (506), totalled more than 500 runs in the series, a first for Australia.
- Allan Border, 8273 runs, moved into second place on the Test run-getters list, passing Geoff Boycott, 8114. His aggregate included 42 half-centuries and 23 centuries. Ahead of him was Sunil Gavaskar, 45 half-centuries and 34 centuries.

Trivia buffs will have a field day with that little lot, but take it from me, it was one helluva team.

TICKLED PINK

The Grosvenor Hotel in London is a pretty swish place and its restaurant, 90 Park Lane, a very elegant one. It's decidedly upmarket, as you would expect of an eatery nestled in the ritziest area of one of the world's most brilliant cities.

Just the spot for 17 deliriously victorious Aussie cricketers to celebrate a milestone in their careers. With us were wives, girlfriends and mates.

You might say this was a 'sponsored night', because after we'd won the First Test at Headingley a telegram had arrived. It said: "Well done; if you can make it two at Lord's the party's on us." It was signed Paul Hogan, John Cornell and Austin Robertson, a good mate of Hogan and Cornell, and my manager. When we made it two-nil at Lord's another telegram lobbed. It said: "Okay, the party's on us. When and where do you want it?" Clearly this generous offer from Crocodile Dundee and Co required a team meeting; it was decided to try to win the six-Test series by a record five-nil, then have the party.

Now our long-awaited night out had arrived. It was totally and brilliantly organised by Daphne Benaud, wife of Richie, and everyone looked a million dollars as we gathered in the foyer of the team hotel, the Westbury.

Merv Hughes caught the eye. For most of the tour he'd looked about one dollar, getting around in a pair of huge green and gold long shorts and a T-shirt with "Party Animal" on it. Plus a pair of dreadful long socks. We could see his knees, that's about all. Now he looked stunning in a brand new suit, crisp shirt, paisley tie, shiny black shoes. He's probably only ever looked smarter on his wedding day.

Boon, who was standing next to me, tapped my elbow and said, "Do you think he's got those shorts on underneath?" Then he added, "Worse still, you don't think he's just wearing the suit so he can get into the joint, then he's going to strip down to those shorts?"

Our transport arrived, not the XXXX coach with the fridge that had taken us from one end of England to the other, but limousines, 'Rollers', 'Mercs' and Bentleys.

Upon arrival there was champagne, but for a change, at this celebration we drank it! The menu was brilliant, if a bit hard to pronounce. We ate foie gras terrine, John Dory, carre d'agneau, cheeses, and for dessert fresh berries. We washed it down with a choice of either Mersault white wine or Lynch Bages red. Some blokes didn't forget their origins and stuck with the good old 'sprig of wattle', cans of XXXX.

I made a short speech of thanks to my team during which I read out the latest missive from Crocodile Dundee and friends. It was a fax, and said: "What can we say? It's all been said and done. By you blokes. Thrashing England is a lot like climaxing and having your feet rubbed at the same time. You should all feel proud of yourselves. As for you AB, you deserved every winning minute. Delighted you didn't cry."

As I sat down, Merv got up. "I'm the master of ceremonies for the night ..." he began. I looked across at him and thought, 'That's funny, I don't recall anyone appointing you MC.'

He kept talking: "We've heard from AB and we've had a real gutful of him getting up and going on. We want to hear from ..." and he went right through the team.

It was just after midnight when the ladies issued instructions for the rest of the celebration: "On with the dancing shoes, boys."

The limos dropped us at Stocks, a popular nightclub in London's famous King's Road in Chelsea. Dancing is not my go and Jane was back home, so I was with the other 'single' blokes having a beer and talking about how good the tour had been.

Suddenly, at my side, I heard a sweet female voice say, "I need to dance with the captain." It was Jane Alderman. I immediately told her about my knee injury, my other injury, and anything else that would stop me dancing. I can tell you Jane was as persistent about a dance as her husband Terry was with his length and line all tour.

So, I danced. The sheer historical element in this appealed so much to Long Tom Moody that he picked me up and hoisted me onto his shoulders. As you can imagine my head was, if not in the clouds, then certainly a very long way above the dance floor.

So far in fact that my head carved a swathe through the fancy lighting arrangements! This startled Tom, who put me down, but he did it too quickly.

Tom was wearing one of those then fashionable shimmering suits with the wide shoulders and the thin pants. The pants were tight numbers and Tom split them from you-know-where to breakfast time and for the rest of the night had to dance around with his 'Reg Grundy's' in full view.

The guys will never again see a 'team dinner' like it, a special event for a special bunch of blokes.

The bill must have been colossal. We may yet see a Crocodile Dundee III—just to pay for it.

Chapter Eight

THE CRUEL SEA

Cricket in St. Kitts, but it's tougher than it looks.

White sands, turquoise water, blue skies; coconut palms and bougainvillea; throbbing steel drum bands, swaying limbo dancers, powerful rum punches, slow balmy nights; friendly people. The Caribbean is all of those, and more. But a cricket tour of the Caribbean is tough, and Australia's tour there in 1991 was tougher than most.

'CRACKER', WHERE ARE YOU?

The Frank Worrell Trophy signifies supremacy when it comes to cricket between Australia and the West Indies. It's only natural that it doesn't have quite the aura that is attached to the Ashes, but in February 1991 as we headed off for the five-Test series in the Caribbean, it was with the knowledge that Australia hadn't held the Worrell Trophy aloft in victory since 1975, when Greg Chappell's team won a six-Test series by five rubbers to one. When you've been out in the cold that long it's thought-provoking.

Our just-completed three-nil Ashes win over England was a confidence boost, as was the fact that we'd beaten Pakistan in a short series the summer before. I felt the time was right for us to beat the West Indies. Our side had developed, we were winning, and the West Indies' great players were getting on a bit, plus they'd had a couple of close-run series in the Caribbean against England and Pakistan in recent times.

It's not just the Tests that make the Caribbean a tough tour. In every game there'll be a couple of good young fast bowlers, or a couple of very good batsmen whose ultimate dream is to play for the West Indies. Success against the Aussies is seen as the stepping stone to glory. Whichever island you're playing they're after you.

Travel is not just a case of hopping on the team bus. The cricket venues are far-spread, from Jamaica to Guyana on the tip of South America; and you can end up spending long hours in airport terminals.

Part of our planning was to make sure the team expected life to be tough; they all knew that for three months they would have to come to grips with what they would perceive as frustrations, but the Caribbean people considered normal.

The other part of planning was to try to get the team right, and to that end moves were made secretly behind the scenes to lure legspinner Trevor Hohns out of retirement.

'Cracker', as we called him, had been a successful member of our great 1989 Ashes-winning team, but upon returning home had announced that at 35 years of age he preferred to devote more time to his family and his sports agency business.

Queensland talked him into a comeback in the 1990–91 summer, the Queensland captaincy being part of the deal. And Cracker made it clear he was not available for Tests against England, who were to tour.

Well, naturally Queensland were happy, but there were others in Australian cricket who were a bit displeased and felt that Trevor had lost nothing in his year off, and was sorely needed for the Tests against England and then the West Indies tour. There was a feeling among the selectors that we should have a spinner in the West Indies who could take the ball away from the bat, that there was historical evidence to suggest it could trouble them.

Trevor was phoned by Laurie Sawle, the chairman of the Australian selection panel, and Jim Higgs, another selector, spoke to him, but because I was playing with Queensland I had the closest contact. He was adamant: "The only reason I've come back is to try and help Queensland. It fits in with my scheduling because I'm not going to be away from home or my business too much." He never wavered.

I thought it was a real shame, because he'd spent long years trying to get into the Test team, then when he finally got his chance on the Ashes tour he retired. He would have been ideal in the West Indies, a strong character and a steadying influence, a real sticker with the bat.

Jim Higgs, as usual, threw a 'curve ball': "Why don't we take Tim Zoehrer as the legspinner?" he asked his fellow selectors. Zoehrer was Australia's second wicketkeeper. Higgs had been impressed by Zoehrer's style in a casual nets session, and it was about this time Zoehrer began exchanging the gloves for the worn ball during Shield games.

Now that would have been a mighty big gamble on the part of the selectors, none of whom I'd ever noticed had a compulsion to suddenly gulp down a beer at the end of a day's play at the Gabba, then shoot out the door saying "Excuse me AB, got to get to Jupiters (the casino on the Gold Coast)!"

So the Higgs 'curve ball' finished up out of the park, so to speak. When things like that crop up the mind naturally gets a little curious: 'A bloke has enough trouble,' I thought, 'just working out when to change the bowling, now I'd have to work out when to change the bloody wicketkeeper as well!'

The selectors had little option but to choose two offspinners, the old rivals Peter Taylor and Greg Matthews. I was nominated as the bowler to come from the leg.

Others said if I had bowled more in the Caribbean the bottom line could have been different. Well, as we all know, hindsight improves any bottom line.

A SNOWMAN, THEN 'BOVVER'

Australian teams traditionally travel to the Caribbean via the United States—a night in San Francisco where a beer at Lefty O'Doule's Bar and Grill was always appreciated, a bus trip that took you over the Golden Gate, then the next morning, around the corner from the hotel for some hash browns and "How'd yo like yo eggs, suh, easy, real easy or over easy?"

But the 1991 team went via London, which was a strange feeling because any other time I'd flown into Heathrow with an Australian team it had been summer. Now it was February and freezing. Our arrival brought puzzled frowns to the faces of the locals, who just a few days before had been watching us, via the satellite, whack England in the Fifth Test. In that one moment I was reminded of the frantic pace cricket has begun to move at in my era.

There aren't too many cricket tours that offer the players the temptation to do something with lots of snow, but London in February did. McDermott, Marsh, Healy, Mark Taylor, Mark Waugh and I made a whopper snowman and dressed him in pads, gloves and a bat—and, of course, the Aussie baggy green cap, just for fun.

Heading for the Caribbean, via a London winter. With Geoff Marsh, and 'Snowy'.

That night we got into a bit of 'bovver'. As often happens when you're on tours there was an invitation to a night out. It might be dinner at someone's place, a party, a show or a sporting event, like a race meeting.

The directors of the Arsenal Football Club had invited us along to watch their team do battle with Leeds, and had accorded us honorary Arsenal fan status for the night by giving us all club caps.

So there we all were up in the directors' box enjoying ourselves to the fullest when, as has been the case with certain Australian cricketers in the past, there was some bother over betting. Nothing quite so generous as the 500-1 Rod Marsh and Dennis Lillee managed on the 1981 Headingley Test match, but the odds Ladbrokes were offering about Leeds were good enough for some of the boys to invest.

Of course they couldn't help themselves and started cheering through their pockets, which brought a few grumbles and black looks from our Arsenal hosts! "Sorry, just kidding," we said, to smooth things over.

Outside the ground, after the game, our next predicament was a bit tougher. We were all pretty jolly, making a big thing out of our sparkling new Arsenal caps as we strolled back to our bus, when this bloke looked at Terry Alderman and said to his mates, "I can smell something real bad around here, like shit ..."

He was wearing a scarf with 'Leeds' knitted into it. Worse, our bus was parked right in the middle of all the Leeds buses! We all beat a hasty retreat.

JUST A TASTE

The prisoners from the jail adjacent to Warner Park, Basseterre, St Kitts, had laboured hard on the pitch for our first game. It was as hard as rock, and the outfield, although the colour of straw, was certainly not as soft.

Warner Park, I had been told, was named after a sea captain ancestor of Pelham Warner, who captained England at cricket about the turn of the century. Pelham was known as 'Plum' Warner and had come to Australia as assistant manager of Jardine's 1932–33 team, when Bodyline became notorious. That was one for the omen-merchants, a mention like that on a tour to the Caribbean!

Our opponents were the President's XI, a strong side captained by Richie Richardson.

There were three fast bowlers, Patrick Patterson, Tony Gray and a new face, Kenneth Benjamin, whose middle names were Charlie Griffith. Now, no matter what any of us might have thought of coincidences like Unlucky 13 and Ancestral Links To Bodyline, it did raise a few eyebrows to learn we were to play against a fast bowler whose parents had seen fit to name him after one of the world's feared fast bowlers.

Drying the pitch, West Indian style.

Simmo knew 'the feared Charlie Griffith' well, having spent a good deal of time during the 1965 Caribbean series against the West Indies trying to read his swaying, jerky action then taking evasive action against the lethal deliveries. So, of course, the 'new Charlie Griffith' was the perfect starting point for a lot of hype about their fast bowlers.

There are plenty of theories about the best way to handle the West Indies pace barrage. Ian Chappell talks about going out there and taking them on— boom, boom, boom. It is not as easy as that. I'd been facing them since 1979 and, yes, some days you'd go out there feeling good and attack and play well.

But you just can't attack all the time—boom, boom, boom. You have to give their bowlers respect, they are just so relentless and when they're bowling consistently well it's sometimes hard not to get into a defensive frame of mind.

On previous tours the first game at St Kitts had been played against the Leeward Islands, an 'island game' if you like. But this President's XI had quite a few players in it who were keen to put their names in front of the West Indian Test selectors, especially the fast bowlers.

Even on the last day there was an intimidating presence about Patrick Patterson.

Mark Taylor scored a gutsy hundred and getting there he had to survive Patrick's idea of a triple-play. Ball one was a bouncer that 'Tails' evaded, but in doing so finished on the seat of his trousers. That fired the small crowd into taunts like "Hit him next time, Patrick." Ball two was short around the off stump and Tails got up on his back foot and smashed it through the covers for four.

Patrick went around the wicket for ball three. It slanted in at Taylor's jugular. Fend for one.

Reacting to an over-the-top crowd in St. Kitts.

I was angered by the crowd on that final day; perhaps they had come along anticipating we'd get beaten, and were frustrated by our fightback for a draw. Even so I didn't think that was any excuse for the abuse hurled at me as I walked off after being run out. It was really nasty, taunting sort of stuff. Totally uncalled for. I did something I'd never done before in my life—I gave them the finger. That led to the local media accusing me of being "inciting". I found that a bit amusing.

There had been laughter at a pre-match function when a local official told a story about Bruce Yardley, the West Australian spinner in the 1978 team, which had had to deal with such fast bowlers as Andy Roberts, Joel Garner and Colin Croft. Bruce had been asked by a West Indian fan, "What's your name, man?" and Bruce had replied, "Yardley." The fan flashed a toothy grin and said, "Man, when we finish with you you'll be Inch-ley."

And when we had first touched down in the Caribbean at St Lucia, en route to St Kitts, we'd overheard a security man, with a wide grin and a deep laugh, tell Patrick Smithers, cricket writer for the *Age*, "You'll be doing a lot of writing about broken arms and heads, man."

We knew the 'duck' season was just around the corner.

DRAWING FIRST BLOOD

Kingston, the capital of Jamaica, is a tough place; on the day we arrived, the front page of the local paper, *The Daily Gleaner*, told us so by way of a Murder Toll item, sort of like those Road Toll updates Australian newspapers used to run.

You wondered if Dirty Harry himself might pop up around the next corner, so constant were the headline references to crime. The cricket team was insulated from that. You knew it must be there, but you didn't go where you might be touched by it.

Beyond Sabina Park, where we were to play our next three matches, the beautiful Blue Mountains were the support act for the anti-crime street posters that said, "Tourism is our business, let's protect it."

The three games, in order, were: against Jamaica, against West Indies in a one-day international, and against West Indies, First Test. Viv Richards arrived and when he was asked about his team's chances in the upcoming clashes, said that West Indian success in the first one-day international would be like "drawing first blood".

Courtney Walsh, the West Indian fast bowler and Jamaican captain, didn't just talk about drawing first blood. If you ever watch the telecasts of the motorcycle grands prix, you'll know that when one of the riders makes a sudden move you'll hear commentator Barry Sheene say so-and-so's "turned up the wick". Well, Courtney turned up the wick.

First he gave Dean Jones a peppering, something like near ten bouncers in a few overs. Then Mark Waugh had to come off dazed after a short one got 'big' on him.

Courtney's quite sharp and his bouncer is a bit quicker. The one that hit Mark came from over the top of the sightscreen, 'out of the stand', and hit him about the temple area. Certainly he was wearing a helmet, but it was still a bad one.

There was a feeling in some quarters that this was intimidatory bowling by Walsh, but I don't think there's really such a thing over there. The bouncer situation in the Caribbean is totally different. They dish it out, teams dish it out in return and the result is a lot more bouncers are bowled.

Still, Walsh did go a bit silly in this game when Craig McDermott came in at No. 9—in the 20 minutes he was in I'd guess Craig copped 15 bouncers, which is a lot. One, Craig tried to hook and the ball forced through the gap between the grille and the helmet peak, and sliced him above the right eye.

So Errol Alcott, the team physiotherapist, was running on again—he was sure earning his dollars that day.

When Craig got back from hospital, with 12 stitches, he said, "You know, the only reason I got hit was because the ball came off so slowly I was through with my shot." I looked at his swollen eye and thought, 'Nice try Craig, if it was so slow how come it forced by the grille?'

The umpires warned Walsh off for bowling excessive bouncers, an action that I heartily endorsed. Obsessive short pitched bowling, and it was four, sometimes five an over to Craig, can ruin the game. Or worse, kill a player.

But I wasn't going to hold my breath about the umpires' actions being repeated anywhere else on the tour. Nor did I think the umpires, Messrs Gaynor and Bell, would be sitting by the phone waiting for a call from the West Indies Test appointments panel.

So, why did Courtney Walsh do it? Had the West Indies decided to target Waugh and McDermott, both of whom had come into the Ashes series against England in the final Tests and done extraordinarily well? Or was it just the frustration of being captain of a team, Jamaica, that was going to be beaten and he'd had a gutful?

Amongst the crowd at Sabina Park after our win in the first one-day international.

Happy after our Sabina Park win, although Dean Jones looks like he's lost his bat!

SCHEMOZZLE AT SABINA

Big Merv Hughes has a nice talent for putting a crisis into another perspective. One of the turning points in the twisting First Test at Sabina Park was the rain farce played out over the fourth and fifth days, and at the centre of all the mud-slinging was the head groundsman.

His name was Charles Joseph, but the players called him 'Joe'. Watching Joe and his workers preparing the Test pitch—rolling and rolling, or down on their knees with their tins of water, slightly wetting the top to help the rolling bring up a sheen you'd swear you could see your reflection in—you knew it was a labour of love. In fact there was a story around that Joe so loved Sabina that when he got married he had the reception in the pavilion.

When a tropical storm burst over Sabina on the night of the Test rest day, it didn't only drench the arena, it swamped Joe with all the blame, which prompted the comment from Merv: "My mum told me a workman is only as good as his tools—and these blokes didn't have any."

New covers were being used, but for the first time, and they leaked at the seams. When we went back for the fourth day the place was an absolute mess, the bowler's run-up at one end was a quagmire, the pitch surrounds were a mudheap and on a good length at one end there was a big damp spot with a footprint in the middle of it—like the one Robinson Crusoe found on the beach!

Joe and his men used grass clippings and spare topsoil to try to dry the surrounds; then they even tried a can of kerosene slopped liberally onto the wet areas, and lit.

For enterprise it rated highly, but the fact was all it did was add to the farce. These events at Sabina must have raised a laugh from the administrators of some of the sports threatening cricket.

The Test was being televised live, at least to Australia, and for all I know England. That's a lot of revenue for the game, but I don't think too many promoters or sponsors would have been too happy with what they saw—and didn't see—on the Test's fourth day, which was eventually abandoned without a ball being bowled.

Richie Benaud made the suggestion that the ICC, the ruling body of world cricket, introduce legislation stipulating that every ground where an international, Test or limited-overs is played should have covers to protect the whole square and 18 metres (20 yards) beyond each side, plus extended run-up covers 22 metres (25 yards) from the bowling crease and the width of two pitches.

Clive Lloyd wrote to the ICC suggesting some of the profits from limited-overs series worldwide be put into a general revenue fund to ensure the poorer cricket venues around the world have adequate facilities.

It's a nice gesture but it might leave the way open for some authorities to rort the system. What's the definition of 'poor'? Who's going to check the books? Would we have a sort of Cricketing Means Test? I think any country that has been able to develop cricketers good enough to compete at international level should be able to develop its ground facilities likewise.

Play didn't even get underway on time on the fifth day, the real problem being the damp spot on the pitch, so it was clear the only result could be a draw. If it hadn't rained in this Test I think we could have won.

They batted and we had them 6/75, which must have been a huge shock for them because it certainly was for us, even though we had gone into the game fancying our chances. We just had a niggling doubt about how well McDermott could bowl in tandem with Hughes. The answer, of course, was bloody well!

We could have had them out for 80. Craig bowled Gus Logie a fearsome bouncer which he tried to hook, but missed and the ball squeezed through the grille then ricocheted up in the air, bounced, hit the stumps, but didn't knock the bails off. They'd have been seven-for.

And Jeff Dujon hooked one off Whitney, low and hard towards Craig McDermott at fine leg, where it can sometimes be a bit hard to pick the ball up off the bat because it gets 'lost' in the crowd background. It cleared Craig by a whisker and went for four.

Their 'tail' stayed with Dujon until Logie got back from hospital where he'd been stitched and taped, then that pair used up all their experience to get the total up to 264. For us, it was case of 'what if …?'

We batted and got 371, which was a lead of 107. There were some very good signs for us: Geoff Marsh's 69 came off 110 balls; Taylor copped one to the jaw from Marshall but put on 139 for the first wicket with Marsh; Boon got a hundred, although his chin was sliced open by a Patterson bouncer at 98.

There were some ominous signs: our 'tail' didn't wag. We were cruising at 5/329 but all out 42 runs later. Their fast bowlers went after our 'tail' in a major way, particularly McDermott, and so much so that he'd come back in shell-shocked. He's quite a handy batsman but once he'd been hit in the eye in that Jamaican game I think they were always going to go after him. They saw him as the Australian bowler who was a real threat to them.

The collapse of the 'tail' and the rain led to a sort of domino effect that undid much of the positive work we'd done, and probably gave them some breathing space, a chance to think harder about our challenge.

This was how the dominoes fell: Patterson takes 4/19 to blast out the 'tail'; Haynes and Greenidge come out, faced with a deficit of 107, and by stumps have belted 187, and a handy lead; rain; nobody wants to play on the last day.

If this had been a fight then I thought we'd won on points—but I knew they'd got up off the canvas a couple of times, and that was disappointing.

INTO THE RECORD BOOKS

Terry Alderman shouted at the top of his voice that it was the best bus trip he'd ever been on. The team mini-bus was hurtling along the narrow streets of Bridgetown, the capital of Barbados, taking us from Kensington Oval to our hotel, The Rockley Resort.

Terry had a point. As we shot past, the locals would stop and stare at the 'moving jukebox', our bus, from which came a raucous, repetitive, tuneless "Three-one, three-one, three-one".

Ten minutes earlier our dressing room in the Sir Garfield Sobers Stand at Kensington had been reverberating to the sounds of 'Underneath the Southern Cross I Stand', and 'I Still Call Australia Home', courtesy of the Aussie cricket team choir, led by David Boon and Peter Taylor. The local beer, Banks, was flowing in copious quantities. We tend to celebrate fully and we had just beaten the West Indies in the fourth one-day international, which gave us an unbeatable three-one lead in the best-of-five series.

It was the first time the West Indies had been beaten at Kensington since England beat them there in a Test in the 1930s; it was the first time they'd lost a one-day series on their home turf; and in the previous five seasons they hadn't even lost a one-day international at home.

This loss to us at Kensington was their third in a fortnight, and it could have been four but for some fickle weather in Trinidad, where rain interfered with the double-header.

Because Trinidad's dry season had "sprung a leak", as the local paper put it, rain reduced the first match to 42 overs a side. But the West Indies only managed to bowl 34 overs. Viv gave a shrug of the famous shoulders and said, "We did our best …" I thought, 'Yeah, best to what?'

Maybe the time has come for the ICC to act on this. Australia acted after the 1992 World Cup semi-final fiasco when South Africa only bowled 45 overs, not 50, to England. The next summer the rule was that if the team bowling first had only completed 45 overs at 'time', then they had to keep bowling. What's more, when they batted they only got 45 back. There was a rider clause to stop any time-wasting shenanighans from the team batting first. But countries shouldn't have to act one out.

The problem is that when the team bowling first goes slow it is then quite impossible for the batting team to organise their progressive run rate, and of course that is a very important ingredient in the approach to the short form of the game. It's a bit like doing a shopping list but not knowing how much money you can take with you.

The upshot was the West Indies had 34 overs to get our 172, a 'false' target really because through gamesmanship they had deprived us of the 'slog' overs,

ABOVE: *Boon leads us in the team victory song in Barbados.*

With my vice-captain, Geoff Marsh. 'Swampy' and I saw some sweet times together.

the 20 per cent at the finish when the batting team up the pace.

And, as any cricketer will tell you, it is easier to chase a low total from a low over base than a high total from higher overs, simply because the bowling side has less overs, therefore less chance, to bowl a team out.

When we took the field we were an angry team. We felt we'd been cheated because at the start of the tour the management officials of the two teams had met and had agreed that it was not just the letter of the laws that mattered, it was the spirit.

Malcolm Marshall was their last man out, caught by David Boon, diving, one-handed at point. Boon never shows emotion in an extravagant way, even when Dean Jones shouts him a beer, but now he raised a fist that said 'Up yours'. It clinched a win for us by 45 runs, a win that Simpson said rated among the top ten since he took over as coach, and which I rated almost up there with the 1987 World Cup.

It's always good to win, but when you know you've beaten the odds it makes it so much better.

The rain in Port Of Spain seemed to fall mostly at Queens Park Oval, and affected the third game in the series, too. Because there was a downpour at the end of our innings, our 245 off 49 overs—run rate five—became, under the local rain rules, 181 off 36 overs for West Indies.

It was academic, but if we'd been playing under the Australian World Series rain rule—the one, incidentally, that caused such dramas at the 1992 World Cup and was modified for the next Australian summer—our 36 highest scoring overs would have become the target. That was 218, or six runs an over, which would certainly have made for a more interesting, and hopefully closer match.

They won with seven wickets in hand and 15 balls to spare.

Barbados is an island it seems of more churches than Adelaide, the city of churches, and the locals will happily tell you that "there are forty-nine different religions—the fiftieth is cricket!" They have had some good ones go forth to spread the message.

One, Sir Garfield Sobers, was to judge the Man Of The Match in the fourth game: he duly handed it over to Geoff Marsh for his 113 off 140 balls, a stunning innings because the early West Indian bowling was scary.

The pitch had good life, a true bounce and real pace, all good for fast bowling—but equally good for batsmen who are looking for some consistency to allow them the confidence to play shots. It was clear from the first ball the West Indies had moved up a cog.

The bouncer rule in one-day cricket in the Caribbean isn't as restrictive as the one in Australia, where if the ball goes over shoulder height it's called a no-ball. In the Caribbean a bouncer is all right unless it's so far over the batsman's head it's a wide.

Hot work in Barbados.

*Taking it easy between Tests
in the Caribbean.*

They stuck it right up us and Marsh and Jones both copped nasty ones early; we were worried Marsh may have suffered a broken rib when Ambrose got one to climb in the third over.

At 2/27 I was in, the 10th over, and not quite the scoreline we'd been hoping for. A bit like getting a chihuahua for your birthday after you'd hinted you wanted a German shepherd.

But, it just so happened this was one of 'those days'—I felt good from the first ball, I attacked, and it came off, the hooking, the cutting, all the shots that once you've turned 35 you describe as 'vintage'. I stayed for 89 balls and got 79 runs, and with Swampy added 146, going past the 150 total mark in only 31 overs.

Talk about sweat! There was a heatwave inside my helmet and the moisture leaking down my face felt like someone was emptying the contents of a boiled kettle over me.

Marsh short-arm jabbed a shortish one from Malcolm Marshall over mid-wicket, over the boundary, and over the ground fence, out into the street.

I asked him, "How did you do that?"

He said, "I don't know, I'll have to have a look at the replay on the television tonight."

Up until that day Australia's best score against the West Indies in a one-day international had been the 274 scored by Ian Chappell's team in the very first World Cup final, 1974. Our 6/283 here eclipsed it.

The West Indies made 246. In accepting his Man Of The Match award Marsh said, "The crowd noise gets you going. If you're batting against a lot of people who want to get stuck into you, it makes you want to really compete. It lifts you because you're not going to give in."

Which was ironic, because before the game the authorities had announced a ban on the 'musical' paraphernalia fans commonly brought to the game—drums, cymbals, clackers, conch shells—on the grounds they "lacked discretion and just created incessant noise".

The fans ignored it. The show must go on … enter Swampy.

OIL, AND TROUBLED WATERS

Trinidad's 'second ground' is Guaracara Park at Point-a-Pierre, about a good hour by road from Port Of Spain. It is a flat expanse surrounded by an oil refinery and all the delightful aromas such an establishment can provide.

I've never played there on either of my tours to the Caribbean, 1984 with Kim Hughes's team, or in 1991, but there's a fair amount of feedback to suggest I only missed a nightmare.

The 1984 game against Trinidad and Tobago, as I've related, ended in uproar because Hughes resented the local captain's decision to bat on during the last day, rather than making a declaration. Hughes's frustration had probably been brought to 'simmer' a little earlier in the game by his fast bowler Rod Hogg.

Rod had teed up twelfth man Carl Rackemann to sub for him after a drinks break, but when he was still missing after ten minutes, Kim, who wanted him back to bowl, began to get a little agitated. "Where the hell is he?" he demanded of Carl, and naturally got a shrug of Carl's big shoulders in reply.

Another ten minutes and it was "Where the f—'s Hoggy, Carl?" and an order that Carl leave the field and get him. When Carl got to the dressing room he found Hoggy stretched out on a bench seat, and totally unmoved by any suggestion from Hughes, via Carl, that he should go back out into the heat.

"What'll I tell him?" asked Carl.

"Tell him that Hogg has passed away," said Hoggy.

There was a brief pause, then Carl said, "I don't know that I can go out and tell the captain that, Rod."

"Then go and tell him that I'm f—ed!" said Hoggy.

Carl said he didn't think he should tell the captain that either, and Hoggy repeated, "Then go and tell him Rodney Hogg has passed away."

So big Carl went back out and told Kim that Rodney had passed away, at which point Kim threw a major wobbly and ran off the ground himself to get Hoggy back on.

Nothing like that happened in 1991, although frustration was 'trumps'. The three-day game against Trinidad and Tobago was hit by rain, abandoned, and became a limited-over 'slogathon', hardly inspiring for Bruce Reid and Terry Alderman, who had been having fitness problems, or Greg Matthews and Peter Taylor who were vying for the one spinning spot in the Second Test team.

When the team bus arrived back each evening the boys would fall out, still in their creams, eyes red from the refinery pollution, and say "Tonguein' for a beer AB" in reply to the non-playing captain's query about the day's proceedings.

On the evening of the last day they looked a bit sheepish. Swampy told me Simpson had handed out a tongue-lashing: "… fielding was slack, bowling careless, and the batting …" Apparently the coach had been lost for words. He was probably searching for "nightmare".

THE REVERSE WHAMMY

Guyana 1991 had fallen upon desperate times. A lot of the beautiful wooden buildings that I recalled from my 1984 visit were in disrepair, paint peeling away, or just rotten. The currency was worthless. In 1984 one US dollar would get you twenty guyanese, now the official rate was 1:125. When we arrived our team manager, Laurie Sawle, was met by local officials keen to hand over our money for that leg of the tour. Laurie was, Terry Alderman said, "awash with the dosh". A conservative estimate was Laurie had about 670,000 guyanese.

At Guyana the West Indian players' body language was meant to intimidate and their appealing was more precipitant in the Second Test. I'd reached about 30, and with Swampy Marsh had started to turn our first innings around after we'd lost Taylor and Boon cheaply, when I got a little inside edge on one from Malcolm Marshall, but was given not out. I thought, 'You beauty, some luck.'

Malcolm, hands on hips, also had a few words to say about my luck. Strong, but brief. Dessie Haynes came from somewhere on the onside, calling me

Malcolm Marshall thinks he's got me caught behind during the Guyana Test.

BELOW: *In dispute with Desmond Haynes over the 'loose ball' incident at Bourda.*

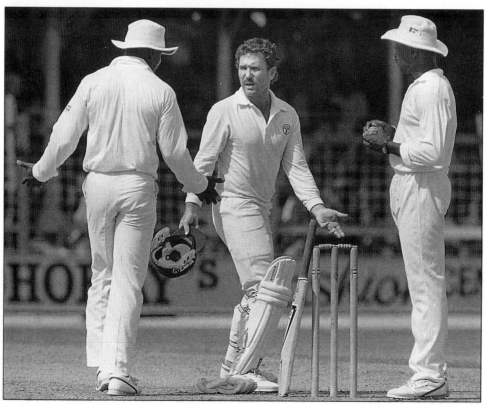

everything under the sun and eyeballing me. Thereafter, for the rest of the series, every time I came out to bat Dessie was there, and into me. These days that stuff's all part and parcel of the 'psych' in the game. We use it too. You tend to get used to it.

But there does need to be a line drawn so that some of it doesn't get too personal. When I captained a World XI in England in 1987 Dessie and I travelled together in the same team for a month. We'd had a good rapport over the years, so what started in Guyana left me feeling just a bit strange.

The 'reverse whammy' came on the second day of the Test. We were all out 348 and had immediate success when we bowled, Craig McDermott beating Gordon Greenidge with cut and sheer pace. Then Richie Richardson came out swinging, playing shots from the word go, hitting everything in the middle.

He said at the end of the day, "Sometimes you see the ball and you know you're going to get a hundred. From the time I started batting I felt like I was going to get a hundred and nothing was going to stop me."

I didn't expect anything like Richardson's innings. We had blokes in defensive positions but Richie was hitting so hard and so well that he was, as he said, unstoppable. It all began to unravel a bit for us. The bowling got ragged, too short, too wide, too full—but that's often the way when a bloke's 'going' like Richie was. Eventually we lost the plot totally. They took control of the game in that day hitting 226 runs off 54 overs. And Richie's hundred had come off only 116 balls.

The scoreboards at the end of the West Indies' first innings, early on the fourth day, showed just how their tactics—slow in the field, fast with the bat—had worked:

Australia 348 off 116.4 overs in 588 minutes.

West Indies 569 off 153.5 overs in 654 minutes.

Should we also have been slow in the field? As you can see the 37 or so overs extra we bowled to them took, in effect, only 66 minutes. The point is, to enhance your chances in a game where your opponents get 500 plus, it's best to make sure it takes a fair time to get them. At Guyana two days would have been better than one and a half.

But even if 'slow in the field' had been our pre-game plan, it wouldn't have worked. Because our frontline bowlers were under such pressure, I had to bowl 30 overs, and off my short run a slow over rate is totally out of the question.

Unless of course Richie and company had been belting me out of the ground into the canal that runs in the streets outside, thus holding up proceedings for fetched balls. They weren't. I got 5/68, including my mate Dessie Haynes. It was the bowling spell that prompted demands that I bowl more.

The 'fast batting' tactic left the West Indies with the best part of two days to force a win via their lead of 221 runs. For us it was always going to be a difficult

Success with the ball at Bourda, but others have a higher opinion of my bowling than I do.

assignment, because we clearly couldn't force a win. We had to save the game, and that meant surviving.

That can be the time when the siege mentality surfaces. They bowl, relentless stuff designed to wear you down, and you just try to play sensibly. It's not quite like batting in a straitjacket as you still have to be mindful of playing balls on their merits, but there is the ever present thought that you don't want to do anything stupid. And if there's any good luck around, you hope it will come your way.

We had reached 73, with Jones and I trying to make a fight of it, when Courtney Walsh bowled a very good yorker which Jones played over, and was bowled, tilting back the middle stump.

But, because I'd heard a call of "no-ball" I thought, 'You beauty, thank God for that!' Jones, though, hadn't heard the call, which can happen when you're wearing a helmet with the jaw guards that also come over the ears, and he had tucked the bat under his left arm and started to walk off.

Straightaway I started yelling to him that he wasn't out, it was a no-ball, and to get back, but of course once the crowd saw he'd been bowled they went berserk, ranting and raving, war dancing and all the rest of it—major noise— because they had a sniff of victory.

What followed took only seconds, but to me, standing helpless, as it turned out, at the other end, it seemed to unfold ever so slowly.

Jones, head down, kept walking. The West Indies team had started to run towards Walsh, then realised the umpire, Duncan, had his arm extended signalling no-ball. Hooper at second slip had the ball.

For a moment I thought, 'I could run at Jones and push him back,' but on second thoughts, 'They could throw to my end and run me out.' I wasn't sure, but clearly I was thinking Jones could be run out.

Suddenly Jones responded to my yelling. His head jerked up as if to say, 'Uh, what's going on?' He started back towards his crease and dived for the line, but Hooper, ball in hand, had whipped the middle stump out. The West Indies appealed again, the square leg umpire, Cumberbatch, signalled Jones out, and the crowd rejoiced again while I just stood there dumbfounded.

Of course, we all knew not long after that umpire Cumberbatch was terribly wrong, that according to Law 38.2 "If a no-ball has been called the striker shall not be given run out unless he attempts to run."

So, if the umpire didn't know the rule, who did?

Well, as I've indicated in my description of the incident I feared Jones could be run out, or I wouldn't have been urging him to go back with such urgency. Clearly nobody in our team knew the rule or they would have been out on the field waving the rule book before Jones was even halfway off. Once the next batsman, Mark Waugh, had faced his first ball that was it. Coach Bob Simpson had approached the umpires at the tea interval with a view to having the decision reversed, but realistically it was more a communiqué of displeasure.

Cumberbatch gave this explanation: "It was really a matter of whether the batsman was trying to take a run, and from my angle, the way he left the crease suggested to me he was doing that."

I see … Jones had been clean bowled middle stump by a yorker, but he decided there was a run in it. 'Deano' is certainly a positive thinker but I don't think he'd ever have thought of that!

What the crowd thought of the umpire's decision to give Dean Jones out, run out.
Next day they hanged his effigy.

The Bermuda Bikies. From left, me, Jones, Marsh, Boon, Reid, Veletta.

SQUARE PEGS, ROUND HOLES?

Word from home told me we'd come under heavy artillery fire over the team we had picked for the Third Test in Trinidad, mainly because we left out offspinning allrounder Greg 'Mo' Matthews for batting allrounder Steve Waugh. The Chappell brothers, Ian and Greg, on the tour for television and newspaper commitments, led the charge.

Both thought that to bat Waugh at No. 7 was a negative move for a team that had to win a match, not save it. Greg, a former Australian selector, wanted Peter Taylor in for Matthews, because he believed the former was "mentally tougher".

Greg also said it was his belief, via what he called team "sources", that coach Bob Simpson was having too much sway in team selection.

Well, there were four of us who picked the team on the tour: me; Simpson; Laurie Sawle, the team manager and, of course, chairman of the Australian selection panel; and Swampy Marsh, the vice-captain, sat in on discussions.

True, we didn't agree on everything. What selection panel does? It's all a matter of opinion. Laurie might have thought one person should be playing, while Simmo might have thought someone else, but in the end consensus was reached.

In hindsight we probably should have picked Terry Alderman for the Fourth Test in Barbados; he had been laid low by a virus early in the tour but had taken a 'five-for' in the lead-up game to the Test. There was concern expressed that he could have been spending more time in the nets. The feeling was that his training routine of 'light net session, then run back to the hotel' should have been 'big net session, catch the bus back'.

Still, the bottom line was that Terry had been around for a long time—and very successfully—so you accepted he knew what he was doing. The other consideration about Terry's selection was it meant we would have McDermott, Hughes, Alderman and Reid as the last four in our batting line-up.

On the performance of the 'tail' up until then, that was a combination that prompted the thought, 'If they make five between them I'll do a nuddy around Kensington Oval'.

Okay, it was a negative thought process—we knew we had to bowl out the West Indies twice; but we considered McDermott, Reid and Hughes would do the bulk of the bowling. Alderman or Steve Waugh would therefore only play a minor role.

So we went for Waugh. Obviously he wasn't going to bowl as well as Terry might, but we knew his aggression had worried the West Indians at times, plus he would bat No. 7, Healy No. 8 and forget the rest. If we needed spin, I was going to do it. The two offspinners were struggling and I looked as likely to get wickets as anyone.

All the good vibes of our historic one-day series win at Kensington came flooding back on the first day of the Test. The scoreline read: West Indies 149, McDermott 4/49 and Hughes 4/44; Australia 2/56. The second day was all heartbreak. Briefly, this is what happened: Curtly Ambrose got Mark Taylor leg before early, then he broke my left thumb with a 'lifter'; Malcolm Marshall bowled me with a 'shooter'—it hadn't happened to me too often in any form of cricket. It just ran along the ground. My 29 runs turned out to be top score in the innings.

We lost our last seven wickets for 39 runs, and by stumps the West Indies were 153 runs ahead with Gordon Greenidge on his way to a double-hundred— 'reverse whammied' again!

I had to watch it all from the 'sick bay', a cane chair in the dressing room. We lost the Test by 343 runs, and stood two down in the series. I knew the hangover from our one-day victory celebrations had finally arrived.

At the end of a tough tour.

Chapter Nine

OUR CUP, THEIR CUP

Winners of the World Cup, 1987.

After Pakistan won the 1992 World Cup in Australasia their captain Imran Khan 'bagged' it as "the worst organised of the five so far". It occurred to me, as the captain of the Cup defenders, and eventual losers in our own backyard, that if anyone was likely to have a whinge it was us. Sad to say our 1992 World Cup demise was all our own work.

MIRACLE IN MADRAS

Sometimes one good game can change your cricketing fortune forever. Well, almost forever; cricket, I've come to learn over the years, is no respecter of those who claim permanency in the game.

My 'good game' arrived on October 9, 1987, in the Chepauk Stadium, Madras, India. When cricketers are invited to fill in those personality questionnaires Madras is rarely listed in the space "Place Most Like To Visit". Even the shortest cricketing stint in Madras can make it instantly clear why a curry powder manufacturer chose to call his product 'Madras'. I still have a picture in my mind of Dean Jones, during the famous second tied Test in Madras in 1986, sitting on the ground during a drinks break, taking off a boot and wringing the sweat out of his sock.

This Chepauk Stadium game was Australia's opening match in the 1987 World Cup, which was share-hosted by India and Pakistan. The bookmakers had rated us an 18–1 chance of winning the Cup, a bit short I thought because Australian cricket was in a deep trough, or what any bloke on the old SCG Hill might refer to as deep something else …

There were the bans over the South African Rebel tours, we'd lost the Ashes at home, we'd been whitewashed in a limited-overs series in Sharjah and there was blood on the floor under the selection table.

Despite all that I thought we were showing signs of being reasonable! We'd get ourselves into a position to win games, then lose. There were a lot of 'ifs' and 'buts' when we assessed our performances.

So it was against that backdrop that we squared up to Kapil Dev's India, who were favoured not just to win the Madras game, but also the Cup outright. It is history now that it was Australia who won the Cup.

If you ask me for my best memory of that 1987 World Cup win, even today I will say it wasn't only being chaired, trophy held aloft, around the ground before all those cheering thousands in the final crowd. I will tell you the celebration party after the first game against India, the 'good game', was a stirring moment, as well.

The game was a thriller, full of drama—which one of my games isn't full of drama? I sometimes wonder—and when we arrived back at the team hotel it was as if all of Australia was there to greet us. Australians who were on trips around just seemed to lob and mingle with the team and our associates. It was a marvellous spontaneous moment that remains forever in my mind as the springboard of a new spirit in a team that, until that day, had been painted as a team of losers.

We had won a game we should have lost; the result was the closest in World Cup history, more nerve-tingling than the West Indies win over Pakistan at

Edgbaston in the 1975 Cup, 9/267 to 7/266, with two balls left.

We made an absolutely brilliant 270 off our 50 overs, with Geoff Marsh getting a century. That was the good news. The bad followed pretty quickly—India 2/207 and there were still 13 overs to go. The equation, as they like to say these days, read: 64 runs to win and 78 balls to be bowled, eight wickets in hand. We were in more strife than some of those blokes used to get into in the Minties ads.

Then India got scragged by cricket's glorious uncertainty in the bustling, beautiful form of Craig McDermott, whose four wickets in his second spell reduced them to their last pair and still six runs needed to win, with the last over to be bowled by 'The Iceman', Steve Waugh.

With his fifth ball he bowled India's last man, Maninder Singh—who was also India's last man in the 1986 tied Test—as he tried desperately for the two runs needed for victory. They had succumbed to our pressure, no 'ifs', no 'buts' about it. We had hung in there for a one run win against all odds and it was a bloody marvellous feeling. A fluke?

Ten days later we met New Zealand at Indore in a weather-reduced 30-over game, in what players call a 'slogathon', after the ground had been flooded in knee-deep water. I called on The Iceman to again bowl the last crucial over. New Zealand needed only seven runs to win with four wickets in hand, one of them the great Martin Crowe, who in 1992 was to be The Man Of The Cup Down Under.

Crowe, 58 off only 47 balls, was caught first ball; he got Smith with the next and went for singles off the last four. We won by three runs. Madras was no fluke.

EDEN—HEAVENLY, THEN HELL

By a strange quirk of cricketing fate two of the most telling World Cup matches in my cricket career were played on grounds named 'Eden'—Eden Gardens in Calcutta where we won the 1987 final, and Eden Park in Auckland where we opened the 1992 contest.

There were 80,000 in at Eden Gardens, a simply awesome sight, when we beat Mike Gatting's Englishmen in that final. Even on the way to the ground the adrenalin was pumping as the team bus threaded its way through the most extraordinary jam of people, buses so full passengers seemed to be hanging out of every window, and cars whose horns honked endlessly.

If we hadn't experienced the vastness of the MCG with about the same number of people, it might have been easy to 'choke' in front of the sea of people massed under the blue and yellow Meccano-like tops on the main stands.

Tosses don't generally worry me too much, but I wanted to win that toss as badly as I ever have in my time as captain—the pitch was slow, to dead slow, and

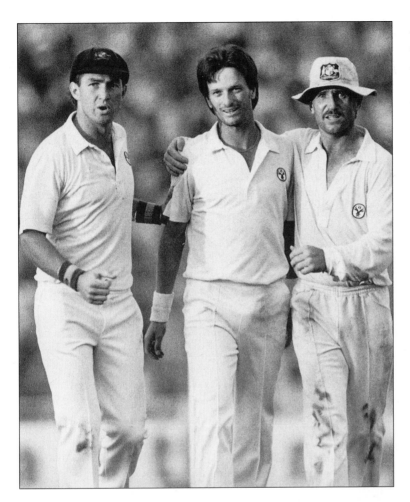

Steve Waugh, centre, 'The Iceman' in our 1987 World Cup campaign.

Cricket in India is different. The Indore ground on the eve of our game against New Zealand.

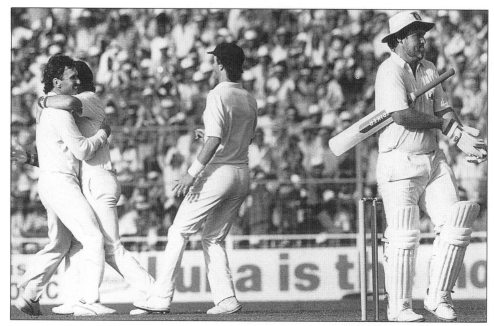

The turning point in the World Cup final — Gatting out, caught reverse sweeping, bowler Border.

at that stage in the Cup the team batting first had a 70 per cent win record.

I won the toss, we batted first and squeaked in by seven runs, thus slightly improving that win percentage of the team batting first. In our innings of 5/253 there was, in the light of arguments over our tactics in 1992, an interesting statistic—after only ten overs we were 52. Whatever happened to our much-touted steady build-up?

Well, the fact is there were plenty of bad balls there to be hit—DeFreitas and Gladstone Small bowled short to David Boon, and on his legs, which is a bit like giving a starving dog a big juicy bone.

When England batted, the tough edge and never-say-die spirit we'd generated in those first few games in the tournament were to help us through some mighty hairy moments. McDermott got a wicket with the third ball of England's innings, O'Donnell got Graham Gooch leg before, Steve Waugh, deep at third man, misfielded, recovered and with a bullet throw gained a run out when the batsmen chanced another run—the last mentioned being an incident that had a remarkable encore in the 1992 Cup!

So far so good ... and when I got Gatting with my first ball—trying that reverse-sweep!—we were looking bloody beautiful. England needed about eight runs an over with ten overs to go, then it was 36 runs from three overs. Twelve an over, impossible!

DeFreitas hit four, six, four off successive balls in the 48th—I'm no medico but I imagine my pulse rate swelled as much as the crowd's roar. England needed 19 from 12 balls. I thought, 'Please, don't let anyone bowl a no-ball!'

O'Donnell, Moody and Dyer give new meaning to the term 'chairing the captain'.

BELOW: World Cup winners, a wonderful feeling.

The 49th over was bowled by Steve Waugh and just as he had so often in the Cup, The Iceman came through. He got DeFreitas, but more importantly England only scored two runs.

Winning brings with it a wonderful feeling of joy and relief, almost a light-headedness. I wouldn't say there were any tears about the place, but there was certainly a nice shine on a few faces and I'm not sure it was all sweat. I spent some time on the shoulders of Jones and McDermott in a victory lap, the Cup held aloft, and by the time the photo session was finished the sun had gone. In the twilight they put on an extraordinary fireworks display whose explosions threatened to deafen us. I can't recall anyone complaining.

Our celebrations went long into the night at the Oberoi Grand Hotel, and in the team room I sat, legs crossed, in the middle of the floor, soaking it all up, sipping on a beer, and dared to wonder, 'Is this the start of something big?'

And the next night, as the team bus moved slowly away from the hotel, heading for the airport, still escorted by hundreds of cheering fans, I sat up front, nursing the Cup in my arms, and thought, 'A new era!'

That heroes' farewell seemed light years away when, in February 1992, we were given a 'ginger' welcome to Eden Park, Auckland by 35,000 Kiwi fans, eager to see us go under to New Zealand in the opening encounter of the fifth World Cup.

Every last one of them seemed to have a hooter which made a noise like a baritone duck being throttled. And there must have been a special deal—buy a hooter, get a scorecard. These weren't regular cricket scorecards, they were squares of yellow cardboard with a black number, either a four or a six. When New Zealand batted every time they gave the ball a belt, no matter where, or how far it went, there'd be roars galore, thousands of bright yellow cards held up, all to the accompaniment of the 'ducks'.

A bloody pain, but it sure beat The Wave. And, of course, it must have been a great 'psych' for the Kiwis. After struggling early, they went whooshka, and at the same time indulged in some unique tactical ploys that probably caught us a bit off guard and may even have fractured our concentration.

During their innings some of their batsmen started 'sledging' our bowlers and the one who copped most of it was The Iceman, Steve Waugh—"You can't bowl, we're slogging the shit out of you!" Sledging is normally the other way around—the bowler seeking to upset the batsman's concentration. Whether the New Zealand 'reverse sledge' ploy caught us on the hop I'm not sure, but it is a fact that our bowlers were too short on a dead slow pitch and Martin Crowe gave us a hiding.

In the lead-up to the Cup a lot was made of a so-called Australian 'winning formula'. Much of the credit for the formula had been given to coach Bob Simpson. Simply, it revolved around the openers, or top order, ignoring the early

The 'other Eden' — Eden Park, New Zealand, 1992.

overs enticement of vacant spaces over the top of the circle; instead the emphasis was on sharp running between the wickets to steadily build the total to 90 off 25 overs. The next ten overs would see consolidation, then in the last 15, 'The Happy Hour', anything goes.

With the ball, bowlers were encouraged to utilise change of pace, the theory being it made it more difficult for batsmen to maintain their timing, therefore reducing their hitting ability. Somebody pointed out that since winning the 1987 Cup Australia had won 75 per cent of its limited-overs contests, more or less using 'the formula'.

Martin Crowe, and the rest of the New Zealand cricket brains trust, decided to challenge 'the formula', but to do it successfully they had to hope the Australian players would stay programmed.

They gave the new ball to an offspinner, figuring neither Marsh nor Boon would hit over the top, and because the pitch was such a slow, marshmallow they gave their fastest bowler only four (expensive) overs and left it to a bunch of medium and slow medium bowlers—our trick, hard to hit!

They were shock tactics. When we saw the offspinner Patel take the new ball the reaction in the dressing room was, "What's going on here?" But at that stage there was no thought about hitting out. And we had been looking fairly comfortable in the chase for 248 when we were nearing 100 with only Marsh out and Boon and Jones in command.

It was only in hindsight, when we had lost by 37 runs, that the critics came out of the woodwork and wondered why we hadn't been slogging Patel all over the park. From memory I don't think anyone collared Patel in the Cup, and there were at least seven chances to do that after our opening game.

So we went home a bit down, not shell-shocked or nonplussed. Disappointed.

There's always a dark feeling about losing, but losing to the Kiwis is ... well, a bit like losing to England. The Kiwis really like beating the Aussies. There's a lot of feeling between us, probably still being dredged up out of the past—the little cousin across the Tasman, the under-arm, and so on. You know in your heart they'll be talking about it for the next ten years ... "What about when we thrashed you in that World Cup game at Eden Park, eh?"

It grates. They just don't let go. They're like a bloody bull terrier.

MR WESSELS, I PRESUME

The loss to New Zealand, headlined with words normally associated with acts of God, brought even greater pressure on the team—it was victory or the pits. I had tried to be realistic about our winning chances before the Cup. That is my way of doing things, I'm not given to confident outbursts just because I'm the captain. I like to give both sides of the picture, I like to be a bit measured.

So, even though I knew no host country had ever won the World Cup, I still rated us a good winning chance. But it was reasonable to anticipate the game against New Zealand, and the next against South Africa, would both be tough games. New Zealand had the cushion of home ground conditions, South Africa had a real point to prove after 21 years out of the 'official' arena.

Ian Chappell seized on my qualifications as "pessimism" and likely to make my team "jittery". I couldn't go along with that—this was a team that had survived some mighty tough times. Not long before they'd beaten the West Indies four-one in limited-overs in the Caribbean, the first time that had ever happened. Chappell's point said little for the character of the team.

Other critics attacked the selectors. The national panel, Laurie Sawle, Jim Higgs, John Benaud and coach Bob Simpson picked the squad of 14. Once the Cup started the team was chosen on tour by Simpson, myself and vice-captain Geoff Marsh, unless we were in a selector's home town—Sawle Perth, Higgs Melbourne, Benaud Sydney, and then that selector would contribute.

The main problem, as I saw it, was that we couldn't seem to settle on a stable combination. There was mainly confusion over whether to play two of the four faster bowlers—Reid, McDermott, Whitney, Hughes—plus three allrounders, or vice-versa.

Plenty of water passed under the bridge between meetings with Kepler Wessels.

The three allrounders were Tom Moody, and the Waugh twins, Steve and Mark. Simon O'Donnell's absence because of his shoulder injury was a blow to us—there's no doubt we missed his late-in-the-order big hitting, and his first change bowling.

Kepler Wessels had played his last game in Australia at the SCG, for Queensland in the 1986 Sheffield Shield final. At least he had supposed it was to be his last because he left his boots in the middle of the ground at the end of the game, when he announced he was returning to South Africa to work in a university. There was certainly no hint the ban on South Africa would be lifted.

Now, about a month short of six years later, Kepler was back; he'd left Australia as Queensland captain and returned as captain of South Africa. In between times he'd played with Kim Hughes's Rebel Australian team, then played with Eastern Province to qualify for South Africa.

In fact, when I recalled that Kepler had also played some cricket in England with Sussex, in Sydney with Waverley, in Brisbane with Valleys, with Queensland, and for Australia, I was tempted to rib him about the territory he'd covered by mimicking the greeting of Sir Henry Morton Stanley to his fellow explorer, "Dr Livingstone, I presume?"

From the very first ball, when Geoff Marsh controversially survived an appeal for a catch behind, to the very last swig of the teams' after-match drink, that World Cup contest between Australia and South Africa was not your average limited-overs game.

Kepler's XI ran onto the SCG like a Springbok Rugby XV, jinking, side-stepping and sprinting.

South Africa won easily, losing only one wicket in passing our disappointing 170 innings total, and anyone who stayed for a drink in the bar in the old Members' Stand at the SCG after South Africa won that historic day/night event—Wednesday, February 26, 1992—would have thought he was in a Rugby ruck. There was a lot of shoving and grunting and shouting.

From the bar, if you look out through the giant glass windows to the playing field, to the right is Australia's dressing room, to the left South Africa's. Afterwards they all came straight over to our room, shoving through the back-slapping crowd, for a chat and a beer, which doesn't happen much anymore.

Ali Bacher came up to me; Bacher had been captain of South Africa's last official Test team, the one that whipped Bill Lawry's team back in the 1969–70 season. He had been a moving force behind the invitations to Rebel teams to tour South Africa, and now was in Australia in his official capacity as the managing director of the newly formed United Cricket Board of South Africa. He was ecstatic.

The infamous 1992 World Cup scoreboard at the SCG.
It led to an amendment in run-rate calculations.

Ali introduced me to a tall, solidly built chap at his side, Steve Tshwete from the African National Congress, then said, "Allan, this was a result that had to happen."

I knew what he meant: all the hard work that had gone into trying to break down the apartheid barrier, that had gone into actually being accepted in the Cup, the sheer enormity of it all—and with the eyes of the world upon them. In Ali's mind South Africa had been destined to win.

I looked at him as straight-faced as I could and said, mock gruffly, "Oh, I *am* pleased I could do the right thing by you Ali!" and we all laughed.

After they'd all gone I sat for a while, trying to assess our performance. I sensed a little bit of apprehension in the team. No-one seemed to be in any sort of consistent form in any facet of the game, batting, fielding or bowling.

I started to wish we'd gone into a camp before the Cup, rather than playing in Sheffield Shield matches and 'mickey mouse' practice matches. That would almost certainly have concentrated our minds more and given us some Cup sparkle that was missing.

THE INDIAN ROPE TRICK

When we began our search for that missing magical spark in our third Cup game, against India, everything seemed to go wrong that could go wrong. It seemed like we'd played Azharuddin's team about a hundred times during the summer, but it was actually *only* 11—five Tests, four preliminary World Series games, and two finals.

Healy tore a hamstring, so Boon, himself worried by a chronic right knee injury, took the gloves.

Boon is round and short and has a brush moustache, and when some of the boys saw him in the gloves and shorty pads, they noted the similarity to a former Australian gloveman and started taking the mickey, calling him 'Rod', after Rodney Marsh.

Boon just knitted his eyebrows, and fixed them with a stern look that said, 'Yeah, well let's just wait and see.'

And there was a domino effect on the batting order; it was a bit tough to ask Boon to open after keeping for 50 overs, so Mark Taylor came into the team to open, Boon went to No. 3, Dean Jones, regular No. 3, dropped a slot and I finished up at No. 7!

Miraculously, at the end of all that shuffling, we found the winning formula in a sequence of events that were so similar to our 'miracle in Madras' in 1987, it was breathtaking.

We made 237, but rain reduced that to 235 off 47 overs. At one stage India needed only 43 to win with five wickets in hand. When we came to the last over, the 47th, I realised I'd made a complete balls-up of the bowling changes. I'd forgotten that because it was a reduced-overs match only two of my bowlers could bowl ten overs.

The scoreboard told me Mike Whitney had bowled ten, Steve Waugh had bowled ten. Now with one over to go I had the option of bringing in an 'untried' bowler, or giving the ball to Tom Moody, who had already taken two wickets, but at a high cost.

Believe me, the Gabba was no place for faint hearts during that last over from Tom. There were two full tosses—and two fours—three wickets—two of them run out—and there was the 'banana skin' …

When Tom began his gangling run-in for the final ball India needed four to win, on strike Srinath, their fast bowler who was as much a beanpole as Moody.

Bowled by Botham in the World Cup match against England.

The Gabba is small and not a great place to defend the threat of a boundary hit. I was at mid-wicket, and Srinath hit it up, over my left shoulder. I thought to myself, 'Geez, he's hit that well. Well enough to go for six … shit, we've lost this one, too!'

But once I turned fully I could see Steve Waugh, running around from long-on, had the catch covered.

So there was no panic. 'He doesn't drop them,' I thought. But he did. And when he did my mind raced: 'Oh, he's dropped it … but surely he can get it in quickly enough to stop them running three and tying the match?'

Waugh was ice cool, resisting the urge to rush and risk taking his eye off the ball before he picked it up, the most common mistake in pressure situations like that. His low throw catapulted in at what seemed a million miles an hour. The greasy ball skidded once on the greasy turf; it was like a rocket taking off. But it was slightly wide of the stumps where stand-in wicketkeeper Boon was waiting.

So Boon had to judge the flight, pace and direction of the throw, then make ground to his right and anticipate the skid-bounce.

He took the ball handsomely as Raju, the non-striker, charged towards him on the third run, then stepped quickly to the stumps, broke them, and gave a little victory skip as Raju was adjudged out, a fraction short of safety. A miracle.

No-one in the team was silly enough to call Boon 'Rod'. 'God' seemed more appropriate.

BLAST FROM THE PAST

In cricket it's funny how some things will come back to haunt you again, and again. Australia have been bitten by the Botham bug a few times.

Ian Botham was part of England's 14-man Cup squad, but had been chosen specifically to open the batting, his mission to execute a blitz.

Our losing start in the Cup had led to criticism of our programmed approach, the steady start and so on; coach Bob Simpson hit back, claiming the other teams were winning because they had copied our approach that had been successful over a long period.

But the truth was that the two top teams, New Zealand and England, were not copying our tactics. Certainly their bowling attacks were capable of subtle pace changes, but each had recognised the importance of the batting net-run-rate, the 'NRR'.

They had installed batsmen at the top of the order who could 'go for it'.

The Cup rules said: in the event of teams finishing on equal points the right to play in the semi-finals will be decided by the most wins in the preliminary matches, or if still equal, the highest net-run-rate in preliminary matches.

I confess we were so intent on sticking to our normal game plan we hadn't even thought about the 'NRR'—until we were about to play England. It was clear what bad shape we were in:

Team	P	W	L	NR	Pts	N/R/R
New Zealand	4	4	-	-	8	1.0790
England	3	2	-	1	5	0.5682
Sri Lanka	4	2	1	1	5	−0.0270
South Africa	4	2	2	-	4	0.0499
West Indies	4	2	2	-	4	−0.0983
India	4	1	2	1	3	0.2260
Pakistan	4	1	2	1	3	−0.0326
Australia	3	1	2	-	2	−0.3208
Zimbabwe	4	-	4	-	0	−1.0760

So, there we were, Steve Waugh and I, completely in charge at the SCG, and England starting to struggle, when England's captain Graham Gooch threw the ball to his beefy opening batsman. There were about 40,000 people in, and 39,500 of them seemed to be Poms, and very noisy ones at that.

It was about the time Prime Minister Keating announced his theory that Australia might make a nice Republic, and about the time of a visit by the Queen. Royalists among cricket fans had clearly decided the SCG on that day was a good spot to show the flag. There were Union Jacks everywhere. Union Jacks on old bedsheets, Union Jacks on faces, and when an Aussie fan waved the flag, up would go a chant: "Union Jack on the Aussie flag, do-da, do-da ... "

Amazing scenes, and in the middle of it Botham bowls me through 'the gate', between bat and pad, just as his South African look-alike Adrian Kuiper had done in the previous match.

We were 5/145. I took the long walk back, up the stairs, past the other blokes in the viewing room, out into the change room, threw my bat and gloves into my 'coffin'—cricket bag—tore at the clasps of my pads, got up, had a drink, and— heard a terrific roar.

Ian Healy had lobbed the first ball of Botham's next over to mid-wicket. We were 6/155. Suddenly we were in free fall. Peter Taylor missed one, McDermott lobbed a catch and we were 8/155. Botham had taken four wickets in seven balls and we hadn't scored a run off him.

Then he came out and belted 53 off 79 balls to set up England's win. They made him Man Of The Match and he announced: "I did it for the Queen."

I had to laugh—there's no stopping Both. I made a mental note to ask Paul Keating at the next Prime Minister's XI game later in the year what he thought of Botham's performance as the Queen's envoy Down Under.

That match against England was the fourth and we'd had a different team for every one of them, and by necessity a different batting order. I said, "We're making too many changes."

Was it panic? Did we think that because it was a condensed eight-match competition we didn't have time to allow one combination to settle? Or maybe the selectors should have had a phone link-up with Simpson and me before each game. I like a settled team, so there was more than a trace of irony in the fact that we didn't field the same team in consecutive matches until the last two matches, against Zimbabwe and the West Indies.

There were far greater ironies around the corner. To make the semi-finals, to have a hope of retaining our world champion status, we needed a bloody big favour from—New Zealand! If New Zealand could beat Pakistan while we beat the West Indies we'd go into the semi-finals.

It promised to be a hard day's night; New Zealand were playing Pakistan in Christchurch during the day, while we were playing the West Indies in Melbourne in a day/nighter—and there was a two-hour time difference.

I hadn't even thought about lunch (11.30 a.m. MCG time) when the lunch score came through from New Zealand, and it did nothing for my appetite—the Kiwis all out 166. It was one of the toughest calls I've had in my cricket career. I thought of the great boxer Jack Dempsey's motto: "Kill the other guy before he kills you." If only we'd done more early in the Cup.

There was another twist. If the West Indies could beat us they would get into the semi-finals ahead of Pakistan. So, while the Pakistanis crowded around a television set in Christchurch, we gave them a top-rating performance, thrashing the West Indies 216 to 159. We had done Pakistan a good turn.

The irony of that won't be lost on anyone who has followed closely some of our contests over the years. It certainly wasn't lost on me.

The last three World Cup results, India over the West Indies, 1983, us over England, 1987, and Pakistan over England, 1992, all raised eyebrows because the winners weren't supposed to win.

That makes winning all the sweeter. When you get to hold that trophy up, no matter if it has "hernia" written all over it, you'll be able to handle it as long as the fans cheer and the photographers say "Smile".

The Reliance Cup, which was the trophy Indian and Pakistan officials had struck for the 1987 World Cup winners, was very ornate, and tall enough to be a bit of a handful. As captain of the winning team, I didn't have any trouble holding it aloft in one clenched fist.

And there was no trouble getting it back to Australia, although, as anyone who has travelled knows it is quite possible for luggage marked "Australia" to reach Austria, or if your luck is right out, the Austral Isles, somewhere in the Pacific. On the way home I never let the Cup leave my sight—it was perched up in a seat in business class, seat-belted in. When we landed in Brisbane I carried it off the plane.

The Reliance Cup was one helluva tough trophy. It survived a victory lap of Eden Gardens and the shenanighans of a long, dressing room celebration, although if you ever get the chance to look it over in the Cricket Board trophy cabinet you'll notice there are a couple of diamonds missing from the cricket ball-like sphere that tops it.

I promise, I don't know what happened! But I do know that it's a good thing the teetotallers from Pakistan beat England in the 1992 Cup final. I shudder to think what a rejoicing Ian Botham might have been tempted to do with that $12,000 Waterford Crystal globe the Australian and New Zealand officials had struck for the occasion.

The 1992 World Cup — too fragile for some?

OPPOSITE: A beautiful homecoming to Jane
with the 1987 Cup.

Chapter Ten

MOMENTS
IN TIME

Sydney turned on a ticker-tape parade after we won back the Ashes in 1989.

Life has many great moments to offer us—moments which are of supreme joy, and which are never forgotten by those who experience them. The recollection of these moments becomes more precious as the years roll by.

D J KNIGHT, *Cricket*

BEING THERE

Ask me what day my son Dene was born and I'll tell you April 20, 1984. But the truth is, when it happened I wasn't sure what day it was—I was in St Lucia in the Caribbean, on the other side of the International Dateline, which can suddenly 'turn' night into day, and Dene Michael arrived about midnight.

The point is I missed his birth, a disappointment. Jane had rung me from our Brisbane home early in the evening to tell me something was happening.

Naturally, being an excited first time father-to-be, I sat up waiting for the news—boy or girl, and most important, both well. I sat up all night, and into the next morning. No call. Not long after sunrise the phone rang—Jane! "It's a boy, we're both terrific!"

I said, "Great darling, but you were a long time in labour." There was one of those dead silences you get on phones, then Jane said, "No ... I had him six hours ago." Unbeknown to me the St Lucia telephone exchange shut down at midnight.

I had also missed the birth of my first daughter, Nicole, despite strategic planning any army general would be proud of to be there, when I was trying to save the Test match at the SCG.

But I was present at the birth of our third child, Tara. I'm glad I made it, and it remains the most overwhelming experience of my life.

There were problems because Tara arrived five weeks early. I was heading out to cricket practice when Jane said, "I think my waters have broken." That made me just a little bit nervous. But Jane seemed relaxed. "You take the kids over to your mum and dad's (a five minute drive) and I'll be ready to go to hospital when you come back," she said.

Only when I got back did she tell me that with Nicole she'd barely made it to the hospital in similar circumstances. We arrived at the Mater Mothers in south Brisbane at 3.30 in the afternoon. Then we waited. Jane had a book; I hadn't thought to take one, and when I said, "Why don't you read your book?" she said "I can't really, you haven't got one."

I started pacing the floor. I could see Jane didn't think that was a good idea. Then I went and held her hand. I don't know if it made Jane feel any better but it did plenty for me. I started wishing I'd gone to the ante-natal classes instead of thinking they were only for women.

Tara arrived at half past midnight; she only weighed about 400 grams (four pounds and 14 ounces), and she was only 40 centimetres (16 inches) long. We were taken along to the nursery, and the doctor told us there was a problem with Tara's breathing, but not to worry, as "with babies of this age and weight 99.9 per cent of them get through". So, I went home and crashed, but Jane had a restless night thinking about that part of one per cent that don't survive.

With a couple of very special ladies — Jane, and little Tara.

Tara was on oxygen for a short time, and in the humidicrib for a few days, and was cardiac respiratory monitored, which was probably just a precaution, but we worried. When I went back the next day we just stood and looked at her; we didn't touch her because we were just a bit frightened, she looked so small.

Life has a strange habit of tossing up a few twists; on the staff of the Mater Mothers is Sister Angela Mary. In 1989 when I was awarded Australian of the Year, Sister Angela Mary was one of the other nominations, for her work with premature babies.

Sister Angela Mary was there to help out with Tara on June 16, 1992.

But that's not all. Tara wasn't planned, she was a mistake. But what a beautiful mistake!

'THOMMO', ME, POMS, AND THE BROWN DOG

The traditional Boxing Day Test at the MCG in 1982, the fourth in that summer's Ashes series between Australia and England, was a truly great match.

It was the first match played on a relaid portion of the pitch square, and the expression 'ups and downs' didn't just apply to the fluctuating fortunes in play, but also to the heights at which the balls came through.

There was incredible tension, spiced with almost slapstick humour—in England's second innings, on the third day, their opener Graeme Fowler hurt his right foot while negotiating a full-pitched thunderbolt from Jeff Thomson, and requested a runner.

What should have been a quick-change affair turned into a ten-minute delay before the runner, David Gower, emerged from the dressing room. This was because the Australian captain, Greg Chappell, when he was asked by Graeme Fowler for a runner, had stipulated, "Yes, but he has to be a slower runner than David Gower."

Greg's little idea of a joke! But it was taken seriously in the England camp where Chris Tavare, nicknamed 'Tortoise' because of the pace of his batting, was told to pad up. It took the intervention of the England manager to get the pads onto the speedier Gower.

Fowler may have been limping but England were not, and late on the fourth day, under a grey sky and with rain in the air, they were in a position to win the Test and breathe life back into their defence of the Ashes.

The scoreboard told the story: England 284, Australia 287—we lost our last five wickets for only 26 runs—England 294, Australia 9/218.

At that point Jeff Thomson, or 'Thommo' as everyone in Australia knew him, joined me at the crease. I remember the time on the old Members' Stand clock, 5.14 p.m., the day December 29.

I had only 16 runs against my name, yet I'd been batting a long time; it had taken me 40 minutes to get off the mark, and even before I'd scored I'd almost been bowled by Ian Botham, letting one go that shaved the off stump. Good judgment.

Just joking; the fact was I'd struggled all series and before that innings had scored only 83 runs all up. That, and the sight of Australia's last man, Thommo, coming out to join me, cheered England right up. "Oh well lads, come on then, let's wrap this up," was the message passing between the fielders.

Thommo and I are fairly alike when there's a crisis around, particularly if it concerns keeping England at bay. I said to him, "Come on pal, let's get stuck in and see if we can keep Both and these other bastards out."

"F—ing oath!" said Jeffrey, who uses the magic word like an Army private uses 'sir'. And so began one of Test cricket's greatest fightbacks.

Immediately, England captain Bob Willis set deep fields inviting me to turn over the strike to Thommo, and very quickly the notation "Border refused run" became as obvious in Bill Frindall's scorebook, as did 'dot' balls.

My reluctance to run had nothing to do with a lack of confidence in Thommo; it was because the sky was a little greyer and the atmosphere a little cooler. Rain seemed to be about and I figured if I could farm as much strike as possible we had a better chance of getting lucky and being saved by rain.

So keen were England to get Thommo on strike that on the last ball of one over David Gower let one of my hits go for four, so I wouldn't run three and be on strike for the next over. Not only did our partnership develop into a useful one, it was also a humorous one.

We nearly ran one another out a couple of times, and with one eye on the now blackening sky, I told Thommo, "Keep your bloody head down!"

He replied, "Get f—ed, I'm doing the batting at the moment, you just worry about your own score."

Heaven only knows what the Poms thought about it all.

At 5.45 p.m. it started to rain lightly and I thought, 'Beauty, if we can hang in here just a bit longer and it pisses down tomorrow, we'll have saved the game and won the Ashes,' because we were leading the series two-nil.

Five minutes later it bucketed down, and off we went—to be met in the dressing room with a few "Well done, boys," and more than a few sheepish grins, the cause of which was the confession that while Thommo and I had been saving the side in the middle, half the rest of the team had tossed in the towel.

As soon as Thommo had gone out to bat they had departed the viewing room saying "Oh well, we've lost the bloody Test," and gone downstairs to the change room to pack their kits and drown their sorrows.

It must have been quite a funny scene as our partnership blossomed and the crowd started "oohing" and "aahing". The boys downstairs would call to those upstairs, "What's happening? ... What's going on?" and the message would come back, "Oh, silly Thommo's just tried to run out AB."

But the rain didn't last and we were back on with two overs to be faced before stumps. The boys stayed upstairs and downstairs—superstition, you know!

I took every ball, the only drama coming on the third last ball of the day when Thommo was almost run out taking a risky two runs to keep me on strike. I could only imagine what sort of an outburst that provoked in the dressing room. At stumps we'd added 37 runs, which meant that next day we only needed that many again to win the Test! I was happy to settle for more rain.

The fifth, and final, day dawned overcast, one of those yuk, grey, Melbourne days—but no rain for the wishful thinkers. There was an air of resignation, if not pessimism, among the others who gave Thommo and I a hit-up before play. Their "Good luck, boys" was prefaced with "Oh well ...", a dead giveaway.

The gates had been thrown open to the faithful among the public, and there were a few shouts of "Hang in there," from among the few thousand present before play. "F—ing oath," promised Thommo.

I'd hazard a guess that soon after play began the crowd had swelled to 15,000, but it sounded like 50,000. The looks on the Poms' faces said, "It's only a matter of time boys—the second new ball's just around the corner." But the looks were of panic as our score mounted, and once Bob Willis tried to get his sweater off the umpire after bowling only five balls, thinking he'd finished his over.

And two of their fieldsmen collided head-on trying to run out Thommo.

*Pipped on the post, but 'Thommo' and I still had our fans after
our valiant last-wicket fight at the MCG against England.*

Then, with us needing four to win, just one good hit, Willis tossed the ball to Botham, who, like me up until then, had really done bugger-all in the series.

The first ball he sent down was a bit of a loosener, a bit short and a bit wide of the off stump, and Thommo, who usually lathers anything like that, just poked at it. The ball flew off the edge to Tavare at second slip, but he dropped it.

For a moment I thought we'd been given another chance—then Miller, the first slip, caught the rebound. In our dressing room it must have been sheer chaos as the blokes upstairs explained to those downstairs how Thommo had been dropped and caught off the same ball.

Naturally England raced off, cock-a-hoop, Botham had done it to us again. Thommo and I trudged off, him saying, "Sorry mate." Back in the rooms, there were condolences, "Great fight, bad luck, gave it your best shot ..."

Nothing of the sort from Rodney Marsh. He was prowling around the room looking in lockers, under kits, behind doors, when someone asked, "Lost something, 'Bacchus'?"

His reply cheered us all up. "Yeah, I'm looking for four runs," he said.

I still see a lot of Thommo, not just in his role as Queensland coach. By profession he's a landscape gardener, and he once did a lot of work at my place, clearing away heaps of bushes, shrubs, trees and long grass that had invited a series of jokes about 'AB's Jungle'.

My son Dene, who is a 'greenie' at heart, stood with his hands on his hips, drew himself up to all of his eight-year-old height, and confronted Thommo with, "Hey, you're destroying the environment."

I think, when he was playing, a lot of people misunderstood Thommo. He was always portrayed as a vicious fast bowler who loved to see blood on the pitch, loved to see batsmen squirm and loved to sledge.

I've never thought of him that way. He's got a great sense of humour and he's very quick-witted. Yes, he drops the magic word a lot, but people have misconstrued that as sledging. He didn't sledge the opposition so much as he sledged himself. His most-used expression was, "Well f— my brown dog." He used to use it if he bowled a bad ball. Or, as in the case of that Test, if things didn't quite work out for him.

TORA! TORA! TORA!

Golf is an important part of many a cricketer's career; there are times when the competition on the golf course between players is just as intense as it is on the cricket field.

If golf's historians have got it right, where the entrance gates to the famous Sydney Cricket Ground stand today was once the site of the first tee of The

Australian Golf Club. Just a bit of trivia, interesting if for no other reason than before the Fifth Ashes Test at the SCG in the first week of 1983, I happened to be the odd man out in a golf challenge featuring the brains trust of Australian cricket, and the site of this stoush was The Australian.

I was paired with Rodney Marsh, advisor to quite a few Australian captains, and our opponents were captains, Greg Chappell and Kim Hughes. Coming to the 17th hole Rodney and I were in deep trouble, one down with two to play.

Standing on the 17th tee at The Australian is a daunting experience, but just so no-one thinks I'm prone to any of the exaggerations the small, white ball game is notorious for, I'll leave the description of the 17th to an expert—Tom Ramsey, who wrote the book *25 Great Australian Golf Courses.*

Says Tom: "The 17th is 390 metres and it takes the heart of a heavyweight to notch a par at this one. Norman Von Nida said he had not managed a par on the past five occasions he had played it. There are trees down the left-hand side and a bunker on the right, 220 metres out.

"The second shot into the prevailing wind is always a long iron or wood, which has to carry water and a bunker. I rate it a par four-and-a-half."

So, there you are. My partner Rodney played the 17th in a fashion that would have brought tears to the eyes of his illustrious golfing brother, Graham. He was still short of the green after three shots.

And Border? Well, I had sliced my tee shot left, into what Ramsey described as "trees", but what in fact was trees and deep rough. I was in so deep I didn't have a shot to the green.

The enemy had fared much better; Greg Chappell was on the green in the regulation two shots, a worry for Rodney and me because Greg's putting was legendary.

I looked down at my ball in the tufts of long grass, I peered through the tree trunks hoping for a sight of the green, and realised I was doing what is commonly called 'considering my plight'. Rodney had come back to help me.

I decided to chip out onto the fairway, hoping to hit my third onto the green close enough to the hole to one-putt for a half. Rodney got fairly fierce about that idea, and the fighting spirit that made him one of cricket's toughest competitors suddenly surfaced.

"Don't you want to win?" he barked. "Get out your four-wood AB, this calls for Tora! Tora! Tora!"

Hype out of the way, he then got down to tactics. "Hit the ball through that eight-inch gap between the trees, fade it, coming around the lake, and lob it onto the green."

Chappell and Hughes, also back to help me consider my plight, thought this was a great lark and were rolling with laughter as I drew the four-wood from the 'holster', and—whack!

The ball went through the needle-eye opening, faded, negotiated the lake safely, lobbed on the green and rolled to a stop a foot from the pin.

Chappell and Hughes stopped laughing about the same moment Rodney and I started. It was the shot of my life. Rodney was galloping in ever increasing circles shouting "Tora! Tora! Tora!"

I tapped in for the birdie, Greg two-putted for a par, and the match was all square going to the 18th. Rodney won that, we won the match and Chappell and Hughes bought the drinks.

WHEN 87 WAS LUCKY

Superstition has been known to play on the minds of cricketers; for a while mine was keeping a beard during a Sheffield Shield match or a Test match. When I had made my first-class start in 1976 I hadn't shaved for three days—the day of the morning I did I had a 'shocker'. So I took to growing a lucky beard. A load of old rubbish, I suppose; must have something to do with soothing the nerves.

The superstition that bobs up most regularly for Australian cricketers is when the scoreboard ticks over—or, these days, flashes up—to any score with 87 in it. That's because back in the 50s a few remarkable incidents happened on that score. And it just grew.

The classic story was in 1961, a Sheffield Shield match between NSW and South Australia. A couple of other Mosman boys, Ian Craig and Gordon Rorke, both of whom also played for Australia, were in the NSW team.

The South Australian captain, Les Favell, had reached 87 in the first innings, and as Craig and NSW captain Richie Benaud walked past Favell, Craig heard Benaud say, "Have you seen the scoreboard, Les?"

Favell, clearly not superstitious, looked up at the 87 and said, "We'll soon fix that!" But promptly got out next ball.

At the start of the South Australian second innings Favell was facing Rorke, who was pretty quick. A NSW player said to Favell, "Do you realise you're still on 87, Les?" He was out first ball.

Whenever I'm asked to recall the Australian tour to England in 1985 just about the first picture that pops into my mind is of a ball of string unravelling. Yet, in the early stages of the Second Test at Lord's there was just no hint of the nightmare that tour was to become.

In fact, the superstitious Australian players had reasoned that an incident just before stumps on the second day of the Test was a sure sign that we were on the verge of doing great things.

The second day was one of those rotten, grey days that England can turn on with a change in the wind direction; there was no rain, but the light was so bad

Rodney Marsh said "Thread the needle," and I did.

there had been four stoppages during our innings.

Still, bleak though it was I had been cheered by the fact that after sending England in to bat we'd rolled them for 290 early that second morning, I had had the honour of meeting the Queen that afternoon, and, just before stumps, Greg Ritchie and I were in control, having lifted the score from 4/101 to 4/180.

However—my score stood at 87.

England's captain was David Gower, and because the light had weakened again he had the spinners John Emburey and Phil Edmonds operating.

Despite this poor light, and the closeness of the day's end, I decided not to depart from my natural game, fearing that to just defend might get me into trouble, if not 'out'. By my 'natural game' I mean I determined to play every ball on its merits—a full-toss is a full-toss and should be dispatched. So, whenever the time was right I would skip down the pitch, trying to either reach the ball on the full, or to smother any spin.

Gower was fielding under my nose, at bat-pad on the offside. Mike Gatting's nose was sniffing out any chance of a bat-pad catch on the onside. He was so close that if I had reached out with my bat I could have cuffed him on the peak of his helmet.

Edmonds flighted one up, its line at my legs; I advanced a couple of skips to meet it, aiming to reach it on the half-volley and flick it away, past Gatting and through the vacant mid-wicket area beyond him.

I didn't quite hit it right; instead of going past Gatting the ball hit him in the midriff, expansive enough in 'Gat's' case to perhaps be called a bread-basket!

Gatting's reflex act was to 'grab for the pain', in this case the ball. For a split second it seemed to have stuck. I thought, 'Just my bloody luck—out on 87!' and I took my first step back towards the Lord's pavilion.

Then, to my left, there was a sudden flurry. The ball was in the air, just over my left shoulder. Gatting was diving trying to catch it.

Suddenly Paul Downton, the England wicketkeeper, dived forward from behind the stumps—only to catch, not the ball, but the rolling Gatting, who had also failed to grasp the ball which had bobbled harmlessly away, along the ground, to Gower.

When stumps were drawn my score had advanced to 92 not out. The next day I went on to make 196, my highest score in Tests at that point in my career.

Australia made 425, a lead of 135; England made 261, leaving us to make 127 to win, which we did despite being 3/22.

Oh, and just for the superstitious—that 196 was my 13th Test century, so who said 87 was unlucky!

OPPOSITE: The catch that wasn't. Gatting looked
like he had me at Lord's in 1985, then spilt it.

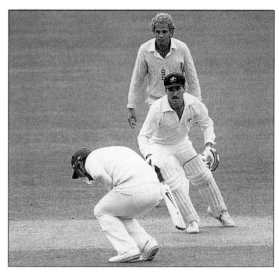

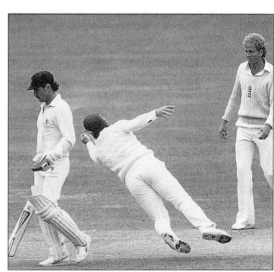
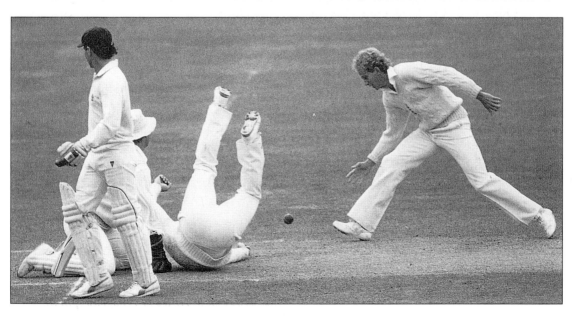

THE TIE

The Madras Tied Test in 1986 was a fantastic game of cricket, and it remains one of my great disappointments that the game has never achieved the same recognition as did the first tied Test played out between Australia and the West Indies at the Gabba in 1960.

People point out to me that the second man on the moon never rated Neil Armstrong status either, but unless you have figured in what I suppose is a 'milestone' you never really know the feeling it can inspire.

The Madras game had everything: weather as hard on players as you could get, humidity the 'killer', temperatures in the 30s; brilliant batting, hard-nosed bowling, individual battles that added to the tension; and the closest possible result achieved on the last, but one, delivery.

I was pleased that Bob Simpson, our coach, who had watched at Madras and played at the Gabba, rated our Madras finish the more fascinating because, as he said, "we came back from the dead".

The circumstances building up to each tie were very different, except that both happened on the final day of the First Test in a series.

At the Gabba Australia had been 6/92 chasing 233 to beat the West Indies, but there were only a few thousand fans there to see history made. In the Chepauk Stadium in Madras, Australia were in the field trying to bowl out India for less than 347, and at the same time put a cork in their scoring rate. And there were 30,000 fans in to watch it unfold.

That crowd factor, and the fact we had to take wickets, not score runs, gives Madras the edge in my book. The Madras tie had everything, mostly drama.

We were seven out for 574 when I declared our first innings, Boon having made his third century in four Tests against India. I made 106, but it was Dean Jones's 210 that spurred us on to our best Test start for a long, long time.

The story about Jones's almighty battle with the oven-like heat, nausea and dehydration—some of us called it 'meltdown'—are all on record, but what is not generally known is the kerfuffle that arose over the type of boots he wore during his marathon innings.

This Test was something of a window of opportunity for Deano because he'd been out of the Test team for a couple of years. In this comeback Test I put him at No. 3 in the batting order, a fair test of his mettle, but I knew Jones's reputation for using his feet to the spinners, and the pitch, dull brown, hard and flat, a 'belter', told me he was sure to get some practice.

Then, drama!

Deano started to use his feet, as often as possible dancing a couple of quick steps down the pitch to negate the bowlers' spin and flight. But he had spikes on his boots, not the 'rubbers' often favoured by players in India, and the Indians started to moan about him damaging the pitch surface.

Out of the blue the umpires had a meeting and told Jones, "You will have to change your boots, your spikes are damaging the pitch." Jones didn't know any different so he came wandering off with the message that he had to change his boots and why.

Then we had Simmo running onto the ground saying, "Bullshit, he's in the act of playing his shot and that's all that matters." Bad luck India. Mind you, I think his boots were the only thing Deano didn't change in that innings; every other item of his gear 'retired drenched' at some stage!

When India batted the game reached a hump—they struggled to 7/245, still a big 130 short of avoiding the follow-on, the only real hope of doing it in the hands of their captain, Kapil Dev.

It was a hurdle of sorts for us, too. We had arrived in India with Australia's Test cricket fortunes at a low ebb. We were in the midst of the Rebel tours to South Africa, we had been thrashed by England and beaten by New Zealand. To make India follow-on might just have pushed a smile through my worry lines.

More drama!

India's last three wickets put on 152, more than a hundred of them off the flailing bat of Kapil. So when we began our second innings there were five sessions of play left, not all that much time to force a result, although we did have a lead of 177 runs.

It was that run cushion, plus the fact that we'd made such heavy inroads into their first innings, that set us thinking that maybe we could win. "Let's throw the bat for a couple of sessions and see where we are at the end of the day," was our game plan.

Another drama!

We mucked it up a bit and by stumps hadn't scored as many runs as we had targeted; we were 5/170 when we thought something more like 200 or 220 would have allowed a declaration and the push for a win.

It was a 'tough' dressing room that evening, steamy, the heat and humidity still a blanket despite the cooler time of day and the slowly circulating ceiling fans above.

I had a beard, and it was a bit prickly, whether from the humidity or the 'heat' in the match situation I couldn't be sure. The tough decision to be made was whether we should bat on the next morning or decide 'Bugger it, let's go for it,' and declare at our stumps total.

Our lead was 347, so statistically things were in our favour—that's a very big ask in a fourth innings even in normal conditions. This Madras pitch was now worn enough for our spinners, Ray Bright and Greg Matthews, to get a bit of bite and bounce.

We knew if we declared straight up we had to bowl 87 overs—so their run rate would be about four an over. But the outfield was very fast. I had a long talk about it with Simmo and Swampy Marsh, the vice-captain, in the room after play and continued the discussion over dinner back at the hotel. There was a lot of "umming" and "aahhing". I was a bit wary about an immediate declaration. It wasn't as if the team had been playing like winners, exactly; even in the first innings we'd choked when we had our foot on their throat.

When I went up to Kapil next morning and told him, "You can have another bat," he looked surprised, and by the looks on the faces of the other Indians when he told them, I think they fancied their chances.

Drama!

We were frustrated by the concentration and technical genius of Gavaskar; it was Sunny's 100th Test in a row, and by tea we had a distinct feeling that he was doing his best to celebrate the occasion by batting India to an historic win.

The scoreline was India 2/193, which really demanded a stiff drink rather than a pot of tea. Gavaskar was within a few good hits of his century and had us on the ropes. I had to now defend a declaration that I had hoped would lead to a first-up win in the series.

Drama!

We grabbed a couple of quick wickets—including Gavaskar for 90—then another, and India were half out for a few runs past 250. I thought, 'They'll pack up shop now, I can go back on the attack.'

I brought the field back in. No sooner had I done that than Shastri, who was playing cleverly, would start bopping the ball over the top again. The beard was getting a fair old scratch. For whatever reason—the tension, the heat, the constant field changes—the last 20 overs took more than two hours to bowl, but it seemed like 20 minutes!

Let's face it, it wasn't one of those occasions when time is all that important, so I wasn't checking the clock. And, of course, there was no slow hand-clap from the crowd, which might have normally been the case; the huge crowd had their minds on the Indian run chase.

Suddenly there was a new drama.

One of the umpires came over to me and accused me of time-wasting. I was incensed and reminded him things were bloody tight, not the sort of situation in which you rush around making snap decisions.

And I mentioned India's slow over rate the previous evening which had halted our run charge for a declaration. "How come you didn't do something about that?" I asked.

He then threatened to send me off, to which I replied, "You can't send me off. Don't be so stupid!" And I turned towards David Boon, who had been standing quietly by my side during the whole episode, and whispered, "He can't do that can he 'Babs'?" The reply was typical Boon: "Buggered if I know."

India reached the stage where they needed 18 runs off the last five overs, with four wickets in hand, and the experienced Shastri leading the way. The tension was incredible.

Drama!

Greg Matthews bowled virtually unchanged through that last day in unbelievably trying conditions, but a performance that is sometimes forgotten in all the tumult was the bowling of Ray Bright, known as 'Candles' for obvious reasons, the left-arm spinner from Victoria.

He was ill and had been on and off the field all day, and now late in the day he had yet again dragged himself back into the fray, ignoring the dehydration that was playing merry hell with his stamina.

When Bright had Sharma caught in the deep, and then bowled More straightaway, making India 8/334, we all thought that was the end of India—that they'd definitely shut up shop this time. They didn't.

Bright was bowling the second last over of the match when Yadav was bowled off his pads, fourth ball, making India 9/344. Their last man, Maninder Singh, played out the last two balls of Bright's over.

Watching from the other end was Ravi Shastri, who had controlled India's innings since the fall of the sixth wicket at 291.

Now, the final drama!

Who should I get to bowl the last over? Well, at no stage did I consider taking Greg Matthews off, even though Shastri had hit some big, and telling, sixes in earlier overs.

So … the last over of the match begins, bowled by Matthews; India need four runs to win, Australia need one wicket. Shastri is on strike.

The decision for me is quite simple: everyone on the boundary except a few blokes floating in the mid-outfield, hoping to stop the batsmen taking a two.

The plan is to give Shastri one run, then bowl at Maninder. After all my deliberation amidst the nerve-shattering noise from the near-frantic crowd, Matthews delivers the first ball. Shastri dances down the pitch, but is cramped by the ball turning into his pads. No run. His thoughts must have been, 'I'll end it with one big hit.'

Second ball he dances down again and plays a big heave to the onside. The ball pitches and turns slightly and Shastri gets a thick inside edge that races out to the mid-wicket boundary area where Steve Waugh is fielding.

Steven races around and gathers the ball, but fumbles slightly, and much to our displeasure the batsmen scamper through for two runs. The crowd goes wild.

More arm-waving from yours truly, sending players scampering to new fielding positions, trying to make sure every angle is covered. Another mid-pitch pow-wow from the batsmen to discuss their latest options; India now need two runs off four balls. Shastri knows if he takes a single India cannot lose.

But then again, 347 runs is a lot to make in the last innings of a match—and, in a day!—and not win. So, the game can go any one of four ways: we can win, India can win, it can be a draw, or it can finish in a tie.

Shastri simply knocks the third ball slowly out to me at mid-wicket for a single, which ties the score with three balls remaining.

India cannot lose the Test, and now all that has to happen in the next three deliveries is for Maninder to take a single, and the Test is theirs.

It takes an eternity before Matthews is ready to deliver the fourth ball of the over. Through frantic discussions with just about every player we finally settle on what we hope is the right mix of attacking and defensive fielding positions, hoping to catch any attempt to loft the ball into the outfield. Maninder blocks and the boys dive on it as if their very lives depend on it.

The fifth ball is slightly quicker, and flatter, and pushes Maninder on to the back foot. The ball turns sharply and catches Maninder on the pads, which brings a huge shout from the fielders—and, incredibly, the umpire raises his finger. Out!

Drama gave way to pandemonium.

The boys went absolutely berserk, and just for that fleeting moment when all hell broke loose, I thought, 'Shit, we've won it!' It took a short while for the real result to sink in. A tie. It was as good as a win for us.

When the last ball was delivered I was fielding in at bat-pad on the offside and as the ball hit Maninder's pads it bounced out in my direction. I was that intent on getting the ball I didn't even appeal.

The first thing I saw was the umpire's finger in the air, and Mo Matthews charging towards our dressing room like a lunatic, arms flapping as if he was trying to fly. The Indians weren't as ecstatic, naturally, probably thinking they'd had a certain win snatched from them.

I could identify with that feeling.

During the last extraordinary overs I'd been thinking, 'Here we are in a bloody cauldron, on an Indian pitch, we've declared twice, we've basically bowled them out twice, and we might lose—where's the justice?'

The after-match celebrations were long and boisterous; I quietly gave the ball to Greg. He had done a most amazing job for Australia, and I felt it only right that he receive the ball that produced this amazing result.

And perhaps it will remain one of the great ironies in my career that the final decision happened to involve an Indian batsman being adjudged leg before by an Indian umpire.

More than that, Maninder Singh complained, "I played the ball, I played the ball," meaning I suppose that he had hit it and therefore could not have been out leg before.

I thought, 'Yes Maninder, I've heard it all before. Since about 1979 in fact.'

Matthews gets Maninder leg before, and for the second time in history a Test finished in a tie.

DUEL IN THE SUN

My first tilt with the West Indies platoon of fast bowlers came at precisely 34 minutes after 11 a.m. on December 1, 1979, in the sauna that is the Gabba cricket ground in Brisbane. It was the celebrated occasion of the first 'combined' Australian Test team after the World Series Peace.

It was a great honour to be chosen in that team, but the captain, Greg Chappell, put me in at No. 3, and batting in that spot against the West Indies came as a nasty shock to the Border system. The giant Joel Garner soon made me feel right out of my depth. I spent 20 very uncomfortable minutes on nought.

I just couldn't get the ball in the middle of the bat, and I played and missed a fair bit. I only scored one run before I was caught behind off Garner. While I was going through this torment I could hear a few chuckles in the slips cordon behind me. It was Viv Richards, white teeth flashing, jaws chomping gum, enjoying my discomfort.

It wasn't the most pleasant time of my life, but it was an experience that made me really want to succeed at Test cricket. Desperately so. I gritted my teeth and thought, 'I'll show you, you mug.'

Nothing derogatory, Viv … just that time-worn Aussie expression that says 'One day I'm coming to get you.'

And when the West Indies next visited Australia in the 1981–82 season I averaged about 60 runs an innings. But the really good feeling didn't arrive until a couple of years later, on March 21, 1984, when, on a steaming hot day on the baked clay of Trinidad's Queen's Park Oval, Viv Richards conceded, "Get your century, man, and let's get outta here."

It was the Second Test of the series and we had trailed by 213 runs on the first innings; just about the time of the tea break on the final day we had reached 238, and coming out to join me in my lather of sweat at the crease was our last man, Terry Alderman.

Terry had been in this situation—going out to bat—in Tests 24 times before. He had scored 56 runs in those 24 innings, his highest score was 12 not out, and his average 4.6, not the sort of statistics to make anyone believe anything other than a crushing West Indies win was just around the corner.

Commentators, and spectators, are less than generous too, often describing bowlers with that sort of a batting record as 'rabbits'. However, I've always had a theory about batting with the 'tail' of the team—you have to appeal to the grit-bit in their character. I try to get them believing 'this thing can be done' by reminding them that as bowlers they have sometimes been frustrated by the 'tail' in other teams.

In Terry's case, I also told him, "All you have to do is keep out the ball that might hit the stumps, and leave the rest to me. The longer we can stay out here the less time they'll have to get whatever target we manage to set them."

Terry won't mind if I say he doesn't really look like a batsman. He's one of those blokes who, for whatever reason, just isn't coordinated when he's wielding a cricket bat. But he is fiercely determined. He'll take whatever is dished out to him, and he'll stand up for more. That afternoon in Trinidad the West Indies fast bowlers peppered him.

After the tea break, and when we'd survived plenty of overs, I called Terry into mid-pitch and said, "I think we might get out of this. Hang in there." Viv was West Indies captain, and he was setting deep fields inviting me to take singles, but after farming the strike early, I decided I could leave it to Terry.

I could see Viv and his boys starting to panic, thinking 'Why can't we get this 'bunny' Alderman out?' They took the second new ball and whizzed it around his ears. They tried spin when the pace blitz failed.

Leaving the field with Terry Alderman after we'd defied the might
of the West Indies in a last-wicket stand, 1984.

We held firm. Terry even got adventurous, and blossomed from blocking the straight ones and ignoring the wide ones, to belting cover drives and whipping some off his legs through the onside.

We were still in when the umpires signalled 'last 20 overs', but not safe, as dismissal would have allowed the West Indies batsmen ample time to knock off our lead, which by then was still only 60 or so runs.

Eventually, with only three overs of that final 20 left to be bowled, and the crowd chanting "Border, Border, Border" as if the Test was being played in Australia, Viv brought on Gus Logie. I hit him for four straight down the ground, to go from 96 to 100, and that's when Viv cried "enough".

It was a great series for me, 521 runs at an average of 74 runs an innings, helped a lot by that Test, in which I also made 98 not out in the first innings— kept on 98 for 12 balls by my 'nemesis', Garner!

All up in that Test I batted for nearly ten and a half exhausting hours. I felt like I'd been steam-ironed! But Joel Garner only got me once in the series, in the first innings of the First Test.

There was a lot of personal satisfaction in that result, but I can tell you that the joy of things shared will often mean more than individual achievement, and the 105 minutes and 61 runs I shared with 'Clem' Alderman that day in Trinidad will remain with me forever.

THE ULTIMATE HONOUR

We all have dreams; mine was to play cricket for Australia, but never in my dreams did I imagine that one day I would receive the Order Of Australia, and the next day be feted by tens of thousands of fellow Australians. All in the name of cricket.

The ticker-tape parade, turned on by Sydney people during their lunch hour on September 28, 1989, really touched me. And I know it touched every other member of that great '89 Ashes winning team. There were no tears from the boys during that emotional moment, but I have to confess I had that burning feeling that sometimes comes to your eyes, and I was blinking a lot more rapidly than I normally do. Emotion has a way of revealing itself, and for me and the boys there had been very few days that were without emotion since our return from England.

When you've been playing cricket away from Australia, it's often difficult to know the reaction back home to your performance. That's particularly the case in India and Pakistan, and was the case in the West Indies until 1991, when the tour was televised live.

Our 1989 Ashes triumph was beamed live by the Nine Network into living rooms all round Australia, so when we won the reaction was huge. Our London headquarters, the Westbury Hotel, was inundated with faxes and phone calls and special telegrams with hero pictures drawn on them. What stuck in all our minds was the number of congratulatory messages from 'ordinary folk', messages signed Sam and Pete, Ipswich, or Jack and Mary, Albury.

So we had an inkling that we'd touched the hearts of a helluva lot of Aussies, but none of us imagined those same hearts would pour out so much affection in this ticker-tape parade a few weeks after we'd grabbed the Ashes in that historic moment at Old Trafford.

The night before the ticker-tape parade we had been in Melbourne for the '89 Ashes Victory Dinner, so when we arrived in Sydney for the parade, about department store opening time, we were all just a little bit the worse for wear. There had been a lot of Ashes action replays over the after-dinner ports. Plural 'ports' I'm sorry to say.

We gathered at the Regent Hotel, which is at the Harbour Bridge, or Mosman, end of Sydney, and sought relief from the coffee pot while some Government officials ran through the details of the parade.

Through the window I could see that the sky looked overcast, and a bit threatening. I thought, 'Gee, I hope it doesn't rain for this.' And there didn't seem to be very many people in the street, either. I thought, 'I hope this isn't a non-event.'

Then the time came to go downstairs and out to the cars which were to form the motorcade; the weather was quite bright. That's the trouble with those modern tinted hotel windows, you get a false impression of what awaits you in the outside world. But the best news was that gathered around the cars was quite a crowd, and they were all cheering.

George Street is Sydney's main street, and runs the length of the city. The Regent Hotel is at its northern end and is located just beyond a sweeping bend, so if you are standing outside the Regent it is impossible to see right along George Street.

So we set out from the Regent, heading south, Swampy Marsh and I sharing a bright red convertible BMW, perched behind the driver. As we came out of the bend I was struck speechless.

I managed to instinctively grab Swampy's blazer jacket sleeve and say, "My God, have a look at this." For, as far as the eye could see there were people lining George Street. From up in the buildings people were tossing down whatever paper they could find onto us as we passed below. A snowstorm of paper.

Rolls of paper came swirling down along with coloured streamers and confetti; a band played 'Waltzing Matilda'; I saw a sign saying "Border For PM" draped above the famous Woolworths Corner, where I used to meet Jane sometimes when we were courting.

I suppose we were halfway along George Street when I thought, 'I've never experienced anything like this—and I'm bloody unlikely to ever again!'

The faces out there were all so positive; there were kids wide-eyed with fascination, there were girls squealing, older people just smiling and waving; some people rushed over to the cars and reached for our hands and some kissed us. Someone even kissed Merv Hughes, rough, tough, gruff Merv. Well, later he told me, "AB, that was real lump-in-the-throat stuff today."

Jane and I flew home to Brisbane a couple of days later. All the way it was hard not to keep thinking back to the astonishing ticker-tape parade through Sydney, and a little boy named Robert Smith.

Robert caught my eye when the motorcade was about a third of the way along George Street because he was in a wheelchair, and his smile was as wide as anybody's in that sea of faces. His dad was waving to me, and called out, "Can you say 'hello' to the young bloke?"

And we just stopped the car and had a bit of a chat. Moments like that make life a bit more worthwhile.

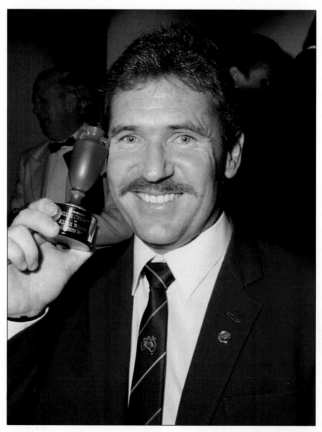

Every Australian cricket captain's dream ... to hold the Ashes.

*ABOVE: Sydney's
ticker-tape parade.*

*With Dean Jones,
and the key to the city
of Sydney, 1989.*

Chapter Eleven

OTHER MOMENTS

An odd place for a cricket team — the desert outside Sharjah.

*Cricket develops character, and I'm glad to say
attracts different characters. That can lead to some
original situations, some muddle-headed,
some memorable, some moving.*

TWO MEN, ONE AIM

Being named The Australian Of The Year in 1989 was a special moment in my life, but a very humbling experience, too. When I went up onto the dais at Admiralty House to receive the award, I followed a young man named Brenden Borellini. Brenden was 21 years old then, and had been named The Young Australian Of The Year. He is deaf and blind, but he reads braille, and communicates by finger spelling.

His mother was by his side during the awards presentation, and it was amazing to watch her, holding his hand palm up, and spelling out, interpreting, for him just what was being said. When Brenden was 10 he knew about that many words, but with the help of a teacher he was able to attend school and get the Higher School Certificate. His aim was to go on and study Asian languages at university.

I took a walk with Brenden that day and the thought crossed my mind, 'Allan, what are you doing here?'

I knew the answer was that Brenden and I, in our completely different ways, were something of an inspiration to other Australians: if you are prepared to work hard enough when the going is tough, then you can achieve plenty.

But at the time I couldn't help thinking young Brenden had done a bit more than me.

PLAY IT AGAIN, AB

There were a lot of records broken when Australia played the Kiwis in the Second Test at Adelaide Oval in 1987. The Test was in the middle of December and in the middle of a heatwave.

The temperature reached 40.7°C, which from memory wasn't a record, but if anybody had bothered to check how many buckets of sweat I lost it would have been a record.

The cricket records arrived on December 13, when I went past Sir Donald Bradman's Test runs record, 6996; and on December 14, when I went past Greg Chappell's Test runs record, 7110. On that day I also reached my highest score in Tests, 205.

Ground announcers have a field day when there are records looming, and get very excited when they are actually broken. When they come one atop another, as they did on the 14th, there is a lot of 'blah-blah' around.

Martin Crowe was in the New Zealand team and he eventually became a bit unsettled by all the action at the microphone.

He had started out relaxed enough. "You've got 'The Don'," he shouted when I reached 71 and the crowd cheered on the 13th.

Borellini and Border.

*Going past Bradman —
and the Kiwis don't look
as happy as I do.*

*BELOW: Tom Lowrey's
'wagon wheel' of my
highest score in Tests.*

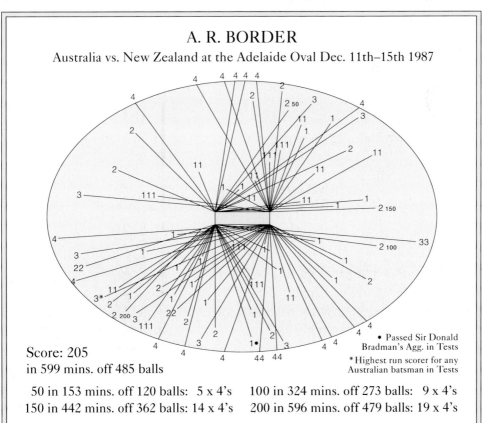

A. R. BORDER

Australia vs. New Zealand at the Adelaide Oval Dec. 11th–15th 1987

• Passed Sir Donald
Bradman's Agg. in Tests

*Highest run scorer for any
Australian batsman in Tests

Score: 205
in 599 mins. off 485 balls

50 in 153 mins. off 120 balls: 5 x 4's   100 in 324 mins. off 273 balls: 9 x 4's
150 in 442 mins. off 362 balls: 14 x 4's   200 in 596 mins. off 479 balls: 19 x 4's

Then, the next day came the announcement that I'd passed Greg Chappell, then one about passing my previous highest Test score, 196, then the 200, at which point Martin said, "Hey AB, I'm getting the shits with this—any more milestones we can help you out with?"

MAN OF FEW WORDS

Curtly Ambrose got me with the 'throat ball' in the gripping Adelaide Test, near the end of our see-sawing series with the West Indies in the summer of '93.

The 'throat ball' generally pitches just short of a length, then rises sharply with a steepling bounce, and at extreme pace if delivered by the very tall Curtly.

Normally you react to a ball of that length by setting yourself for the back defence, but the wicked bounce forces a reflex toss back of the head, and that means the eyes leave the ball.

When the head jerks back the gloves and bat jerk up like a soldier raising his shield. It's called self-preservation!

Curtly is a man of few words. Whenever I passed Curtly off the field he was always brief: "Skipperrr."

My reply was as brief, and as respectful: "Curtlyyy."

The only other words I can remember from him were, "How's that?"

In the middle he's stopped and given me the stare on occasions when things haven't gone his way, but he's never said a word.

He controls it very well.

He's in my list of four best West Indian pacemen: Malcolm Marshall, Joel Garner, Michael Holding, and Curtly.

WAYNE'S WORLD

After our disappointments in the 1992 World Cup I needed to get away from it all. Show me an Australian cricketer and I'll show you a frustrated championship golfer prone to wild dreams about playing the Masters at Augusta.

I made it to the azalea-fringed fairways of Augusta in 1992, not, of course, to play in the Masters, but for a nine-handicapper from Down Under it turned out to be the next best thing.

I'm good mates with US PGA winner Wayne Grady, who hails from Queensland, a terrific bloke with no airs or graces, who loves to drop into the Gabba for a beer with the boys. Wayne organised a ticket for me to follow the Masters, but more than that he invited me to caddie for him in the Par-3 tournament Augusta holds on Masters' eve.

I had 205 good reasons to cool off.

Nothing sinister, just a bit of fun photography.

In the group were Ian Baker-Finch and Nick Price, from Zimbabwe; in the group in front of us was the great Arnold Palmer, and following the action a crowd, would you believe, of about 60,000!

I had to wear long white overalls that made me look like a lab technician. 'Grades' laughed at me, "Hey AB, you're nervous. You're all the same you cricketers, stick you in the middle of the MCG on a dark night facing Curtly Ambrose and a crowd of 80,000 and you're okay. Take you out of your element in front of 60,000 close-up here and you go to water!" He was right, I admit it.

Grades had four birdies, but missed a couple he should have got—I *did* tell him he should have aimed for the bottom lip!

It was one of *the* great days of my life.

ELTON, MOLLY AND US

For some reason cricketers and showbiz people seem to get on well; back in 1932 an Australian team, with Don Bradman in it, played in Hollywood. Ian 'Molly' Meldrum puts on a big barbecue for the Australians every summer. Elton John has been known to go a fair bit further.

Elton is a sports fanatic, and a very generous bloke. I get the feeling he likes to be around us cricketers, where he's not the centre of public attention, but there's still a lot of hype.

Cricketers and their families can be separated for long periods of time. Time for a get-together is often the day before the traditional Boxing Day Test. Christmas in Melbourne, 1991.

A bit of fun at training camp—Jones and Greg Matthews consider our fate.

During the Perth Challenge in 1986 Elton rang the rooms to invite everyone in the team out to dinner, but he was greeted with the news that most of the blokes had their wives over.

No problem—Elton invited everyone, and it was bigger than Hollywood, pink champagne, corsages, the works.

Elton likes to bet on England versus Australia matches, usually with Dean Jones; Jones backs himself to get 50, and the kitty is one of Deano's bats to one of Elton's gold records.

It never seemed like a fair swap to me!

ANOTHER DAY, ANOTHER DISASTER

When I was playing with East Lancashire back in 1978, also over for a season in the League were John Dyson and Andrew Hilditch, and we were all invited to play in a League pick-up side which was to travel to the south of England, Bristol, for a week of cricket, drinking and general fun.

This was quite traditional, as any Australian who has played in the League will testify; and who were we to break with tradition?

As luck would have it one of the matches was at the Downend ground, where I had played in 1977 during my stint with Gloucester.

So, the match begins, and enter Andrew Hilditch, who over the years had become a master of disaster, an accident waiting to happen.

A Downend player hits the ball out into the covers and runs; two of our players, one of them Andrew, swoop on the ball, but collide.

The other bloke's leg is accidentally gashed by Andrew's spikes, there's blood everywhere and the game is stopped while he's taken off.

The game resumes, and two balls later another one goes into the covers, and Andrew swoops. No-one goes within cooee of Andrew this time, so he simply picks up the ball and underarms it back to the bowler.

But Andrew's radar is out, and the ball starts heading directly towards the umpire's head. Andrew yells, "Look out, ump!"

The umpire, who is quite elderly, turns slightly to see what he should be looking out for, sees the ball hurtling towards him, and collapses. Naturally all the players rush to him, but no-one's really got a clue what to do. He looks very still and pale, so much so that someone says, "I think he's dead," which creates total panic.

Enter Hilditch. He steps forward, bends over the stricken umpire and belts him in the chest with the heel of his hands.

And the umpire comes to, much to the relief of everyone. He had only fainted, but as a precaution he was helped off the field and an ambulance was called. The game resumes.

Meanwhile the player with the gashed leg needs stitches, and it's decided he should wait for the ambulance, too.

But the umpire decides he's all right, and wants to go home. He gets on his mo-ped—yes, mo-ped—and rides out of the ground just as the ambulance is arriving.

As the umpire turns out of the ground into the traffic he is bowled over by a passing car, which hurts him but not seriously.

The ambulance has picked up the injured player and on leaving for the local casualty goes to the rescue of the luckless umpire.

Just another day in the life of a Lancashire League cricketer!

WHO PULLED FRANK'S LEG?

My man from Gloucester, Frank Twiselton, was back in Australia in 1988, this time to manage the England team that had played in the 1977 Centenary Test in Melbourne.

The game plan was that the same players who contested the 1977 match would go round in a series of 'encores' to help raise money for the Australian Olympic Appeal fund. And it was a huge success.

But there was one problem for Frank, and to this day he's not too sure who to blame—Dennis Lillee or Rod Marsh.

On the flight out Frank had been lucky enough to travel 'economy in style'— instead of four seats across, there were only two, allowing Frank some leg room. Anyone who's ever spent the best part of a day flying London to Sydney will know that's a big break.

Frank was so impressed he decided to see if he could get the same seat on his way back home, and approached Dennis Lillee about it. "Dennis, you know just about everyone in Qantas, can you have a word …?"

Dennis said, "No problem."

But Frank was worried that Dennis might forget, so he asked Rod Marsh, too. Rod assured Frank there would be no problem.

On the return trip, half an hour out of Heathrow, Frank was enjoying a nice leg-stretch, when the steward came down the aisle checking a list against seat numbers.

He reached Frank and inquired, "Mr Frank Twiselton?" He then told Frank not to worry, because "when we land the wheelchair will be brought right to your seat."

Lillee or Marsh had arranged Frank's seat and told Qantas that he was a war hero with a 'gammy' leg.

SO LONG, RODNEY

I'm not the kind of bloke who's likely to burst out crying when there's some emotion around, but I have been known to get a lump in my throat on certain occasions.

The end of the 1983–84 season was one such occasion; there was a lot of emotion around, because the Big Three of Australian cricket, Greg Chappell, Dennis Lillee and Rodney Marsh, were all retiring.

Chappell and Lillee bowed out at the end of the Fifth Test against Pakistan at the SCG, Chappell scoring 182 to go past Bradman's Test run record, Lillee taking his 355th Test wicket, ironically caught by Marsh, also his 355th Test victim. We all had a few hundred drinks with Greg and Dennis that night, January 6 it was.

But Rodney, or 'Bacchus' as we all knew him, decided he wouldn't go until after the finals of the World Series in which we were to play the West Indies.

In my career Bacchus was the teammate I most admired; after the peace between the Cricket Board and World Series Cricket he became a sort of 'father figure' in the side, spending hours passing on his knowledge of the game to the new, young blokes like me.

I first played against Lillee and Marsh in an interstate one-day match; Lillee bowled me a bouncer first ball—what else?—then later I caught him on the mid-wicket fence to win the game.

The selectors were about to choose the first Test side to include both Cricket Board and World Series Cricket players, and after the game Marsh made a point of coming into our room, introducing himself and having a chat. We hit it off straightaway, I felt like he was a senior player who was going out of his way to bring me into the fold.

He was a very tough competitor, and a fiercely proud one, which might explain why he opted to have one more crack at the West Indies—we'd never beaten them in the finals of the World Series.

The first final was at the SCG and we got absolutely belted; we went to the MCG for the second final, and before the match, Greg and Dennis in 'civvies', and Rodney in the green and gold of World Series, bid their farewells to Australia's cricket fans, 42,000 of them in at the MCG that day, February 11.

It was an emotional moment, and an inspirational one for the Australian team, particularly as Rodney was to play that day. We went out and held the West Indies to 5/222—and you wouldn't want to know, got 9/222 ourselves. It was the first tie in international limited-overs history!

Well, because the West Indies had lost fewer wickets we thought that was it—goodbye World Series Cup, goodbye Rodney. So, we had a few drinks to drown our sorrows, then a few more to farewell Rodney.

ABOVE: Rodney Marsh went out of his way to welcome me into the fold.

Lillee, Greg Chappell, and Marsh say their last farewell.

Rodney made an emotional speech—lump in the throat—during which he officially handed over to me duties of leading the team in its victory song—when appropriate, of course! Then we had a very big drink indeed.

In the middle of all this the phone jangled, and the 'roomie' shouted, "Rodney Marsh, telephone!" It was Rod's wife Roslyn, calling from Perth.

Rodney was very close to tears when he came back and sat down next to me, and told me about the call.

"Ros—she asked if I was sure I was doing the right thing by retiring. Great lady, AB. She badly wants a family life, but here she is asking me am I sure. I'm sure AB. That's it."

I put an arm around his shoulder and all I could think of to say was "She'll be right, mate."

YOU CAN TAKE THE BOY OUT OF MOSMAN...

When Jane and I, and the family, go back to Mosman, as we do quite regularly to visit Jane's parents, I often wander up to Mosman Oval, where it all began for me. I take Dene with me.

There are a lot of memories ... "I used to climb that tree, 'Deano' ... that's where I smacked Uncle Johnno for six ... " Father and son having a few laughs together.

But the most enduring memory was provided by Mosman Council, just a few days after I'd come home from the 1993 New Zealand tour. As part of Centenary celebrations a cricket match was organised: Allan Border captain of mayor Dom Lopez's XI, against Greg Chappell's XI.

Dom's team, despite losing four wickets for no runs at the Chappell total, 289, got up by one wicket. My 160 runs should be judged in the light of these circumstances: I was the guest of honour; the age, if not fitness, of a bowling attack that included Dave Renneberg, Grahame Corling, Gary Gilmour and Ross Edwards, who in his playing days was a batsman-wicketkeeper.

At the end of the day Dom announced Mosman Oval would be re-named Allan Border Oval, indeed a great honour for me.

OPPOSITE: With Mum Sheila and Dad John outside what used to be the family home, 'Omaha', during the Mosman Council Centenary. The Mulligan family, the current owners, entered into the spirit of the occasion.

Chapter Twelve

ON SECOND THOUGHTS

Gathering my thoughts for the media.

When a sportsman has been up for as long as I have incidents come to mind that influence memories of the game and its players. They may even contribute to the future direction of cricket.

WHO SAID WHAT?

In my second innings in the last Test of the 1984 series in the West Indies, the second ball, a thunderbolt from the right hand of the giant Joel Garner, missed my swaying head by a bee's whizzer.

It was about the 400th bouncer that had nearly cleaned me up on tour, but it went the closest to cleaning me up, and I was startled. I looked up at Joel, who had this long follow-through and was standing only a pace or two away, and gasped, "Oh, you big bastard!"

He just looked down at me for a second, then he turned on his heel and strolled back towards his bowling mark ... while I thought to myself, 'Stupid bugger AB, what a dumb thing to say second ball you've faced, especially as big Joel bowled it!'

While I was considering my lack of nous Dessie Haynes, who was fielding at bat-pad, ran down and spoke to Joel. In the half hour that evening until stumps I copped the lot, verbal bouncers as well.

Next morning, the fourth, and following the rest day, I was back, my aim to save the game, although with our score at 7/135—7/29 if our first innings deficit was counted—it was a forlorn hope. Our last three Tests had been nightmares, beaten by ten wickets, then an innings, and now we were looking down the gun-barrel again.

The Sabina Park pitch was very bouncy, which was ideal for big Joel, and it had plenty of pace too, perfect for Malcolm Marshall.

On that fourth morning while I was out on the ground hitting up before play, I felt a hand grip my shoulder. It was big Joel and he was wanting to know what I was doing calling him a black bastard the evening before.

I looked at him wide-eyed, and said, "Joel, you've got to be kidding; what I said was you were a big bastard."

It hadn't been expressed in any sort of an aggressive, or nasty way. It was more an expression of shocked admiration—but how do you explain to a West Indian that in Australia the term 'bastard' can often be used in non-derogatory fashion? Especially when time's short.

Australia's last man out that morning was John Maguire, bowled by big Joel. As Joel came back from his follow-through, to collect his hat from the umpire, we shook hands. No hard feelings.

I've heard of all sorts of bastards mentioned on the cricket field—lucky ones, big ones, jammy ones, poor ones—but I can honestly say I've never heard mention of a black one.

Racism is a worldwide issue that can only be defused by more tolerance. Once racism colours cricket, whether it be black bastards, white cowards, or just plain yellow, then the game has a problem.

PACE ECLIPSE, NOW!

In the summer of 1979–80 when I got the call-up for what might be termed cricket's 'national service'—in the frontline against the West Indian pace quartet—I was still in 'short pants' when it came to Test cricket, having played only 11 Tests.

The fastest bowler I'd faced in that time was a toss-up between Pakistan's Imran Khan and England's Bob Willis. But neither Imran nor Willis had the same reputation for bruising batsmen and breaking their spirit as did the bowlers from the Caribbean.

There was a sort of aura around the West Indian attack, felt not only in the grandstands, but, and this surprised me, also in the Australian dressing room. Now there weren't too many shrinking violets in the room about that time—Greg Chappell, Lillee, Marsh, Thommo, Len Pascoe—but even their acknowledged grit didn't seem to be able to shout down the general chit-chat: "… these guys are just awesome …"

I'd have to say I got overtaken by it a bit. Despite my rookie status Greg Chappell slotted me in at No. 3 in the batting order. It was just too tall an order for me, and I made only 118 runs in six digs and averaged less than 20.

It wasn't my worst Test series—in 1981–82 my tours to Pakistan and New Zealand were shockers—but I know I was a shot duck even before I walked out to bat. Big Joel Garner gave me no end of trouble. Think of it this way: I was five foot, nine inches (172 cm), drawn up to my full, imposing height; and he stood six foot, nine inches (202 cm). If we add on the length of his right arm—which seemed long enough to scratch his knee without bothering to bend—say another two foot-plus (60 cm), then big Joel was ripping the ball down at me from a height of about nine feet (270 cm)!

Balls from Joel seemed to alternate around the Adam's apple, from just short of a good length, or around the feet, the well disguised yorker.

The others supporting Garner then were Michael Holding, Andy Roberts and Colin Croft, and because I was only at the crease a short while I had plenty of time to sit back in the easy chair at the Gabba and do a bit of forward planning: next time, how can I see off an attack like this?

Holding was very, very quick, nicknamed 'Whispering Death', because of his softly-softly graceful run to the crease.

Roberts was clever, able to set you up with a 'slow' bouncer which you might hook for four, then next ball, with no change in his action, let you have one a yard quicker that would frighten the life out of you.

When Colin Croft was bowling I always had the thought running through my mind that 'this guy doesn't really care how he gets me out, even if he has to knock me out.'

They were relentless. The dictionary defines 'intimidation' as: "to frighten into action, to cow, to inspire with fear." I never felt fear facing the West Indian fast bowlers. I was never intimidated. But I will say the pace and the pressure can unsettle a batsman, and one or two failures can suddenly destroy confidence.

That happened to Greg Chappell in the 1981–82 season when he got seven ducks, some of them one, or two ball jobs. He became so depressed that after one failure he came back to the room, tossed his bat into his locker, and announced it was time for him to quit. Rod Marsh changed his mind for him pretty quickly.

There were a lot of technical opinions floated as to the reason for Greg's dreadful run of outs, but Greg himself was in no doubt: "Mental."

Having faced up to the West Indies in 31 of my 141 Tests I'd have to say it was a lot tougher near the end, in the 1991 Caribbean series, than it was in the beginning.

Look at it this way: Joel Garner is one of nature's gentlemen and in the 80s I never had any impression other than Joel was trying to get batsmen out; in 1991 I had a feeling it was a slightly different ball game.

In the Caribbean it just seemed as if the 'edge' of a West Indies versus Australia series had been overtaken by a lot more 'venom'.

A FEW BRIGHT IDEAS?

I like Test cricket and Sheffield Shield cricket just the way they are—almost. And one-day cricket? Well, if it ain't broke, why fix it?

When I was in short pants I used to run home from school, across Mosman Oval, to watch the Sheffield Shield on television. True, they only used to televise the last two hours, but it was often the best action session of the day, when tired bowlers were getting belted or a new innings was starting.

I hope down the line, with Australian television about to undergo fairly dramatic change, I'll be able to watch the Sheffield Shield final live, and even the last two hours of a day's play once again. With the commercial channels, the ABC, Sky and Pay TV I'm sure the Cricket Board could negotiate a deal for the Shield, especially as all the Shield teams have big money sponsorships these days, and would love a TV profile.

Any call for the Shield to be televised generally leads to an airing of the theory that it's too boring to inflict on the audience, and a demand that we pay homage to the great god, Brighter Cricket.

What is 'brighter cricket'? Is it batsmen belting balls all over the park, or is it bowlers taking hat-tricks willy-nilly? Is it exciting cricket, or entertaining cricket, because there's a fair old gulf between those two.

I'm always a bit wary about calls to jazz up the game too much, because once you start fiddling around with what is really a simple format you can lose the plot totally. I don't think playing Sheffield Shield at night is an option, simply because we don't have a white ball, or one of any other colour, good enough to ensure a proper game. Even when we use two white balls in World Series they don't stay white for that long. There is an ugly sighting time for batsmen when day is turning to night, and the lights haven't quite taken over.

The lights themselves are not always the best, and changeable atmospheric conditions—heavy dew—are also a factor that can increase the degree of difficulty in playing a four-day/night match.

My concern would be that given all those variables, rules would have to be changed to reduce the danger of physical injury to batsmen, and therefore disadvantage the bowler. A major part of any fast bowler's weaponry is his need to dig the ball in short, to keep the batsman thinking, but such deliveries would be exceptionally tough to handle in the longer match format. Packer's World Series Cricket had exactly that problem in the day/night SuperTests, and the white ball hasn't changed since then.

But cricket wouldn't be cricket if the bowlers were told, "No aggression please, fellas, it's night-time."

And, I don't think it would be cricket if we went down the track of mixing limited-overs into the Sheffield Shield format. There has been a call to limit the first innings of each side to a set number of overs, then let them play for an outright result over the final two days.

I just think that's bastardising the game.

However, I do agree that we need to address what is called the "first innings win mentality", where one side might take two days, or more, to scrape together 450, then the other team goes about its chase as diligently as an owner-builder laying the bricks in a 40-square mansion.

All for two points. I'd like to see first innings points scrapped and a return to the bonus points system of the 70s. The bonus points would operate in the first innings up to a cut-off stage, say 100 overs; that's not to say the captain couldn't bat on after that point if he wanted, but there would certainly be less incentive to do so.

There's no doubt in my mind the bonus points system makes batsmen more aware of the need to score runs at a reasonable rate, and bowlers more aware of trying to take wickets. But more than anything it gives the captains the option of opening up the game and going for the outright win, and the maximum points that go with that.

I'd like to see only the slightest tampering with Test cricket. After all, it's only when you get a deadly, deadly dull series that the critics say, "Test cricket is dying, something must be done." Then along comes a series like Australia's last one with the West Indies and everyone says the Tests are the best.

Test cricket is ebb and flow, food for the brain stuff. My only concession to the merchants of brighter cricket would be to suggest a tasteful splash of colour be added to Test players' white clothing, something like that worn at Wimbledon, where the basic white is retained, and a moderate amount of colour, say that of the country, is added for contrast.

I think it's important when making changes, particularly to a format that is relatively successful, that the timing of change is right. Any changes to World Series would, I think, need to be very carefully thought through. The timing of any change would probably revolve around either strong player disaffection, or a drop-off in crowd support.

The 'wide rule' has become a bit overdone; if the ball is way down legside, fair enough, call it, because it is harder for the batsman to hit a ball slanting that way. But now we've reached a point where batsmen are making to play at balls outside the off stump, then not playing and staring at the umpire as if to say 'Hey ump, that's a wide.' And the umpires have started calling "wide" for balls that might be only 45 centimetres (18 inches) outside the off stump.

Now that's wrong, because any batsman should be able to play a reasonable shot at that ball. I think a bowler should be allowed a little bit of width outside off—and that's coming from a batsman!

Some time in the future the 'interchange' could be introduced. There have been suggestions as many as four players could be on the bench and called into the game at various stages to pinch-hit, or bowl in a particular way.

I'd resist that, because it could get as busy as your local shopping mall two days before Christmas. But I would support the twelfth man taking an active role in World Series, rather than his traditional passive role.

In the end, it doesn't really matter what changes the game's administrators make; it's up to the players to ensure that the entertainment factor stays high enough to maintain the public's interest and encourage them to come to cricket.

THE MEDIA

In the main I have been fairly treated by the press, but there have been isolated occasions when they have gone too far. Sometimes today's cricket media is too aggressive towards the game, its players, and even the players' families. It can be overly intrusive, too.

When Jane had Nicole she'd hardly had time to get her breath back before the phone rang. It was a radio station.

Reporter: "Jane Border? Oh good, what did you have, a boy or a girl?"

Jane: "I haven't had time to tell my husband yet, do you mind!"

On Australia's tour to the Caribbean in 1991 a journalist named Fishman took advantage of his friendship with the players Greg Matthews and Mike Whitney to gain entrance to the team's inner sanctum. He was made welcome around the bar, on outings and even rode on the team bus—then turned around and wrote a load of rubbish looking for headlines and big book sales. Diabolical.

When we won the Ashes back in 1989, England's effort, when Marsh and Taylor put on 300, was described so: "Any uninitiated casual visitor strolling into the Nottingham ground would have been forgiven for thinking the Australian openers Geoff Marsh and Mark Taylor were playing a joint Benefit match ... not against fellow professionals, well paid, pampered and protected, but against a bunch of well-meaning and harmless country bumpkins. All village idiots."

They are just three examples of why relations between the players and the media have become a bit strained. There was a time when a player could have a drink with a cricket journalist in a bar after a day's play and not have to worry that the next day it would be headlines in the newspaper. That's not always the case these days.

Today's media, not just the cricket media, no longer respects the privacy of the public figure. You're public property, therefore anything goes. In cricket, expectations have been raised higher by the hype surrounding the one-day game. Night cricket, and all its trappings, has created a new audience, and the media feels obliged to satisfy the fans' every curiosity.

When I came into the Australian team in 1979 I was just another short-back-and-sides bloke, nickname 'Pugsley', about whom the most exciting line was "He's another Neil Harvey." When Shane Warne came onto the cricket scene in 1991, spiked fair hair, nickname 'Hollywood', and the first legspinner since ... well, you'd think since Clarrie Grimmett, then nothing was left to the imagination. Mother's name, father's name, girlfriend's name, social likes—you name it. The media build-up, and, via that the public's expectation of Shane, was totally over the top. It's that expectation that can create problems when the hiccup comes along.

My nickname in the media has ranged from 'Grumpy' to 'Captain Cranky', and I concede I do get surly at times. That was particularly so in the early days of my reign as captain, when I was under constant media bombardment.

Some blokes might have been less tetchy. But my philosophy has been to try to be as honest as possible with the media. I expected a fair go in return, and as a general rule they did respect me for that, but not when we lost.

The 1991–92 season was a case in point. We beat India four-nil in the Tests, beat West Indies and India in the World Series, but because we went under in the World Cup, which was the main focus of the media and the public, the season was painted as a disaster.

The pre-Cup media hype was that Australia were the best one-day side in the

In the media spotlight ...

... sometimes the going can get tough.

world, we were unbackable odds-on favourites, and why were the other teams even bothering to turn up. So, when there was a hiccup early the media turned on us—champs to chumps in the space of a couple of games. I'll concede we hadn't played at our best, but the criticism was over the top.

When Australia wins a day/night match we are rarely pestered the next morning at the airport, but lose one and every television channel is there.

After our Cup loss to England at the SCG, next morning I was on the walkway at Sydney airport, not happy naturally, heading for the Golden Wing, sanctuary and breakfast, when a reporter from Channel Seven started shoving a microphone under my nose and talking about "the worst Australian World Cup team ever, will you retire, and Botham's come back to haunt you again."

I considered his approach intrusive and his questions silly, and refused to go on with an interview.

That night Channel Seven's news played the confrontation back, portraying me as the biggest prick of all time. They couldn't be bothered doing the decent thing and just saying "Allan Border wasn't talking today." So I told Channel Seven they were unwelcome at the next pre-match media conference.

And, I think well within my rights to do so. My point is this: if the bloke had come up to me at the airport and said, "Excuse me Allan, do you mind if we have a chat somewhere less crowded about last night's game? I know it's tough, but would you mind …" then okay, I'd have thought about facing the music.

But I just couldn't cop him catching me on the run, in a very public place, and making some totally crass comment about me retiring. I mean, quit in the middle of the World Cup—have you ever heard such rubbish?

The expectation of retirement had been created by another section of the media ringing up Neil Harvey, who'd been out of the game for 30 years, and quoting his statement that I should give the game away. In the eyes of the media Harvey's throwaway line—he'd said it two years before, as well—became some sort of self-fulfilling prophecy.

As our Cup crisis deepened 'worry photos' of me started to appear in the newspapers, photos of me with my hands covering my eyes, head bowed, or with my eyes closed and a look of anguish on my face.

The captions underneath were about "the worried Allan Border, frustrated by his team's poor form". It reached a point where I'd go to the photographers at net practice and say, "Which face would you like today, fellas—the worried one or the happy one?" They'd say, "Sorry Allan, just doing our job."

One of the shots of my scrunched up face had been taken while I was doing the warm-up stretches. It was the look of a man thinking to himself, 'Shit, I think my hammy's going to pull!' But the caption said I was showing the strain of losing games.

Criticism is always hard to swallow, whether it's justified or not, but I can wear it; what I can't wear is the 'cheap shot', nor do I think I should be expected to tolerate the fools among the media, just as the media don't expect me to tolerate a sloppy performance from my team.

I've had media blokes come up to me with, "I usually do the horse racing, but I got told to come out here and ask you when you're going to retire." About 25 times, every year for the last five years, I've been asked by the media, "When are you going to retire?" It reached the stage where I began thinking to myself, 'The next time I hear that bloody question I'm going to say, 'I'm not going to retire, ever!' '

TIME BANDITS

After our 1991 tour of the Caribbean, when I was back into family harness at Chapel Hill, there was a cricket item in one of the newspapers, a revelation by the West Indies Board that they had suffered a half million dollar plus loss on our 1991 visit.

With it came a suggestion from their Board that the days of five-Test series in the Caribbean were probably finished.

It took my mind back to the first day of the Second Test in Guyana—and prompted a thought that the day might not be all that far away when no country would be too keen on a five-Test series.

On that day the West Indies bowlers managed to bowl only 83 overs. Before the series began it had been agreed in the tour conditions that 90 overs were to be bowled in a day. Simple enough? Play starts at 10.25 a.m. and finishes at 5.25 p.m., and in that period the fielding team will bowl 90 overs.

Wrong. The West Indies maintained we could call it a day only when the 90 overs had been bowled.

On that first day when stumps were scheduled to be drawn, after six hours, the West Indies had managed to bowl only 74 overs. In the next hour they bowled only another nine, when stumps were drawn because of bad light. It was reasonable to think it might have been bad, after all the day was well into overtime.

This West Indian idea of a day's play is no problem for a bowling team; but it is a problem for the spectator in terms of value for money, and it is a problem for the batting team.

The wickets of Matthews and Jones fell after the scheduled time of stumps. Geoff Marsh was out about the same time. The 'slow' fast bowlers create a psychological edge because when the scheduled time of stumps draws near, the batsman, instead of being able to think *finis* as has been cricket's tradition, now has to think, 'Hell, there's another sixteen overs to go.'

Geoff Marsh had already batted for five and a half hours, 'a day' to all intents and purposes—should he have been expected to bat another 16 overs?

The West Indian tactic, and it has been successful, has been to use four fast bowlers, each in six over spells, or 12 an hour, sometimes less. They were prepared mentally for overtime, because that was their game plan.

On the other hand you could say the batting team had a bee in its bonnet about slow over rates lengthening the day, and was therefore mentally unstable. In hindsight, in this series at least, we should have sat down, recognised we were going to do some overtime, gritted our teeth, and adjusted mentally to that scenario.

Wonderful thing hindsight; but in this case just a piece of sticky tape that would in the end do nothing to help the game overall.

The West Indies weren't cheating, but it was gamesmanship stretched to the limit. And when this is recognised and new rules are framed the West Indies display a persecution complex, implying "you're all just jealous".

Not at all. Winning is nice, but should it be so all-encompassing as to promote the disintegration of the game? Do teams have to win before they can question the tactics of opponents?

TEA WITHOUT SUGAR

After the West Indies had won the Test series in the Caribbean in 1991, their captain Viv Richards hardly had his 'hands back around the Frank Worrell Trophy'—actually, it had been lost—before he set about 'bagging' Bob Simpson, calling him among other things "a poor loser".

Post-match press conferences are generally tame affairs for captains—unless your younger brother has just bowled one underarm!—and the one at Kensington Oval reached flashpoint out of the blue. One moment Viv was answering a question about Gordon Greenidge's 226 in the second innings of the Test, in the next breath he was telling everyone "Bobby Simpson is a moaner." It wasn't as if one of the questions had been, "... okay, so Australian coach Bob Simpson said earlier in the tour he thought the West Indies were beatable, what do you think about that ...?"

Viv's was an extraordinary outburst, the captain of one country coming out and saying such bitter things about an official from the visiting country. Why?

Of course, in any Test series as hard-fought as this one had been, there were going to be frayed tempers and the odd bust-up. But I wouldn't have thought it could have got down to a slanging match, with "I don't like so-and-so ... he had a crack at me ..."

And yes, Simmo had been on the front foot about a few things—the West

Indies slow over rates and how they were against the spirit of the game, the Jones run out and why it was against the rules, and, like a few hundred others, he'd suggested early in the tour the West Indies were under a bit of pressure.

All Viv needed to deliver, if anything, was a throwaway line: "Tough luck Simmo, we're still the kings."

Instead he hurled a bomb, going on about having little respect for Simpson, and "Bobby Simpson ain't our cup of tea." It was irrational. You'd have thought Viv had just lost the series and was sour, instead of being two-and-one.

Look at it this way: what if, at the press conference, I'd come out and said Lance Gibbs, the West Indian manager, wasn't our cup of tea etc.? The West Indies administration would have gone berserk—demanded my resignation probably.

When our manager Laurie Sawle registered a complaint the West Indies Board side-stepped his demand for a public apology from Viv, and instead issued a statement saying Viv regretted any embarrassment he may have caused.

"May have". I wouldn't have thought there were any 'ifs' about it.

IN HOT WATER

During the Fifth, and series-deciding Test against the West Indies in the 1992–93 season, Australia's rookie fast bowler, Jo Angel, who was making his debut, was no-balled for short-pitched bowling.

It prompted me to make a gesture, with my left hand, towards the umpire, Col Timmins, a gesture which in effect said, 'Given the amount of short-pitched balls the West Indies have been allowed to bowl at us during the summer without an umpire stepping in, that is the most ridiculous call of all time.'

I didn't hurl my hat on the ground, I didn't kick the ground, I didn't wave my fist—I made a cynical gesture that I doubt any member of the public could have seen. I was cited under Code of Conduct rule 1(e) which says: "Players or officials shall not use crude or abusive language ('sledging'), nor make offensive gestures."

I had to appear before the ICC match referee, Donald Carr, who told me I should have known better than to make such a gesture to an umpire. Probably right, but to be quite honest this situation was almost laughable.

I made this point to Donald: "In other words, you're saying to me, that it is okay for the West Indies to appeal for a catch behind the wicket and all rush up to the umpire in an intimidating fashion, and when they don't get the decision, fall down on the ground or just stand there with their hands on their hips staring in disbelief."

I said: "How come none of them are in here for obvious dissent, but I am for this ridiculous charge over a gesture nobody in the crowd saw, and was misconstrued to boot?"

I asked him: "Tell me Donald, is this code of conduct thing protection for the umpires, or protection for the game?" His answer left me in no doubt it was the game—the way the game is perceived.

I said: "Well, what am I doing here? This is the most trivial thing I can think of." As far as I'm concerned if the umpires were offended, it was something that should have been sorted out on the field, at the end of the over.

By coincidence, one of the umpires, Steve Randell, was also the umpire at the centre of a report on me in the First Test in the series, when the West Indies had managed to hang on for a draw. It was very frustrating because Richie Richardson was using his pad more often than his bat as his main line of defence. Naturally we were hitting the pads a lot, not just Richie's either, and there were a lot of appeals for leg before. Some said maybe there were too many appeals, but I was convinced some should have been upheld.

On one occasion I walked past Randell and said to him, "You were giving leg before decisions yesterday, aren't you making them today?" A bit cheeky, but hardly offensive, certainly not "showing dissent", certainly not bringing the game into disrepute.

Surely umpires haven't become so precious that they can't handle a comment like that without putting a player on report. If that can't be laughed off on the field then I'd say we're in danger of all out war breaking out between umpires and players.

When I was told I'd been cited I was so incensed I chose to ignore the hearing convened by the ICC match referee, Raman Subba Row. I regret that, it was poor form on my part, and offensive. I deserved the $2000 fine, and was probably lucky I didn't get a game or two suspension as well.

I concede that we need to preserve the spirit of cricket, and I appreciate how important to that end a good relationship between umpires and players is, but it is equally important we don't turn umpires into some sort of protected species.

I think the problem with umpires in Australia is that not enough of them have a 'feel' for the game because not enough of them have played the game at senior level. If the pay was better, past players could be more inclined to stay in the game. England have the best umpires simply because most of them have spent 20 years or so on the playing side before turning to umpiring.

Australian umpires get too bogged down in the mathematics of leg before decisions—you know, the stumps are so many centimetres high, and if the ball bounced a centimetre outside the leg stump it might have missed by half a centimetre.

In England they don't worry about that; if they think it would have hit, you're out. And that leads to consistency.

And they don't take kindly to batsmen who just shove their pad down the pitch, tucking their bat in behind trying to make out they're playing a shot. If a batsman does that in England the umpires have a quiet word. "Start using your bat son, because if the ball is going to hit the stumps, I'm going to give you out, because I don't consider you are playing a shot." One of two things can happen, either the bloke starts making some runs, or he thinks the umpire is bluffing and he gets out leg before. The game comes alive.

In Australia we're trying to encourage spinners, yet all the time we see batsmen being allowed to get away with that sort of bat-behind-pad nonsense. That doesn't do too much for the way the game is perceived.

Ridiculous stoppages for bad light is another blight on the game. My understanding of the rule is that play is stopped if the batsmen are in physical danger. On the last tour to Sri Lanka in 1992 we came off in a Test when the Sri Lankans were facing the 'spitting cobras' of Shane Warne and 'Moey', Greg Matthews, spinners!

Everyone is clamouring for neutral umpires and a third umpire, via the video. The 1992 World Cup was played with neutral umpires, but I saw just as many mistakes made. Neutral umpires don't necessarily improve the standard, they just take out the 'home-town' influence.

I thought the 'third umpire' via video replay worked very well in New Zealand on our 1993 tour, even though I had been sceptical. I now think everyone should press ahead with this idea.

A West Indian appeal which seems to have ended in disappointment.

Chapter Thirteen

MAN FOR ALL SEASONS

Getting older, but looking younger! Ready for a television appearance before the 1992-93 season.

---

*C*ricket is the summer game, and the anticipation is of dry, hot days under a clear blue sky. Yet, more than in any other sport cricketers have to cope with all sorts of variable conditions, and not just when they play in some faraway country. Sometimes there is only cold comfort in the cricketer's own backyard and other times the sun shines on a cricketer's fortunes in distant lands.

SUMMER IN COLOMBO

In Colombo, the capital of Sri Lanka, the traffic is a noisy rabble of old trucks, ever-stopping buses, spasmodic ox carts and hundreds of thousands of pedestrians, all of which move slowly.

One evening, early in our tour there in 1992, the boys decided that a change from the local fare was in order, and chose Italian at a venue about a kilometre down the road from our hotel. There were ten of us, and to get to our destination we needed five of the local taxis, a motorised three-wheel rickshaw-like vehicle called a *bajaj*.

The *bajaj* had a driver seated up front at the handlebars, and carried two passengers, three at a pinch; there was no roof. I was travelling with my vice-captain, Mark Taylor, known in the team as 'Tubbsie'.

While we were waiting for our hotel doorman to whistle up five taxis a bit of the 'boys will be boys' came out in us, and there was a lot of discussion about the slowness of the traffic, and the local speed limit, 32 km/h, which of course seemed ridiculous to us.

But we'd noticed that the *bajaj* drivers had an extraordinary ability to weave their way out of the most tangled traffic jams; then somebody mentioned the word "race". Tubbsie and I got our driver away to a smart start, and with a good deal of egging-on, and even a suggestion that money could change hands in the form of a 100 rupee bonus if we arrived first, we retained our lead.

There was a large, busy roundabout only a short way from our destination, and we had to take the second exit. Suddenly a car cut in front of us to take the first exit. Our driver reacted, wrenched at the handlebars—and flipped!

We flipped onto Tubbsie's side; I grabbed for the side-rail and fell on top of Tubbsie, so I had a soft landing. He wasn't so lucky.

I had just dragged myself out of the mangled mess—one back wheel was still spinning—when the rest of the boys came upon us. They weren't exactly white-faced, just wide-eyed. They said that coming from behind it had looked like a real horror smash, sparks flying everywhere as the *bajaj* skidded along on its side.

I survived, but Tubbsie was limping from a twisted ankle. We were checking him out when the driver emerged from the huge crowd that had gathered about us, came up to me and said, "What about my bonus?" I looked at him. Then I looked at Tubbsie hobbling, and thought, 'I should tell this bloke to piss off, he's nearly killed us.' But the truth was, I suppose, it was self-inflicted.

We were lucky, and it's probably not drawing too much of a long bow to say Dame Fortune smiled on us on the cricket field, too.

Playing cricket in Sri Lanka is a hot and sticky business, like playing in a steam bath. When I went there in 1983 the pitches were typical subcontinent—brown and dry, only for spinners. But in 1992, possibly because we were there at

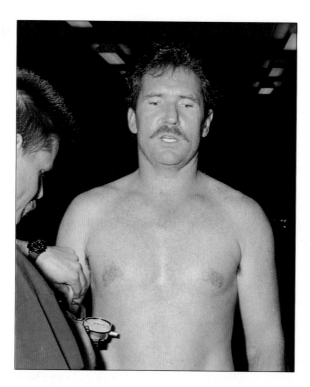

Hard yakka, getting ready for the tour to Sri Lanka.

the tail-end of the wet season, they were juicier, and that, along with the high seams on the hard balls, made conditions ideal for the pacier bowlers.

The 1992 tour was a 'quickie', the type of tour that promises to be more and more part of an Australian cricketer's lot. While we continue to invite three overseas teams to Australia every summer, we face the likelihood of having to undertake six or seven week tours before, and after, our season. They are circumstances in which it is easy to be caught on the hop, as has happened with tours to Pakistan a couple of times.

We had come out of our winter, had a few days practice in Sri Lanka in indifferent conditions, had a trial game which was basically a washout, then straight into the big stuff. No real match practice, and that's when you are at your most vulnerable. And, more often than not, that can be the experience on a 'quickie' tour.

And Sri Lanka are not weak. Make no mistake—given a couple of strike bowlers this cricket-crazy nation will be a force down the line.

We lost the one-day series, and as a sidelight, ran a poor last in the fashion stakes as well! For the night cricket Sri Lanka were decked out in splendid gunpowder blue with a white band. We wore salmon pink with a blue band, can you believe! It didn't sit all that well with the baggy green caps.

I had come to Sri Lanka with a losing record as a Test captain on the subcontinent, and when the last day of the First Test dawned in Colombo, I didn't look like changing it. Sri Lanka needed only 181 to win on a pitch that had already served up over 1200 runs, and in the stands the spectators were singing those black spiritual numbers in anticipation of a win.

Mid-afternoon the scoreboard read, Sri Lanka 2/127, and it looked all over for us. Then their best batsman, Aravinda De Silva, hit one over my head at mid-on, but not so well that I didn't have a chance of catching it.

I turned, ran back, dived, and just missed the chance.

Three balls later he played the same shot, only a little bit higher and a little bit further. Again I turned and started running.

I plucked off my white hat, then I flicked off my 'sunnies'; it must have looked like a cricket strip-tease. I caught it. One hour and 20 minutes later they were all out; they'd lost 8/37, and the Test. Greg Matthews and Shane Warne bowled magnificently. The grandstand was stunned silence, and the fat lady had sung for us.

My captaincy record wasn't the only aspect of my play making headlines before the tour; there was much being made of the fact that I hadn't scored a century for Australia for four years, since my 113 not out against Pakistan in Faisalabad in 1988.

Strangely enough a statistic like that plays less on my mind than it seems to on the minds of others. My attitude to batting has always been simple: score as many runs as I can. If I score a hundred, that's good. But let's face it, during that drought of hundreds it wasn't as if I had been failing, or letting the team down.

I'd played in eight Test series, in that time only in the series against the West Indies did my average drop below 40 runs an innings.

Opponent	Runs	HS	Ave
West Indies	258	75	32.25
England	442	80	73.00
New Zealand	129	78*	64.50
Sri Lanka	165	85	55.00
Pakistan	134	62*	44.60
England	281	83*	46.83
West Indies	225	59	34.38
India	275	91*	55.00

* denotes 'not out'

I think I'd played in 34 Tests, and my only regular thought on the matter was, 'It would be nice to know if I can still do it.'

On this Sri Lanka tour I'd been hitting the ball pretty well, just not going on with it. In the Third Test, the last in the series, I went in when we were 4/57, and I hadn't even scored before we were 5/58.

That man out was Mark Waugh, in the middle of an absolute horror run, out for a duck, his third. We started calling him 'Le Specs', and in the second innings, when he got his fourth, we changed his nickname to 'Audi', after the car whose symbol is the four rings. Cricket can be cruel.

It got crueller. Someone reminded Mark if he got another one he'd qualify for the Olympics—five rings!

By drinks in the final session of the first day I'd reached 96, and first ball after the break, off a full toss from their spinner Anasurai, I belted four to reach my 24th Test hundred. I suppose it was a relief personally, but from the team's viewpoint it had taken us well past 200, and out of danger.

It hadn't been an innings of endurance, either; I had batted aggressively, and maybe played just about every shot that's in the book, and a few that aren't.

But the most satisfying aspect of the trip to Sri Lanka was that our First Test victory gave us a win in the series.

Greg Chappell's team had won a one-off Test in 1983, but in 1992 our win had been best-of-three, therefore making us the first Australian team to win a series on the subcontinent since Bill Lawry's side beat India in 1969.

WINTER IN ADELAIDE

My 1992 winter was free of cricket, a time to be with Jane and the children, and to play the home handyman role. But it also gave me time to assess my cricket career. I had just turned 37, and because I'd never really been a great one for attending to injuries—I had a 'put up with them, and they'll go away' philosophy—a few niggles were starting to catch up with me. And I was getting a bit more asthma.

I wanted to beat the West Indies, then go to England for a fourth Ashes tour, play South Africa at home, then captain the Australian team to South Africa, about 18 months of solid cricket.

I knew I had to address my fitness levels; I was not about to use my age as an excuse if I suddenly started playing badly. Nor did I want to just fade out of the game. I had my eyes tested, and underwent a general maintenance program at a local gym, a weights circuit, the step machine and on the bike. And in the nets I worked hard on my technique.

I felt like a new man, so much so that on the second last evening of the First Test against the West Indies at the Gabba, I took on Keith Arthurton for a single to get off the mark—something I might have risked when I was 21!—realised I was a good 'head short' of my ground, stretched out a bit more, and tore a hamstring.

It turned out to be the first link in a chain of events at that time in my cricketing life that I won't recall with any fondness.

At lunch on the final day of the Test the West Indies were 4/9, needing 231 to win, obviously our best chance to knock them over for quite a while.

Then, for most of the rest of the day Richie Richardson played an out of character, front pad down the wicket, blocking game, which was very frustrating, made more so by the rejection of our leg before appeals.

My frustration with the umpiring had cost me a $2000 fine for breaching the ICC code of conduct, and my sore leg eventually cost me my place in the one-day team.

No sooner had we finished the Test than we were in Perth for the World Series, where we were booed and hissed at by the WACA crowd, and Ian Healy and Mike Whitney were pelted with fruit, and even cans. Great! Playing for Queensland at the WACA I don't think twice about bad crowd reaction, but playing for Australia I'd have expected some loyalty.

Because we played so badly in that game—beaten by nine wickets—I made the point afterwards that perhaps the team 'hierarchy', of which I am one, could have improved on the preparation, to my mind a quite realistic observation.

This resulted in a series of headlines suggesting Simmo the coach and I were at loggerheads, an absolute beat-up. Unfortunately, Ian McDonald, the team manager, gave the headlines credibility by issuing a statement with a few sarcastic references about my memory of team meetings. It was a nice old 'serve', and very disappointing to me that it appeared in the media as an 'official' line.

The point was made to me that I should have kept my comments about our preparation in-house. Why? I was asked by the media why we got our arses kicked, and I said we didn't prepare properly.

The expectation from the media towards me is very high; it seems to me if I don't talk to them there's a drama, and if I do there's some sort of strife—it's a pretty thin line. On this occasion the media chose to 'speed it up', and read too much into my use of the word "hierarchy".

My sense of humour didn't improve when I was told in Perth that because I'd twanged my hamstring again, I should miss the next four World Series matches.

I'd have thought I only needed to miss one of the games, then I'd be okay again, but the others in the team hierarchy wanted me to have a longer rest. I didn't think I needed one, and in light of David Boon's problems with a hamstring later in the summer, I think I had a point. He wasn't asked to go home and rest. I thought I could get the necessary treatment, and stay with the team.

But, home I went. It was a week of intense physio, weights, electro-stuff and massage, day in day out. By the time of the Queensland versus Pakistan match, my only hope of proving my fitness before the Second Test, I was close to a hundred per cent right again.

I was still annoyed with the world; bits and pieces were being written that my position in the team was under a cloud, and that my fitness was under question. One journalist in particular was chipping away.

Frustration in the Gabba Test. I'm at first slip because of my torn hamstring.

The headlines said "Should AB stay, or go?" and underneath they had comments from various people. Neil Harvey, one of my constant critics, threw another left hook.

I went into the Pakistan match determined to score a lot of runs and silence the doubters. I thought, 'With runs on the board there can be no question mark over my head.'

It was a good Gabba pitch, good opposition bowlers, Wasim and Mushtaq, and I got a good hundred.

In the first innings of the Second Test, at the MCG, we were in a bit of strife when I went to the crease. Another one of those team crises, 4/115. But I felt good, and my feet were moving. I can always tell. I look down at the crease occasionally and I can see where my front foot is getting to. Sometimes, when you're out of touch, you think you're playing forward, but when you look down you can see you're not, that your feet are still on the crease.

I played all the shots that I hadn't been playing well for a while—the cuts, the cover drive, the old pull shot. If they bowled short I had a bit of a dash at it. I didn't miss too many opportunities to score, and all round it was one of my better hundreds.

I answered any self-doubts I had about my age. I had proved myself, and against the West Indies pace attack. Proved, too, that I wasn't just in the team because I was some sort of figure-head standing on my past record. I was in the team because I deserved to be there. I was happy, I'd got the monkey off my back. And, I'd stuck it up a few people.

And if you're going to do something special in cricket the MCG is the place to do it. The Bay-13 fans are just sensational the way they respond.

On the way to a century
at the MCG.

BELOW: *A nice gesture from
my opposing captain, Richie
Richardson, after I'd passed
my century.*

We had two rookies playing in this Test, Damien Martyn and Shane Warne. In our second innings we were in trouble, 5/90, and Martyn, batting with our tail, which as you know can be pretty ordinary, manipulated the score up to 196. He came of age.

Then, with the West Indies 1/143 and blazing, chasing an unlikely 369 for victory—but with me worrying anyway!—Warne clean bowled Richie Richardson with a 'zooter', his skidder ball.

It was the moment that turned the Test our way on the last day, and gave us a series lead over the West Indies for the first time since who knows when. It was a huge moment for us, and it was expected that we could now go on and win back the Frank Worrell trophy.

But the Third Test at the SCG, where we might reasonably have expected to have another win given the nature of the pitch, turned out to be a run feast with Brian Lara playing one of the great Test innings, scoring 277. The game was drawn and we moved from the Test arena into the World Series.

In past seasons the World Series had often given us renewed momentum for the Tests; even though we went off the boil this time, losing the finals, it made no difference to our thoughts about winning the Test series. There was a good 'edge' to our final practice for the Fourth Test in Adelaide, that feeling of anticipation, 'This is it, we can clinch the series in this game.' And so began one of the greatest Test matches in cricket history.

We made one change from Sydney, Tim May in for Greg Matthews, just offspinner for offspinner, but Adelaide's pitch had been re-laid, and was taking more spin than for some seasons, and it was Tim's home patch of turf.

Then, on the eve of the Test, a big problem for us. A million-to-one practice accident left Damien Martyn with a bung eye, in hospital and out of the Test. All of a sudden urgent messages went out around Australia to find the selectors.

Dean Jones was the obvious choice, a middle-order player and experienced. But Jones had chipped a thumb bone in the World Series and, given a Test match situation where he'd have copped a lot of short balls, that wasn't the right way to go.

So, it got down to two left-handed rookies, Justin Langer who could bat anywhere in the order, or Matthew Hayden, who would have to open, meaning Boon, our most successful batsman, would have to be moved.

Langer it was, and, of course, he did a wonderful job in his debut Test in the face of some torrid short-pitched bowling, being knocked groggy and having his helmet cracked apart.

Ironically it was the 60th anniversary of the infamous Bodyline series, and the public perception after the Adelaide Test, according to talkback radio and letters to newspapers, was that Bodyline was alive and well.

I feel I should make a couple of points about that. Firstly, let me say I think the bouncer rule, one bumper per batsman per over, is ridiculous. It weights the game in favour of the batsman, robbing the fast bowler of the element of surprise and the capacity to build pressure. The old rule, when commonsense allowed fast bowlers to send down three bumpers in two overs, worked well when properly policed.

Secondly, the umpires get so mesmerised by the new bouncer rule, they forget all about the other rule, the one about the bowling of fast, short-pitched balls designed to intimidate the batsman.

The Cricket Board's playing conditions for 1992–93 said in part: "Umpires shall consider intimidation to be the deliberate bowling of fast short-pitched balls which by their length, height and direction are intended or likely to inflict physical injury on the striker. The relative skill of the striker shall also be taken into account."

On the last day when our tail was scrambling for a win, I'd say the West Indies fast bowlers resorted to short-pitched bowling at them. I wasn't aware of the umpires speaking to them about it.

The reason for that is pretty simple: a fast short-pitched ball is defined as "a ball which passes, or would have passed, above the shoulder of a batsman standing upright at the crease."

So, if Tim May had been hit in the throat the delivery might have been illegal, provided one earlier in the over had passed above shoulder height. But he could be hit above the heart six times in the over and that's okay.

Of course, it's just a nonsense to expect umpires to accurately assess marginal deliveries when a batsman is moving his position so quickly. I'd have thought a bit of commonsense, and the old fashioned 'gut feeling' would be the way to go.

Still, that's all academic now. This Test saw some amazing heroics. West Indies made 252 and in our reply Boon took a horrific blow to the left elbow. I could tell from the way he staggered and grabbed his arm that he was in a bad way. I immediately thought, 'He's got a broken arm, he's our best player, he's going to be out—forever! It's not what we need right now.'

It wasn't broken but it had affected the nerves so badly he couldn't grip the bat properly. He doesn't say much, does Boon, but I knew he must have been in real pain.

He went back into bat when we were struggling and got the runs with Mervyn Hughes that kept us in the game, getting us up to 213 in our first innings.

In the West Indies second innings I was keen to get at them with the spinners, May and Shane Warne, because the pitch was definitely going to help them. But I was held up on two counts.

The rain, which had cut short the second day's play, returned, and worse, Tim May, who has a habit of getting injured, so much so I wonder if he hasn't got some hex on him, tried to field a ball at mid-on, but trod on the thumb of his bowling hand instead! It took a big gash out of the thumb and damaged the bottom joint; as I watched him head off the field for treatment I thought, 'Oh well, that's that. Great!' But he came back. Every now and again I'd give him the ball and ask "How's it feel?" and after a few spins he said, "Yeah, yeah, they're coming out well."

He came on and bowled his best-ever spell, 5/9 off about six overs. In the middle of it all he said, "This is scary, AB, they're just coming out so good."

I looked at him for a couple of seconds, then said, "Well, just keep treading on your hand."

So, we had to get 186 on a fourth day wicket in Adelaide to win the Worrell Trophy. You fancy your chances, but of course I'm a bit nervous about Australia chasing runs as I've seen us cock it up many, many times.

We knew the West Indies were going to come at us with everything; it was going to be tough. I didn't sleep brilliantly because I was tossing over all the scenarios. But, win and we were two-up, one to play—that was the scenario that mattered. Next morning our warm-up was just perfect, and positive.

Moments before lunch we were looking good, 50 on the board and Justin Langer and Mark Waugh going along nicely; one ball after lunch and I was in, the score 4/64.

I'd scored one run when Curtly Ambrose sent down the 17th ball of my innings, a 'throat ball'. Sometimes when I get out I can be really disappointed with the shot I've played. Or, perhaps my thought process hasn't been right, the concentration hasn't been there.

This ball caught me by surprise, because the ball before had pitched short too, about the same spot, and stayed down. This one leapt at my face, making me jerk my head and raise my hands in an instinctive defensive movement. The ball caught my batting glove and lobbed to the fieldsman at bat-pad.

When I got back to the dressing room and sat down to think about it I knew there was no way I could have done anything different. Against the 'throat ball' you just have to hope it either lobs over the close-in fielder's head, or goes straight to ground.

We plunged to 7/74. Langer was still out there, so there was a little bit of hope. But with a hundred runs still to get and only Shane Warne, Tim May and Craig McDermott to come, well the expectation was they would just get out.

When they didn't, and our score started to creep up, I started to get nervous. The palms of my hands began to sweat, and I went for the 'worry ball'. I tend to get that way when I'm watching tense periods of play that I haven't got any control over. It was just an old ball out of the practice bag and I must have thrown it from hand to hand 60,000 times while the score crept up.

Eventually the tension enveloped everyone. If someone wanted to move he'd wait until the end of the over, then race off and do what he wanted, then race back. You just don't want to break the spell. Jokes in the beginning, like "What price are we to get these?" later gave way to serious urgings, "Yes, run!" or "No, wait!" In the end we should have won.

With two needed Craig was facing Walsh and pulled one. Dessie Haynes, about three metres away at short leg, made a freakish stop. On the television replay you could see the ball take a bit of a right-angle bounce off the rough and what might have been the tying, or even winning, runs ended up worth nothing. Next ball he was out.

We were on the threshold of a great victory, then it was gone. Unbelievable. I thought, 'It just can't happen like that. Why didn't we get beaten by fifty, then there'd be none of that real ugly feeling in your stomach that comes with being beaten by the smallest margin in history.' Two runs!

There was dead silence in the dressing room for half an hour. No-one knew what to say. The two batsmen, Tim and Craig, were distraught. The first finger on Tim's right hand was a mashed, swollen mess from the hits he'd taken from the short-pitchers. I had to go and do a press conference.

It was very tough.

SPRING IN CHRISTCHURCH

In the first few days of 1993 I was hard at work at the SCG; it was the Third Test against the West Indies, we were leading the series one-nil, and because the SCG had been such a good ground for us in Tests against the West Indies—we had won handsomely in 1985 and 1989—I was hoping we could go two-up.

It was at the SCG that I had made my first-class debut, with NSW against Queensland, 16 summers before. The SCG, 1993, had changed quite a bit from those days. What was once the greenest, smoothest surface in Australia was now a patchwork of brownish streaks, and around the pitch square was bumpy enough to make fielding a nightmare.

The pitch itself, which has been 'exhumed' a few times in a bid to restore life, was as dead as last year's mutton, and offered nothing for any bowler from the fastest to the slowest. Even the odd downpour of rain failed to freshen the pitch surface.

A draw was the result we didn't really need. Something like 1200 runs were scored in the Test, from about 400 overs, and only 16 wickets fell.

One milestone that has eluded me in Tests is a century at the SCG. I've got past the 50-mark 11 times, but never been able to go on with it. It did occur to me over this five-day-long Benefit For Batsmen that I might never have a better chance of cracking my maiden SCG Test ton.

I made 74, and knew in my heart that realistically I could hope for only one more chance at the missing hundred—against South Africa during their tour in 1994. I thought to myself, 'AB, you're going to have to stay fresh, and in mighty good form.'

Nothing could really soften my frustration at the drawn result, but my failure to get a century was offset to a fair degree by the fact that during my innings I passed 10,000 runs in Test cricket, a milestone reached by only one other player, Sunny Gavaskar.

A scriptwriter would probably have had me dancing down the pitch, or playing a mighty hook for six, and a full-house crowd cheering. The reality was I pushed an offspinner, speared in at my legs from Carl Hooper, down to mid-on for a single, and went to 21. Sunny, who was in Cape Town commentating on the Test series between India and South Africa, sent me a fax, welcoming me to The Ten Thousand Club. It read:

> *Congratulations, and welcome to the Club 10,000. It's good to have you as it was getting pretty lonely out here.*
>
> *For your information I am sending you some of the rules of the club.*
> * *Membership is open only to players of restricted height and strokes—you have to be under five feet ten inches and you cannot play the reverse sweep.*
> * *You must have taken at least one Test wicket.*

I was having one of my best series against the West Indies. My batting average against them has tended to move in the same direction as plenty of the rest of the world's batsmen—downwards, when compared to performance against all the other countries.

In the first three Tests I'd hit 278 runs at over 50 runs an innings, yet my overall Test average against the West Indies was almost 40. And, I did feel as if I was in good touch, although I knew there were a couple of bits and pieces that could be tidied up. Nothing really worrying, just that I'd been a bit late on the hook shot now and again, and I'd taken a few to the helmet!

Yet, by the end of the series I'd scored only another 20 runs, 19 and one in Adelaide, and the dread of all batsmen, a pair in Perth. Worse, one of my two ducks was what kids these days bitingly call a 'golden duck'—a first ball job.

I'd been out first ball in a game before, but it was my first pair. Still, I was in good company; Neil Harvey, just to name one, had once succumbed. So had Victor Trumper. And, I was to find out at the end of the season that my 'golden duck' was one of 25 scored by first-class batsmen in Australia during the summer!

This run of outs was a great disappointment to me. From the team point of view, after we'd lost the series, I started to think 'what might have been' thoughts, like 'If only I could have scored just two more runs in that second innings in Adelaide, we'd have won the Test and the Worrell Trophy.'

And, of course, I'd been thinking that if, or when, I went past Sunny's record of 10,122 runs, I wanted it to be in front of an Australian crowd. It just didn't work out that way.

Directly after the West Indies series we flew to New Zealand to play three Tests and five limited-overs internationals. It was the 'sting in the tail' of what had been a very long campaign for us, beginning with the tough pre-season tour to Sri Lanka. My team was showing some alarming signs of wear and tear.

Boon and I were growing older together—our hamstrings seemed to be shortening; McDermott was annoyed by a fickle hernia; Merv Hughes's knees were groaning about the weight they had to carry; even the young buck, Shane Warne, had developed a chronic problem with a foot.

Despite the amount of cricket I'd played in the previous six months I decided I needed to play in the first game of the New Zealand tour, a match against an Emerging XI, to see if I could find some better form.

It was played at the odd-sounding Pukapura Park, a pretty ground in New Plymouth, but so small it could be a bowler's nightmare. In the 1992 World Cup the Sri Lanka and Zimbabwe batsmen had belted 625 runs in a day!

I made another duck, my third in a row, when I top-edged an attempted sweep.

Not exactly what I'd been hoping for! My form, and the fact that everywhere I went some interviewer would remind me just how close I was to Gavaskar's record, made me a little edgy. It was just getting totally out of hand. I recall telling one interviewer, who mentioned the record, "Well, for the four-hundredth time ..."

I went into the First Test at Lancaster Park, Christchurch, my 139th Test, needing just 50 runs to pass Sunny, but my form card read like that of a novice: 19, 1, 0, 0, 0.

I had a few things on my mind. I wanted to win the Trans-Tasman Trophy, the booty for winning the Test series; I certainly didn't want to make four ducks in a row! And, I wanted to make at least 50.

By one of those quirks of fate that cricket revels in, at the game at Lancaster Park was the great Kiwi fast bowler Richard Hadlee, now Sir Richard, in his role of television commentator.

It had been at Lancaster Park that Hadlee had taken his 400th wicket in Tests, thus establishing himself as the world's leading wicket-taker, eventually going on to take 415. That was in February, 1990. Now, three years later, at Lancaster Park, I was in a position to become the world's leading Test run-getter.

Richard could understand my frustration over the constant speculation on the record. He remembered that as he neared Ian Botham's record of 373 wickets, the goal had become dangerously distracting. It had got to the point where he was living the whole thing day and night, even dreaming about how he wanted

The Club 10,000. 'Sunny' Gavaskar and me, 'The Runs Brothers'.

World record holder,
Christchurch, 1993.

A special celebration,
after passing 'Sunny'
Gavaskar's record.

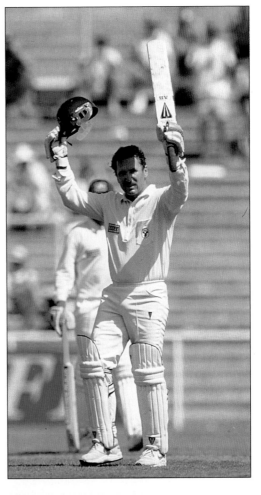

The sweep shot
that took me past
Gavaskar's record.

it to happen. His teammates had said, "For heaven's sake, do it, then you can come back and join the rest of us!"

I wasn't preoccupied by the record, but I did want to get it over with quickly, if for no other reason than to stop the endless speculation from the media.

I didn't have to bat until the second day of the Test, because Mark Taylor and Justin Langer had spent almost all the first day in complete command. I went in when Langer was out leg before to Morrison to the fourth ball of the morning.

I was a bit nervous; the pitch had been difficult to bat on, a strange greenish brown in colour, and a bit moist so the ball was seaming around a bit. And I had to face the second new ball.

Danny Morrison is one of those bowlers who worries me. I don't really know why it is, but if I'm answering one of those cricket questionnaires it's Danny's name that springs to mind when I'm filling in the 'Bowlers Who Trouble You Most' section. Maybe it's because he can swing the ball in, and late. I just never seem to be able to get the best of him.

Early, I was very scratchy. My mind was on the fourth duck, and how not to get it. I got to 20, but had given the edges of the bat a fair workout.

Morrison got one to swing back late, a yorker length, and in my desperate effort to avoid it, and a crushed foot, I fell over, finishing up on my knees. I thought, 'Terrific AB, you didn't even bat like this in the Mosman Under-12s.'

I was nearly run out at nine; I tapped one to the offside and took off, but Steve Waugh sent me back. I was about three metres from the crease, and the fielder had an underarm toss of about the same distance to run me out. He missed.

The crowd, which was around the 6000 mark, must have thought it was cricket's answer to the Keystone Cops!

Once the shine started to go off the ball, and I got to 30, I relaxed a bit more. When I was on 42 I hit a cover drive to the boundary off the left-arm paceman Su'a. So, I needed just four more runs to pass Sunny, and for once I felt homesick. The MCG would have been a much better place to have been at that moment.

The bowler was Dipak Patel, the offspinner, but he wasn't doing too much with the ball, and because of that I was more than prepared to use my feet, coming down the pitch to try to meet the ball on the full or half-volley, and drive.

He bowled, tossed up, drifting into my legs, and down the pitch I came; but the drift and loop deceived me just enough for a little bit of improvisation to creep into my sweep shot.

I thought, 'Oops, I'm a bit in no-man's land here, but, better hit it … oh, oh, that's in the air a bit, that bloke at backward square could catch that!'

As it turned out, ungainly though the shot looked, I'd timed it sweetly, and it went quickly and fell well away from the running fielder, lobbing over the boundary rope on the first bounce.

My batting partner, Ian Healy, wondered why there was a bit more commotion and fist-clenching than a half-century normally brings. I said, "I think that's it, I think I've gone past Sunny." He thought I needed 57 runs.

So that's how low-key the moment was; more a feeling of relief almost, rather than overwhelming elation. The Kiwis told me Richard Hadlee had celebrated his breaking of Botham's record in Bangalore, India, dressed in a silk jacket and turban and drinking champagne.

I had a beer with the boys, and a piece of ice-cream cake that had been prepared a few days earlier, stored in the team hotel freezer, then hidden in the Lancaster Park dining room freezer, waiting on me to 'provide the icing', you might say.

AUTUMN

When, and where will it all end for me? I hope that I can walk away from the game under my own steam, and with my reputation intact. I just want to make sure that I don't overstay my welcome. I don't want someone else to make the decision for me, namely being dropped from the side. I hope I can realise when the time is right to go gracefully.

A lot of people on the edge of the game were lobbying for me to go after the First Test against the West Indies at the Gabba in 1992, when I was out with a hamstring injury, and Mark Taylor took over.

Then, when we lost the series in Perth so badly, and I got my first 'pair' in my life, there were murmurs again. But I hadn't done that badly—third on the aggregates and scored a hundred. One thing is sure, as I get older the calls for my head will become more regular.

I'm the one who knows best how I feel, whether I'm playing well, how my body is coping, and if I'm still playing with the same motivation. The toughest question I will have to answer is: Am I just playing for the sake of it? When I say 'Yes' then it will be time to go.

When I went past Sunny Gavaskar's record there was a possibility my intensity could drop away. It didn't. I have always set goals for myself. My long-term goal is to captain the Australian team to South Africa in 1994, the first 'official' tour by an Australian team since 1969, a 25-year milestone.

I was never approached to join the Rebel teams, and wouldn't have gone anyway, so it will give me a good gut feeling if I can achieve my goal in 1994. I've only played against South Africa once—in the 1992 World Cup. We got thrashed, and I lasted one ball—so, I'd like to go.

EPILOGUE

Beyond Ten Thousand

Retirement. A life, or 31 years of it anyway, spent hitting cricket balls—but it will all have to end sometime. And then I'll have to live like a normal person.

How will I cope? I suppose, at first, with a great deal of difficulty. Most of all, I know I'll miss the camaraderie that goes with the game, being one of the boys, sharing stories, and chatting over a beer in the dressing room at the end of the day's play.

But in its place will be the satisfaction of being able to spend more quality time with my family, Jane, Dene, Nicole and new baby Tara.

The cricket memories will always be there; the really good ones will rise to the surface, Ashes glory, the victory dinner when Prime Minister Hawke honoured me with the Order Of Australia, the ticker-tape parade—the emotional outpouring that came with such long-awaited success.

That was the nicest memory, simply because things had seemed so very bad for so long. Jane maintains the bad times, the captaincy and the pressures they put on me turned me from a fun-loving bloke into an introverted cynic. Hopefully, in the relaxation mode of retirement I'll be able to cast aside the media's mantle of 'Captain Cranky'—how does 'Ex-captain Extrovert' sound?

I have two and a half acres of bush paradise outside Brisbane where I can work outdoors and sharpen my handyman skills, which have so far been a bit rushed, fitted in whilst on 'cricket leave', and once, quite dramatic. Jane and I decided the family car, for safety reasons, should be a big four-wheel drive with a bull-bar. 'Handyman Al' decided to hitch a trailer and take it down the back to clean up after some very heavy rain—but skidded it through next door's post-and-rail fence, flattening it, and doing about $400 damage to Jane's car.

Despite that, Jane's life promises to be smoother, and no longer will she be the 'cricket widow'. A lot of people think that's just a throwaway line, the 'cricket widow', but on my rough estimate I'd say I've only been home, on average, a few months every year since we married in 1980.

Not only has she had to cope with my long absences, but when I'm embroiled in some controversy, or even a good headline, Jane naturally has felt the same public pressure, and, of course, a loss of her privacy.

Yet, she never stopped supporting me. She managed by expanding her own lifestyle, but more than anything she's always understood just how important

At home with the family, April 1993, just before leaving on my fourth, and last Ashes tour.

cricket is to me, and to the family. It has given us a nice home, a good lifestyle, the kids a good education and good prospects for the future.

Dene is a little bright spark, and I know we'll be having a lot of fun together. He's good with the computer—he's already got part two of my life story underway and stored. He loves dinosaurs, so there'll be pin-the-tail-on-the-dinosaur at birthday parties.

He's very competitive, and wants to win all the time—sounds familiar? He gets upset if he doesn't, and I've told him, "You can only do your best." Hopefully he'll come to accept that, but never stop trying to win.

Nicole is a little lady who loves cutting and pasting, drawing, mainly ballerinas, and painting. She pays incredible attention to detail. The walls of the house look like an art gallery. She doesn't get her talent from me. I'm a straight-line man, houses with pointy gables.

It should be a lot of fun. Although Jane says, "This won't be like your big hotels here Allan; in summer it gets very hot and humid, and in winter it gets very cold because we don't have air-conditioning." I think it's a hint.

"... and you'll have to queue for things, the automatic teller machine and so on, just like everyone else. No team manager to do it for you.

"... and you'll have to learn how to stack the dishwasher!" Maybe retiring isn't such a good idea, after all.

SCOREBOARD

As at April, 1993

TEST

Debut: 1978/79 Australia v England, Melbourne

BATTING RECORD AGAINST EACH COUNTRY

Opponent	Debut	M	Inn	N.O	Runs	H.S	50	100	Avrge	Ct
England	1978/79	41	73	18	3115	196	20	7	56.64	49
India	1979/80	20	35	5	1567	163	9	4	52.23	14
New Zealand	1980/81	20	29	3	1319	205	5	4	50.73	28
Pakistan	1978/79	22	36	8	1666	153	8	6	59.50	22
Sri Lanka	1982/83	7	11	1	543	106	4	1	54.30	8
West Indies	1979/80	31	59	7	2052	126	14	3	39.46	19

INNINGS OF MATCH COMPARISON

	Inn	N.O	Runs	H.S	50	100	Avrge	Ct
First Innings	79	8	3583	162	24	8	50.46	46
Second Innings	60	4	2425	205	12	6	43.30	45
Third Innings	73	20	3434	163	22	9	64.79	35
Fourth Innings	31	10	820	123*	2	2	39.05	14

RECORD IN EACH COUNTRY

Country	Debut	M	Inn	N.O	Runs	H.S	50	100	Avrge	Ct
Australia	1978/79	80	137	20	5416	205	33	12	46.29	80
England	1980	19	34	10	1649	196	11	4	68.71	29
India	1979/80	9	16	1	766	162	4	2	51.07	6
New Zealand	1981/82	10	14	2	602	140	3	2	50.17	8
Pakistan	1979/80	9	16	4	743	153	3	3	61.92	10
Sri Lanka	1982/83	4	7	1	290	106	1	1	48.33	5
West Indies	1983/84	10	19	4	796	100*	5	1	53.07	2

* Denotes not out

BATTING

Season	Series	M	Inn	N.O	Runs	H.S	50	100	Avrge	Ct
1978/79	AUS v ENG in AUS	3	6	2	146	60*	1	-	36.50	3
1978/79	AUS v PAK in AUS	2	4	1	276	105	2	1	92.00	1
1979/80	AUS v IND in IND	6	12	-	521	162	3	1	43.42	4
1979/80	AUS v W.I in AUS	3	6	-	118	54	1	-	19.66	1
1979/80	AUS v ENG in AUS	3	5	1	199	115	1	1	49.75	4
1979/80	AUS v PAK in PAK	3	5	2	395	153	1	2	131.67	5
1980	AUS v ENG in ENG	1	2	2	77	56*	1	-	-	1
1980/81	AUS v N.Z in AUS	3	4	-	100	45	-	-	25.00	7
1980/81	AUS v IND in AUS	3	5	-	228	124	1	1	45.60	3
1981	AUS v ENG in ENG	6	12	3	533	123*	3	2	59.22	12
1981/82	AUS v PAK in AUS	3	5	-	84	37	-	-	16.80	3
1981/82	AUS v W.I in AUS	3	6	1	336	126	3	1	67.20	5
1981/82	AUS v N.Z in N.Z	3	3	-	44	38	-	-	14.67	1
1982/83	AUS v PAK in PAK	3	6	1	118	55*	1	-	23.60	1
1982/83	AUS v ENG in AUS	5	9	2	317	89	3	-	45.29	4
1982/83	AUS v S.L in S.L	1	1	1	47	47*	-	-	-	3
1983/84	AUS v PAK in AUS	5	6	1	429	118	2	2	85.80	7
1983/84	AUS v W.I in W.I	5	10	3	521	100*	4	1	74.43	1
1984/85	AUS v W.I in AUS	5	9	-	246	69	1	-	27.33	4
1985	AUS v ENG in ENG	6	11	2	597	196	1	2	66.33	11
1985/86	AUS v N.Z in AUS	3	6	1	279	152*	1	1	55.80	4
1985/86	AUS v IND in AUS	3	5	-	298	163	1	1	59.60	-
1985/86	AUS v N.Z in N.Z	3	5	1	290	140	-	2	72.50	3
1986/87	AUS v IND in IND	3	4	1	245	106	1	1	81.67	2
1986/87	AUS v ENG in AUS	5	10	1	473	125	1	2	52.56	4
1987/88	AUS v N.Z in AUS	3	4	-	288	205	-	1	72.00	6
1987/88	AUS v ENG in AUS	1	2	1	50	48*	-	-	50.00	1
1987/88	AUS v S.L in AUS	1	1	-	88	88	1	-	88.00	1
1988/89	AUS v PAK in PAK	3	5	1	230	113*	1	1	57.50	4
1988/89	AUS v W.I in AUS	5	10	2	258	75	2	-	32.25	7
1989	AUS v ENG in ENG	6	9	3	442	80	6	-	73.67	5
1989/90	AUS v N.Z in AUS	1	1	-	50	50	1	-	50.00	3
1989/90	AUS v S.L in AUS	2	3	-	165	85	2	-	55.00	2
1989/90	AUS v PAK in AUS	3	5	2	134	62*	1	-	44.67	1
1989/90	AUS v N.Z in N.Z	1	2	1	79	78*	1	-	79.00	1
1990/91	AUS v ENG in AUS	5	7	1	281	83*	3	-	46.83	4
1990/91	AUS v W.I in W.I	5	9	1	275	59	1	-	34.38	1
1991/92	AUS v IND in AUS	5	9	4	275	91*	3	-	55.00	5
1992/93	AUS v S.L in S.L	3	6	-	243	106	1	1	40.50	2
1992/93	AUS v W.I in AUS	5	9	-	298	110	2	1	33.11	-
1992/93	AUS v N.Z in N.Z	3	4	-	189	88	2	-	47.25	3
Total		141	243	42	10262	205	60	25	51.05	140

BATTING POSITION COMPARISON

Position	Debut	Inn	N.O	Runs	H.S	50	100	Avrge
3	1978/79	36	3	1554	163	8	4	47.09
4	1981/82	89	13	3792	205	21	8	49.89
5	1978/79	51	10	2239	125	12	7	54.61
6	1978/79	60	13	2505	153	17	6	53.30
7	1981	6	2	152	83*	2	-	38.00
8	1982/83	1	1	20	20*	-	-	-

RECORD AS CAPTAIN

Opponent	Tests	Won	Lost	Drawn	Tied
England	23	9	5	9	-
India	11	4	-	6	1
New Zealand	14	3	5	6	-
Pakistan	6	1	1	4	-
Sri Lanka	6	3	-	3	-
West Indies	18	4	8	6	-
Total	78	24	19	34	1

	Debut	M	Inn	N.O	Runs	H.S	50	100	Avrge	Ct
Non Captain	1978/79	63	111	20	4551	162	27	12	50.01	67
As Captain	1984/85	78	132	22	5711	205	33	13	51.92	73

ONE THOUSAND RUN INCREMENTS

Runs	Date			M	Inn	Runs	Avrge
1000	Dec	14	1979	13	26	1070	46.52
2000	Feb	7	1981	27	48	2051	51.28
3000	Jan	30	1982	39	72	3013	50.22
4000	Mar	2	1984	57	99	4027	49.11
5000	Jun	27	1985	68	120	5012	50.63
6000	Feb	28	1986	80	140	6062	51.81
7000	Dec	11	1987	91	159	7131	53.62
8000	Jly	6	1989	105	184	8001	52.29
9000	Mar	1	1991	121	207	9013	53.02
10000	Jan	2	1993	136	235	10053	52.09

INNINGS ON THE ROAD TO 10 000

Batsman	1000	2000	3000	4000	5000	6000	7000	8000	9000	10000
AR Border	26	48	72	99	120	140	159	184	207	235
SM Gavaskar	21	44	66	81	95	117	140	166	192	212

TEST CENTURIES

Score	Opponent	Venue	Season
205	New Zealand	Adelaide	1987/88
196	England	Lord's	1985
163	India	Melbourne	1985/86
162	India	Madras	1979/80
153	Pakistan	Lahore	1979/80
152*	New Zealand	Brisbane	1985/86
150*	Pakistan	Lahore	1979/80
146*	England	Manchester	1985
140	New Zealand	Christchurch	1985/86
126	West Indies	Adelaide	1981/82
125	England	Perth	1986/87
124	India	Melbourne	1980/81
123*	England	Manchester	1981
118	Pakistan	Brisbane	1983/84
117*	Pakistan	Adelaide	1983/84
115	England	Perth	1979/80
114*	New Zealand	Christchurch	1985/86
113*	Pakistan	Faisalabad	1988/89
110	West Indies	Melbourne	1992/93
106*	England	The Oval	1981
106	India	Madras	1986/87
106	Sri Lanka	Moratuwa	1992/93
105	Pakistan	Melbourne	1978/79
100*	West Indies	Port-of-Spain	1983/84
100*	England	Adelaide	1986/87

BOWLING

Opponent	Debut	M	Balls	Mdns	Rns	Wkts	Avge	5	10	Best	Stk/Rt	RPO	Eco/Rt
England	1978/79	41	944	42	339	3	113.00	-	-	1/25	314.67	2.15	35.91
India	1979/80	20	576	28	226	4	56.50	-	-	2/60	144.00	2.35	39.24
N. Zealand	1980/81	20	398	27	129	5	25.80	-	-	3/20	79.60	1.94	32.41
Pakistan	1978/79	22	540	26	208	5	41.60	-	-	2/35	108.00	2.31	38.52
Sri Lanka	1982/83	7	215	8	100	2	50.00	-	-	1/11	107.50	2.79	46.51
W. Indies	1979/80	31	1066	46	462	19	24.32	2	1	7/46	56.11	2.60	43.34
Total		141	3739	177	1464	38	38.53	2	1	7/46	98.39	2.35	39.15

INTERNATIONAL LIMITED-OVERS

Debut: 1978/79 Australia v England, Sydney

BATTING

Season	M	Inn	N.O	Runs	H.S	50	100	Avrge	Stk/Rt	Ct
1978/79	2	1	-	11	11	-	-	11.00	61.11	-
1979	3	3	-	59	34	-	-	19.67	44.70	1
1979/80	7	7	-	130	44	-	-	18.57	47.97	2
1980	2	2	-	39	26	-	-	19.50	69.64	-
1980/81	14	13	1	450	105*	3	1	37.50	65.79	6
1981	3	3	1	95	73*	1	-	47.50	67.86	1
1981/82	17	16	5	411	75*	3	-	37.36	74.32	4
1982/83	20	17	1	302	54	1	-	18.88	70.40	5
1983	6	6	-	150	43	-	-	25.00	72.46	3
1983/84	17	16	2	372	90	3	-	26.57	61.39	1
1984/85	22	20	5	708	127*	5	2	47.20	79.19	8
1985	3	3	1	188	85*	2	-	94.00	72.03	2
1985/86	16	15	1	356	65*	3	-	25.43	68.33	12
1986/87	21	21	3	698	91*	5	-	38.78	64.15	9
1987/88	19	18	2	364	67	2	-	22.75	82.35	12
1988/89	12	11	1	256	78	2	-	25.60	69.75	14
1989	3	3	-	96	53	1	-	32.00	87.27	-
1989/90	23	20	6	578	84*	2	-	41.29	75.46	16
1990/91	13	13	1	357	79	3	-	29.75	75.48	6
1991/92	18	15	2	280	76	1	-	21.54	72.35	9
1992/93	12	12	3	181	30	-	-	20.11	74.18	6
Total	253	235	35	6081	127*	37	3	30.41	70.31	117

RECORD AGAINST EACH COUNTRY

Opponents	Debut	M	Inn	N.O	Runs	H.S	50	100	Avrge	Stk/Rt	Ct
Bangladesh	1989/90	1	-	-	-	-	-	-	-	-	-
Canada	1979	1	1	-	25	25	-	-	25.00	47.17	-
England	1978/79	41	40	5	1212	91	8	-	34.63	70.71	13
India	1980/81	38	35	9	1104	105*	7	1	42.46	78.19	17
New Zealand	1980/81	48	44	5	857	58	5	-	21.97	63.01	28
Pakistan	1979	34	31	7	647	75*	4	-	26.96	66.56	18
Sri Lanka	1982/83	23	18	3	537	118*	3	1	35.80	94.54	12
South Africa	1991/92	1	1	-	0	0	-	-	0.00	0.00	-
West Indies	1979/80	61	60	6	1546	127*	9	1	28.63	65.51	26
Zimbabwe	1983	5	5	-	153	67	1	-	30.60	73.21	3

INNINGS BY INNINGS COMPARISON

	Inn	N.O	Runs	H.S	50	100	Avrge	Stk/Rt	Ct
First Innings	131	13	3220	127*	15	2	27.29	71.68	70
Second Innings	104	22	2861	105*	22	1	34.89	68.82	47

RECORD IN EACH COUNTRY

Country	Debut	M	Inn	N.O	Runs	H.S	50	100	Avrge	Stk/Rt	Ct
Australia	1978/79	167	155	22	3946	127*	23	3	29.67	68.84	85
England	1978/79	20	20	2	627	85*	4	-	34.83	69.21	7
India	1984/85	22	21	5	671	91*	5	-	41.94	83.46	9
New Zealand	1981/82	15	14	4	220	53*	1	-	22.00	56.56	8
Pakistan	1982/83	5	4	-	53	24	-	-	13.25	58.24	2
Sri Lanka	1982/83	7	6	1	89	30	-	-	17.80	84.76	-
Sharjah	1984/85	8	6	-	160	84	1	-	26.67	77.29	3
West Indies	1983/84	9	9	1	315	90	3	-	39.38	75.90	3

BATTING POSITION COMPARISON

Batting Pos.	Debut	Inn	N.O	Runs	H.S	50	100	Avrge	Stk/Rt
1/2	1980/81	17	1	615	105*	3	1	38.44	63.40
3	1978/79	28	2	656	62*	4	-	25.23	59.10
4	1980	106	13	3125	127*	22	2	33.60	71.77
5	1980/81	31	8	774	84*	5	-	33.65	75.22
6	1979/80	47	8	857	61	3	-	21.97	77.35
7	1978/79	5	3	42	11*	-	-	21.00	82.35
8	1990/91	1	-	12	12	-	-	12.00	44.44

BOWLING

Opponent	Debut	M	Balls	Mdns	Runs	Wkts	Avrge	5	Best	Stk/Rt	RPO	Eco/Rt
Bangladesh	1989/90	1	-	-	-	-	-	-	-	-	-	-
Canada	1979	1	-	-	-	-	-	-	-	-	-	-
England	1978/79	41	374	3	282	12	23.50	-	3/21	31.17	4.52	75.40
India	1980/81	38	338	-	282	8	35.25	-	3/23	42.25	5.01	83.43
New Zealand	1980/81	48	150	1	111	7	15.86	-	3/25	21.43	4.44	74.00
Pakistan	1979	34	398	1	381	9	42.33	-	2/24	44.22	5.74	95.73
Sri Lanka	1982/83	23	238	1	186	7	26.57	-	2/2	34.00	4.69	78.15
South Africa	1991/92	1	24	-	13	-	-	-	-	-	3.25	54.17
West Indies	1979/80	61	792	4	567	20	28.35	-	3/20	39.60	4.30	71.59
Zimbabwe	1983	5	132	1	77	2	38.50	-	1/11	66.00	3.50	58.33
Total		253	2446	11	1899	65	29.22	-	3/20	37.63	4.66	77.64

SHEFFIELD SHIELD

Debut: 1976/77 New South Wales v Queensland, Sydney

BATTING

Season	Team	M	Inn	N.O	Runs	H.S	50	100	Avrge	Ct
1976/77	New South Wales	4	6	-	120	68	1	-	20.00	6
1977/78	New South Wales	9	17	-	617	84	6	-	36.29	7
1978/79	New South Wales	7	13	-	775	135	3	3	59.62	3
1979/80	New South Wales	1	2	-	206	200	-	1	103.00	2
1980/81	Queensland	7	11	2	459	106	3	1	51.00	5
1981/82	Queensland	2	3	-	110	58	2	-	36.67	2
1982/83	Queensland	5	9	1	630	165	4	1	78.75	4
1983/84	Queensland	4	7	1	432	110	4	1	72.00	4
1984/85	Queensland	5	8	2	376	144*	1	1	62.67	7
1985/86	Queensland	4	7	1	568	194	1	3	94.67	4
1986/87	Queensland	7	10	-	472	77	4	-	47.20	10
1987/88	Queensland	8	15	2	738	168	1	3	56.77	4
1988/89	Queensland	7	11	-	248	57	2	-	22.55	6
1989/90	Queensland	3	6	2	272	144*	-	1	68.00	7
1990/91	Queensland	3	4	-	143	79	2	-	35.75	2
1991/92	Queensland	5	8	1	354	196	-	1	50.57	7
1992/93	Queensland	3	5	-	180	71	2	-	36.00	3

Team	Debut	M	Inn	N.O	Runs	H.S	50	100	Avrge	Ct
New South Wales	1980/81	14	24	1	1078	165	4	3	46.87	10
Queensland	1976/77	4	7	-	359	200	1	1	51.29	5
South Australia	1976/77	19	33	6	1797	196	7	6	66.56	26
Tasmania	1977/78	11	17	2	830	144*	5	2	55.33	16
Victoria	1976/77	20	33	2	1456	194	9	3	46.97	18
Western Australia	1976/77	16	28	1	1180	135	10	1	43.70	8
Total		84	142	12	6700	200	36	16	51.54	83

Team	Debut	M	Inn	N.O	Runs	H.S	50	100	Avrge	Ct
New South Wales	1976/77	21	38	-	1718	200	10	4	45.21	18
Queensland	1980/81	63	104	12	4982	196	26	12	54.15	65

CENTURIES

Runs	Team	Opponent	Venue	Season
200	New South Wales	Queensland	Brisbane	1979/80
196	Queensland	South Australia	Brisbane	1991/92
194	Queensland	Victoria	Brisbane	1985/86
168	Queensland	Victoria	Brisbane	1987/88
165	Queensland	New South Wales	Sydney	1982/83
144*	Queensland	Tasmania	Launceston	1984/85
144*	Queensland	South Australia	Brisbane	1989/90

135	New South Wales	Western Australia	Perth	1978/79
119	Queensland	South Australia	Adelaide	1985/86
118	Queensland	South Australia	Brisbane	1985/86
118*	Queensland	South Australia	Brisbane	1987/88
114	New South Wales	Victoria	Sydney	1978/79
113	New South Wales	Tasmania	Sydney	1978/79
110	Queensland	South Australia	Brisbane	1983/84
106	Queensland	New South Wales	Brisbane	1980/81
101	Queensland	New South Wales	Newcastle	1987/88

BOWLING

Opponents	Debut	M	Balls	Mdns	Rns	Wkts	Avrge	5	Best	Stk/Rt	RPO	Eco/Rt
New South Wales	1980/81	14	738	31	326	14	23.29	-	4/61	52.71	2.65	44.17
Queensland	1976/77	4	188	8	97	2	48.50	-	1/16	94.00	3.10	51.60
South Australia	1976/77	19	735	21	373	6	62.17	-	3/24	122.50	3.04	50.75
Tasmania	1977/78	11	246	7	106	2	53.00	-	1/12	123.00	2.59	43.09
Victoria	1976/77	20	442	17	172	9	19.11	1	5/46	49.11	2.33	38.91
Western Australia	1976/77	16	656	23	234	4	58.50	-	2/29	164.00	2.14	35.67
Total		84	3005	107	1308	37	35.35	1	5/46	81.22	2.61	43.53

DOMESTIC LIMITED-OVERS

Debut: 1977/78 New South Wales v Queensland, Brisbane

BATTING

Opponents	Debut	M	Inn	N.O	Runs	H.S	50	100	Avrge	Stk/Rt	Ct
New South Wales	1980/81	7	7	-	174	60	1	-	24.86	54.55	4
Queensland	1977/78	2	2	1	68	57	1	-	68.00	60.71	1
South Australia	1980/81	4	3	1	103	97	1	-	51.50	85.12	2
Tasmania	1981/82	6	6	2	219	68	3	-	54.75	75.78	5
Victoria	1978/79	8	8	3	263	77*	2	-	52.60	79.22	5
Western Australia	1977/78	8	7	1	215	72	2	-	35.83	70.03	5
Total		35	33	8	1042	97	10	-	41.68	70.41	22

BOWLING

Opponents	Debut	M	Balls	Mdns	Rns	Wks	Avrge	5	Best	Stk/Rt	RPO	Eco/Rt
New South Wales	1980/81	7	42	1	22	2	11.00	-	2/9	21.00	3.14	52.38
Queensland	1977/78	2	-	-	-	-	-	-	-	-	-	-
South Australia	1980/81	4	65	-	73	-	-	-	-	-	6.74	112.31
Tasmania	1981/82	6	4	-	6	-	-	-	-	-	9.00	150.00
Victoria	1978/79	8	168	2	94	1	94.00	-	1/33	168.00	3.36	55.95
Western Australia	1977/78	8	114	2	103	1	103.00	-	1/40	114.00	5.42	90.35
Total		35	393	5	298	4	74.50	-	2/9	98.25	4.55	75.83

ACKNOWLEDGEMENTS

I am indebted to many people for their help in the production of this book; Richie Benaud, who very kindly provided the Foreword; my family, particularly my mother and father, who reminded me just what fun the early days were; John Benaud, who came up with the concept, and provided editorial co-ordination; my publishers, Denis Cornell and Austin Robertson; Ross Dundas, the statistician; Robert Craddock, who like me, longs for the day Queensland win the Sheffield Shield.

The photos are from many sources; the family albums, so thoughtfully kept by my mother and Jane; my own cricket photo collection, much of which was donated to me by the very professional cricket photographers who have followed Australia's fortunes to every corner of the cricketing world.

I would like to thank Viv Jenkins, Gregg Porteous, Adrian Murrell, Graham Morris, Ken Kelly and Nikhil Bhattacharya; also, Frank Twiselton, the 'Downend Connection'; Tony Cozier, who organised the Willie Alleyne "Duel in the Sun" photo; Mike Coward, who secured photos of the Madras tied Test, and "The 10,000 Run Men" ('Sunny' Gavaskar and myself) from the *Hindu*, and from *Sportstar* magazine, Madras, India; Ian Kennedy of the *Age*, Melbourne, for "Christmas with the kids"; Bob Finlayson, of the *Australian*, for "The Border Pavilion".

I am also indebted to the following organisations: Australian Picture Library; Allsport UK Ltd; PBL Marketing; Australian Consolidated Press; Woman's Day; News Ltd.; John Fairfax Ltd.